THE SUNRISE SEMESTER LIBRARY

is composed of major literary works published in conjunction with the educational television course, Sunrise Semester. This pioneering program is presented by the Columbia Broadcasting System, and offered for college credit by New York University. Sunrise Semester first appeared in New York during the fall of 1957. Interest in the lectures was so great that the original series has been broadcast over local TV stations throughout the country. *3 Plays by Ibsen* (*Hedda Gabler, A Doll's House, The Wild Duck*) is one of seven literary landmarks selected for discussion by the Sunrise Semester TV instructor, David H. Greene, of the Department of English at N.Y.U. The other titles in *The Sunrise Semester Library* (available as inexpensive Dell Laurel Editions) are:

MOBY DICK. Herman Melville
Introduction by William E. Gibson

CRIME AND PUNISHMENT. Fyodor Dostoyevsky
Introduction by Ernest J. Simmons

MADAME BOVARY. Gustave Flaubert
Introduction by Floyd Zulli, Jr.

SIX CENTURIES OF GREAT POETRY
Edited, with an introduction, by Robert Penn Warren and Albert Erskine

JUDE THE OBSCURE. Thomas Hardy
Introduction by William E. Buckler

GREAT STORIES BY CHEKHOV
Edited, with an introduction, by David H. Greene

The introduction to *3 Plays by Ibsen* has been written especially for this edition by Professor Seymour L. Flaxman, Department of German, New York University.

The Sunrise Semester Library

3 PLAYS BY
IBSEN

Hedda Gabler

A Doll's House

The Wild Duck

With an introduction by
Seymour L. Flaxman

LAUREL
EDITION

Published by
DELL PUBLISHING CO., INC.
750 Third Avenue
New York 17, N. Y.

The name "Sunrise Semester" is
TM, Columbia Broadcasting System, Inc.

Sunrise Semester is a joint television presentation
of WCBS–TV and New York University

Designed and produced by
Western Printing and Lithographing Company

First Dell printing—January, 1959
Second Dell printing—October, 1960

Printed in U.S.A.

CONTENTS

INTRODUCTION

by Seymour L. Flaxman

Henrik Ibsen is the greatest dramatist since Shake-speare. Whether considered from the point of view of his dramatic technique, his impact on the drama, or his ability to create character upon the stage, he is the most significant playwright in the modern theatre. His influence on the drama of the last seventy-five years has been enormous, and it has touched almost every important dramatist from August Strindberg and Gerhart Hauptmann to Eugene O'Neill and Arthur Miller. Even that great French innovator in theatrical technique, André Antoine, who inspired the "free theatre" movement in Europe, used Ibsen's plays for his triumphs on the stage.

Born in the little Norwegian town of Skien on March 20, 1828, Henrik Ibsen was the son of a prosperous business man. But by the time Ibsen was eight years old, his father had lost his fortune. Thus Ibsen's hope of studying medicine had to be abandoned and, at the age of sixteen, he became a pharmacist's apprentice so that he could earn his own living. In 1849 he wrote his first play, *Catiline,* an historical tragedy, disguising the authorship under a pseudonym. The play was received without any great enthusiasm, and no publisher would risk printing it. A good friend of Ibsen's had the play published at his own expense, but some time later, when both Ibsen and his friend were down on their luck, they sold a number of copies to a grocer—for use as wrapping paper.

In Bergen Ibsen found a position in the theatre, success as a dramatist, and a wife, Susannah Thoresen. Six years later, in 1857, he was happy to be appointed director of the Norwegian Theatre in Christiania at twice the salary he had been getting in Bergen, but he soon discovered that the theatre was on the verge of bankruptcy and that he was expected to save it. He struggled to keep it solvent, but in 1862 it finally collapsed, leaving him without a source of income. He supported himself by journalism, but in 1864 he received enough money from the government and some friends to be able to live abroad. He remained outside of Norway, mainly in Italy and Germany, for almost thirty years. Yet as can be seen from both *Brand* and *Peer Gynt,* which brought him recognition in Scandinavia, there is much of Norway in his work. Ibsen could not reconcile himself to political conditions in his native land, and he satirized Norwegian politics and small-town life in *The League of Youth* and *An Enemy of the People.* As Brandes left Dresden, Ibsen told him, "Now you go home to provoke the Danes, while I stay behind to annoy the Norwegians."

Meanwhile, the poor and lonely pharmacist's apprentice had become a respected "pillar of society," complete with frock-coat and gold-rimmed spectacles, who was proud to see his son enter the diplomatic service. Ibsen shrewdly invested his money in securities, and had also become an art collector. He enjoyed an international reputation and world-wide prestige. When he died in 1906, he was given a public funeral, attended by the King.

The three plays in this volume, *A Doll's House, The Wild Duck,* and *Hedda Gabler,* reveal the most important aspects of Ibsen's work and genius. *A Doll's*

House was written in 1879, and it was only four years
later that its American première took place in Louis-
ville, Kentucky. It is often referred to as "a problem
play," but Ibsen was more inclined to ask questions
than to answer them. Here he depicts the typical middle-class marriage of his day, and shows his complete
mastery of the social drama.

Although Ibsen later scoffed at the idea that he was
a feminist, he has woven into his play the ideas that
charged the atmosphere of his time, ideas that were
upsetting the old order of things. The rights of women,
the economic basis of middle-class marriage, the
theory of heredity, the criticism of orthodox religion
—all these challenging questions, which are still very
much with us in our own day, appear in *A Doll's
House*. Thousands of women in Ibsen's audiences felt
Nora's problem to be their own. Ibsen was fond of
looking at the same situation from more than one
point of view, and it is characteristic of him that, in
Ghosts, he should later have shown the terrible tragedy
that might come of living out such a hopeless marriage.

Yet the fundamental problem in *A Doll's House* is
the conflict between warm, vibrant, childish Nora and
her possessive, unbending Helmer. A devoted wife and
mother, who romps with her children, Nora is ready
to dance a tarantella to charm her difficult husband.
Trapped by her own sacrifices to love, Nora is forced
to assert her own dignity and worth as an individual.

The technique of the play owes much to the French
drama of intrigue, but Ibsen proved himself a virtuoso
in the use of analytic exposition. Earlier events, which
have already determined the course of the action, are
slowly revealed to the audience, thus maintaining constant suspense. So effective is the development of the
play that in the last scene, when Nora returns her wedding ring to her husband and tells him that he has be-

come a stranger to her, it seems inevitable that she
should walk out the door and never return. With *A
Doll's House* Ibsen had brought the middle-class tragedy to new heights, and had proved that the failures of
middle-class men and women could be as moving as
those of kings and queens.

In *The Wild Duck*, the tightly knit closed style of
A Doll's House gave way to a looser, more open style,
which could embrace both tragic and comic elements,
and which was to reappear in the dramas of such play-
wrights as Hauptmann, Chekhov, and O'Neill. The
Ibsen who had his characters in *Pillars of Society* seek
only the truth now lets us see the other side of the
coin, for the characters in *The Wild Duck* are in desperate need of their illusions. There is no real hero in
this play, where Ibsen has caught a group of weak, ordinary mortals, enmeshed in the snares of life.

Perhaps the real hero is the poetic symbol of "the
wild duck," which adds numerous romantic associations and interpretations to the play. The modernity
of Ibsen is evident in the inner tensions of the drama,
which are suggested by the skillful ambivalence of this
symbol. Here Ibsen has made an important advance
beyond *A Doll's House,* for the conflict is not only one
of personality and character, but of psychology.

Those accustomed to thinking only of the realistic
Ibsen will be startled to find the romantic Ibsen a master of suggestive symbolism. The attempt to identify a
particular character in the play as "the wild duck" of
the title leads us to new and challenging reinterpreta-
tions of the whole drama, and we are at last forced to
the realization that this mystical bird is not a mathe-
matical constant, but a truly poetic symbol, with a
number of values. How significant a part of Ibsen's
work such symbolism actually is may be judged from
the fact that it is evident from such early plays as
Brand and *Peer Gynt* to *The Lady from the Sea* and
When We Dead Awaken.

In *Hedda Gabler* Ibsen has developed one of those full-length portraits, which, like *John Gabriel Borkman,* shows Ibsen as a master of depth psychology in a way that anticipates Freud. In his picture of young Hedvig in *The Wild Duck,* Ibsen explored the psychology of the adolescent girl, a theme that was to be more fully exploited by Strindberg and Wedekind. But *Hedda Gabler* is a study of a mature woman, with demonic, and almost pathological, masculine drives. Mated with unimaginative, ineffectual George Tesman, she longs for Eilert Lövborg "with vine-leaves in his hair." Jealousy and frustration drive her to burn Lövborg's manuscript and, thinking of Thea, she says to herself, "I am burning your child."

Ibsen had developed a keen sense of the theatre in his years of professional association with the stage, and this striking curtain line at the end of the third act is a typical example of his powerful dramatic technique. He is still the social dramatist, too, and at the beginning of the first act, in the scene with Tesman's maiden aunt, he quickly creates the atmosphere that is stifling Hedda. A more neurotic wife than Nora, Hedda is driven to suicide, and she shoots herself with the symbolic pistols that belonged to her father, the general. Only Brack, but not the audience, finds it difficult to believe that people do such things.

Ibsen was at the height of his fame when he wrote *Hedda Gabler,* and in this play he demonstrated his remarkable ability to give his characters the glow of their passions. The figures in his dramas come to life upon the stage, and Hedda is the kind of role that every actress wants to play. In speaking of this drama, Ibsen flatly stated that he had no desire to deal with problems. Thus Ibsen was not merely the playwright of ideas, of problems, of technique, but was, above all, a writer for the stage. Ideas, problems, and techniques may change, but great characters, like Peer Gynt, Nora, Hedda Gabler, and John Gabriel Borkman, never go out of date. When the lights go down and the curtain rises on the magic square of life, Ibsen's men and women will always hold the audience in their spell.

January, 1959

HEDDA GABLER

PERSONS OF THE PLAY

GEORGE TESMAN
HEDDA TESMAN, *his wife*
MISS JULIANA TESMAN, *his aunt*
MRS ELVSTED
JUDGE BRACK
EILERT LÖVBORG
BERTA, *servant at the Tesmans'*

The action takes place at Tesman's villa in the west end of Christiania.

ACT ONE

SCENE—*A spacious, handsome and tastefully furnished drawing room, decorated in dark colors. In the back a wide doorway with curtains drawn back, leading into a smaller room decorated in the same style as the drawing room. In the right-hand wall of the front room a folding door leading out to the hall. In the opposite wall, on the left, a glass door, also with curtains drawn back. Through the panes can be seen part of a veranda outside and trees covered with autumn foliage. An oval table, with a cover on it and surrounded by chairs, stands well forward. In front, by the wall on the right, a wide stove of dark porcelain, a high-backed armchair, a cushioned footrest and two footstools. A settee with a small round table in front of it fills the upper right-hand corner. In front, on the left, a little way from the wall, a sofa. Further back than the glass door a piano. On either side of the doorway at the back a whatnot with terra-cotta and majolica ornaments. Against the back wall of the inner room a sofa, with a table, and one or two chairs. Over the sofa hangs the portrait of a handsome elderly man in a general's uniform. Over the table a hanging lamp with an opal glass shade. A number of bouquets are arranged about the drawing room in vases and glasses. Others lie upon the tables. The floors in both rooms are covered with thick carpets. Morning light. The sun shines in through the glass door.*

MISS JULIANA TESMAN, *with her bonnet on and carry-*

ing a parasol, comes in from the hall, followed by
BERTA, *who carries a bouquet wrapped in paper.* MISS
TESMAN *is a comely and pleasant-looking lady of about
sixty-five. She is nicely but simply dressed in a gray
walking costume.* BERTA *is a middle-aged woman of
plain and rather countrified appearance.*

MISS TESMAN [*stops close to the door, listens and says
softly*]: Upon my word, I don't believe they are stir-
ring yet!

BERTA [*also softly*]. I told you so, miss. Remember how
late the steamboat got in last night. And then, when
they got home!—good lord, what a lot the young
mistress had to unpack before she could get to bed.

MISS TESMAN. Well, well—let them have their sleep out.
But let us see that they get a good breath of the fresh
morning air when they do appear. [*She goes to the
glass door and throws it open.*]

BERTA [*beside the table, at a loss what to do with the
bouquet in her hand*]. I declare, there isn't a bit of
room left. I think I'll put it down here, miss. [*She
places it on the piano.*]

MISS TESMAN. So you've got a new mistress now, my
dear Berta. Heaven knows it was a wrench to me to
part with you.

BERTA [*on the point of weeping*]. And do you think it
wasn't hard for me too, miss? After all the blessed
years I've been with you and Miss Rina.

MISS TESMAN. We must make the best of it, Berta. There
was nothing else to be done. George can't do without you, you see—he absolutely can't. He has had
you to look after him ever since he was a little boy.

BERTA. Ah, but, Miss Julia, I can't help thinking of Miss
Rina lying helpless at home there, poor thing. And
with only that new girl too! She'll never learn to
take proper care of an invalid.

MISS TESMAN. Oh, I shall manage to train her. And of
course, you know, I shall take most of it upon my-

self. You needn't be uneasy about my poor sister, my dear Berta.

BERTA. Well, but there's another thing, miss. I'm so mortally afraid I shan't be able to suit the young mistress.

MISS TESMAN. Oh well—just at first there may be one or two things—

BERTA. Most like she'll be terrible grand in her ways.

MISS TESMAN. Well, you can't wonder at that—General Gabler's daughter! Think of the sort of life she was accustomed to in her father's time. Don't you remember how we used to see her riding down the road along with the general? In that long black habit—and with feathers in her hat?

BERTA. Yes indeed—I remember well enough! But, good lord, I should never have dreamt in those days that she and Master George would make a match of it.

MISS TESMAN. Nor I. But by-the-bye, Berta—while I think of it: in future you mustn't say Master George. You must say Doctor Tesman.

BERTA. Yes, the young mistress spoke of that too—last night—the moment they set foot in the house. Is it true then, miss?

MISS TESMAN. Yes, indeed it is. Only think, Berta—some foreign university has made him a doctor—while he has been abroad, you understand. I hadn't heard a word about it until he told me himself upon the pier.

BERTA. Well, well, he's clever enough for anything, he is. But I didn't think he'd have gone in for doctoring people too.

MISS TESMAN. No, no, it's not that sort of doctor he is. [*Nods significantly.*] But let me tell you, we may have to call him something still grander before long.

BERTA. You don't say so! What can that be, miss?

MISS TESMAN [*smiling*]. H'm—wouldn't you like to know! [*With emotion.*] Ah dear, dear—if my poor brother could only look up from his grave now and see what his little boy has grown into! [*Looks around*.] But bless me, Berta—why have you done this? Taken the chintz covers off all the furniture?

BERTA. The mistress told me to. She can't abide covers on the chairs, she says.

MISS TESMAN. Are they going to make this their every-day sitting room then?

BERTA. Yes, that's what I understood—from the mistress. Master George—the doctor—he said nothing.

[GEORGE TESMAN *comes from the right into the inner room, humming to himself and carrying an un-strapped empty portmanteau. He is a middle-sized, young-looking man of thirty-three, rather stout, with a round, open cheerful face, fair hair and beard. He wears spectacles and is somewhat carelessly dressed in comfortable indoor clothes.*]

MISS TESMAN. Good morning, good morning, George.

TESMAN [*in the doorway between the rooms*]. Aunt Julia! Dear Aunt Julia! [*Goes up to her and shakes hands warmly.*] Come all this way—so early! Eh?

MISS TESMAN. Why, of course I had to come and see how you were getting on.

TESMAN. In spite of your having had no proper night's rest?

MISS TESMAN. Oh, that makes no difference to me.

TESMAN. Well, I suppose you got home all right from the pier? Eh?

MISS TESMAN. Yes, quite safely, thank goodness. Judge Brack was good enough to see me right to my door.

TESMAN. We were so sorry we couldn't give you a seat in the carriage. But you saw what a pile of boxes Hedda had to bring with her.

MISS TESMAN. Yes, she had certainly plenty of boxes.

BERTA [*to* TESMAN]. Shall I go in and see if there's anything I can do for the mistress?

TESMAN. No, thank you, Berta—you needn't. She said she would ring if she wanted anything.

BERTA [*going toward the right*]. Very well.

TESMAN. But look here—take this portmanteau with you.

BERTA [*taking it*]. I'll put it in the attic. [*She goes out by the hall door.*]

TESMAN. Fancy, Auntie—I had the whole of that portmanteau chock-full of copies of documents. You wouldn't believe how much I have picked up from all the archives I have been examining—curious old details that no one has had any idea of—

MISS TESMAN. Yes, you don't seem to have wasted your time on your wedding trip, George.

TESMAN. No, that I haven't. But do take off your bonnet, Auntie. Look here! Let me untie the strings—eh?

MISS TESMAN [*while he does so*]. Well, well—this is just as if you were still at home with us.

TESMAN [*with the bonnet in his hand, looks at it from all sides*]. Why, what a gorgeous bonnet you've been investing in!

MISS TESMAN. I bought it on Hedda's account!

TESMAN. On Hedda's account? Eh?

MISS TESMAN. Yes, so that Hedda needn't be ashamed of me if we happened to go out together.

TESMAN [*patting her cheek*]. You always think of everything, Aunt Julia. [*Lays the bonnet on a chair beside the table.*] And now, look here—suppose we sit comfortably on the sofa and have a little chat till Hedda comes. [*They seat themselves. She places her parasol in the corner of the sofa.*]

MISS TESMAN [*takes both his hands and looks at him*]. What a delight it is to have you again, as large as life, before my very eyes, George! My George—my poor brother's own boy!

TESMAN. And it's a delight for me, too, to see you again, Aunt Julia! You who have been father and mother in one to me.

MISS TESMAN. Oh yes, I know you will always keep a place in your heart for your old aunts.

TESMAN. And what about Aunt Rina? No improvement —eh?

MISS TESMAN. Oh no—we can scarcely look for any improvement in her case, poor thing. There she lies, helpless, as she has lain for all these years. But heaven grant I may not lose her yet awhile! For if I did, I don't know what I should make of my life, George—especially now that I haven't you to look after any more.

TESMAN [*patting her back*]. There, there, there!

MISS TESMAN [*suddenly changing her tone*]. And to think that here you are a married man, George! And that you should be the one to carry off Hedda Gabler—the beautiful Hedda Gabler! Only think of it—she that was so beset with admirers!

TESMAN [*hums a little and smiles complacently*]. Yes, I fancy I have several good friends about town who would like to stand in my shoes—eh?

MISS TESMAN. And then this fine long wedding tour you have had! More than five—nearly six months—

TESMAN. Well, for me it has been a sort of tour of research as well. I have had to do so much grubbing among old records—and to read no end of books too, Auntie.

MISS TESMAN. Oh yes, I suppose so. [*More confidentially and lowering her voice a little.*] But listen now, George—have you nothing—nothing special to tell me?

TESMAN. As to our journey?

MISS TESMAN. Yes.

TESMAN. No, I don't know of anything except what I have told you in my letters. I had a doctor's degree conferred on me—but that I told you yesterday.

MISS TESMAN. Yes, yes, you did. But what I mean is—haven't you any—any—expectations?

TESMAN. Expectations?

MISS TESMAN. Why, you know, George—I'm your old auntie!

TESMAN. Why, of course I have expectations.

MISS TESMAN. Ah!

TESMAN. I have every expectation of being a professor one of these days.

MISS TESMAN. Oh yes, a professor—

TESMAN. Indeed, I may say I am certain of it. But my dear auntie—you know all about that already!

MISS TESMAN [*laughing to herself*]. Yes, of course I do. You are right there. [*Changing the subject.*] But we were talking about your journey. It must have cost a great deal of money, George.

TESMAN. Well, you see—my handsome traveling scholarship went a good way.

MISS TESMAN. But I can't understand how you can have made it go far enough for two.

TESMAN. No, that's not so easy to understand—eh?

MISS TESMAN. And especially traveling with a lady— they tell me that makes it ever so much more expensive.

TESMAN. Yes, of course—it makes it a little more expensive. But Hedda had to have this trip, Auntie! She really had to. Nothing else would have done.

MISS TESMAN. No, no, I suppose not. A wedding tour seems to be quite indispensable nowadays. But tell me now—have you gone thoroughly over the house yet?

TESMAN. Yes, you may be sure I have. I have been afoot ever since daylight.

MISS TESMAN. And what do you think of it all?

TESMAN. I'm delighted! Quite delighted! Only I can't think what we are to do with the two empty rooms between this inner parlor and Hedda's bedroom.

MISS TESMAN [*laughing*]. Oh, my dear George, I daresay you may find some use for them—in the course of time.

TESMAN. Why, of course you are quite right, Aunt Julia! You mean as my library increases—eh?

MISS TESMAN. Yes, quite so, my dear boy. It was your
library I was thinking of.

TESMAN. I am specially pleased on Hedda's account.
Often and often, before we were engaged, she said
that she would never care to live anywhere but in
Secretary Falk's villa.

MISS TESMAN. Yes, it was lucky that this very house
should come into the market just after you had
started.

TESMAN. Yes, Aunt Julia, the luck was on our side,
wasn't it—eh?

MISS TESMAN. But the expense, my dear George! You
will find it very expensive, all this.

TESMAN [*looks at her a little cast down*]. Yes, I suppose
I shall, Aunt!

MISS TESMAN. Oh, frightfully!

TESMAN. How much do you think? In round numbers?
Eh?

MISS TESMAN. Oh, I can't even guess until all the accounts come in.

TESMAN. Well, fortunately Judge Brack has secured the
most favorable terms for me—so he said in a letter
to Hedda.

MISS TESMAN. Yes, don't be uneasy, my dear boy. Besides, I have given security for the furniture and all
the carpets.

TESMAN. Security? You? My dear aunt Julia—what sort
of security could you give?

MISS TESMAN. I have given a mortgage on our annuity.

TESMAN [*jumps up*]. What! on your—and Aunt Rina's
annuity!

MISS TESMAN. Yes, I knew of no other plan, you see.

TESMAN [*placing himself before her*]. Have you gone
out of your senses, Auntie? Your annuity—it's all
that you and Aunt Rina have to live upon.

MISS TESMAN. Well, well, don't get so excited about it.
It's only a matter of form, you know—Judge Brack

assured me of that. It was he that was kind enough
to arrange the whole affair for me. A mere matter of
form, he said.

TESMAN. Yes, that may be all very well. But nevertheless—

MISS TESMAN. You will have your own salary to depend
upon now. And, good heavens, even if we did have
to pay up a little—to eke things out a bit at the
start—! Why, it would be nothing but a pleasure to
us.

TESMAN. Oh, Auntie—will you never be tired of making sacrifices for me!

MISS TESMAN [*rises and lays her hands on his shoulders*].
Have I had any other happiness in this world except
to smooth your way for you, my dear boy? You who
have had neither father nor mother to depend on.
And now we have reached the goal, George! Things
have looked black enough for us sometimes; but,
thank heaven, now you have nothing to fear.

TESMAN. Yes, it is really marvelous how everything has
turned out for the best.

MISS TESMAN. And the people who opposed you—who
wanted to bar the way for you—now you have them
at your feet. They have fallen, George. Your most
dangerous rival—his fall was the worst. And now he
has to lie on the bed he has made for himself—poor
misguided creature.

TESMAN. Have you heard anything of Eilert? Since I
went away, I mean.

MISS TESMAN. Only that he is said to have published a
new book.

TESMAN. What! Eilert Lövborg! Recently—eh?

MISS TESMAN. Yes, so they say. Heaven knows whether
it can be worth anything! Ah, when your new book
appears—that will be another story, George! What
is it to be about?

TESMAN. It will deal with the domestic industries of
Brabant during the Middle Ages.

MISS TESMAN. Fancy—to be able to write on such a subject as that!

TESMAN. However, it may be some time before the book is ready. I have all these collections to arrange first, you see.

MISS TESMAN. Yes, collecting and arranging—no one can beat you at that. There you are my poor brother's own son.

TESMAN. I am looking forward eagerly to setting to work at it, especially now that I have my own delightful home to work in.

MISS TESMAN. And, most of all, now that you have got the wife of your heart, my dear George.

TESMAN [*embracing her*]. Oh yes, yes, Aunt Julia. Hedda—she is the best part of all! [*Looks toward the doorway.*] I believe I hear her coming—eh?

[HEDDA *enters from the left through the inner room. She is a woman of nine-and-twenty. Her face and figure show refinement and distinction. Her complexion is pale and opaque. Her steel-gray eyes express a cold, unruffled repose. Her hair is of an agreeable medium brown but not particularly abundant. She is dressed in a tasteful, somewhat loose-fitting morning gown.*]

MISS TESMAN [*going to meet* HEDDA]. Good morning, my dear Hedda! Good morning, and a hearty welcome.

HEDDA [*holds out her hand*]. Good morning, dear Miss Tesman! So early a call! That is kind of you.

MISS TESMAN [*with some embarrassment*]. Well—has the bride slept well in her new home?

HEDDA. Oh yes, thanks. Passably.

TESMAN [*laughing*]. Passably! Come, that's good, Hedda! You were sleeping like a stone when I got up.

HEDDA. Fortunately. Of course one has always to accustom one's self to new surroundings, Miss Tesman—little by little. [*Looking toward the left.*] Oh—there the servant has gone and opened the veranda door and let in a whole flood of sunshine.

MISS TESMAN [*going toward the door*]. Well, then, we will shut it.

HEDDA. No, no, not that! Tesman, please draw the curtains. That will give a softer light.

TESMAN [*at the door*]. All right—all right. There now, Hedda, now you have both shade and fresh air.

HEDDA. Yes, fresh air we certainly must have, with all these stacks of flowers— But—won't you sit down, Miss Tesman?

MISS TESMAN. No, thank you. Now that I have seen that everything is all right here—thank heaven!—I must be getting home again. My sister is lying longing for me, poor thing.

TESMAN. Give her my very best love, Auntie, and say I shall look in and see her later in the day.

MISS TESMAN. Yes, yes, I'll be sure to tell her. But by-the-bye, George—[*feeling in her dress pocket*]—I have—for you here—

TESMAN. What is it, Auntie? Eh?

MISS TESMAN [*produces a flat parcel wrapped in news-paper and hands it to him*]. Look here, my dear boy.

TESMAN [*opening the parcel*]. Well, I declare! Have you really saved them for me, Aunt Julia! Hedda! isn't this touching—eh?

HEDDA [*beside the whatnot on the right*]. Well, what is it?

TESMAN. My old morning shoes! My slippers.

HEDDA. Indeed. I remember you often spoke of them while we were abroad.

TESMAN. Yes, I missed them terribly. [*Goes up to her.*] Now you shall see them, Hedda!

HEDDA [*going toward the stove*]. Thanks, I really don't care about it.

TESMAN [*following her*]. Only think—ill as she was, Aunt Rina embroidered these for me. Oh, you can't think how many associations cling to them.

HEDDA [*at the table*]. Scarcely for me.

MISS TESMAN. Of course not for Hedda, George.

TESMAN. Well, but now that she belongs to the family, I thought—

HEDDA [*interrupting*]. We shall never get on with this servant, Tesman.

MISS TESMAN. Not get on with Berta?

TESMAN. Why, dear, what puts that in your head? Eh?

HEDDA [*pointing*]. Look there! She has left her old bonnet lying about on a chair.

TESMAN [*in consternation drops the slippers on the floor*]. Why, Hedda—

HEDDA. Just fancy if anyone should come in and see it!

TESMAN. But, Hedda—that's Aunt Julia's bonnet.

HEDDA. Is it!

MISS TESMAN [*taking up the bonnet*]. Yes, indeed it's mine. And, what's more, it's not old, Madame Hedda.

HEDDA. I really did not look closely at it, Miss Tesman.

MISS TESMAN [*trying on the bonnet*]. Let me tell you it's the first time I have worn it—the very first time.

TESMAN. And a very nice bonnet it is too—quite a beauty!

MISS TESMAN. Oh, it's no such great things, George. [*Looks around her.*] My parasol—? Ah, here. [*Takes it.*] For this is mine too [*mutters*]—not Berta's.

TESMAN. A new bonnet and a new parasol! Only think, Hedda!

HEDDA. Very handsome indeed.

TESMAN. Yes, isn't it? Eh? But, Auntie, take a good look at Hedda before you go! See how handsome she is!

MISS TESMAN. Oh, my dear boy, there's nothing new in that. Hedda was always lovely. [*She nods and goes toward the right.*]

TESMAN [*following*]. Yes, but have you noticed what splendid condition she is in? How she has filled out on the journey?

HEDDA [*crossing the room*]. Oh, do be quiet!

MISS TESMAN [*who has stopped and turned*]. Filled out?

TESMAN. Of course you don't notice it so much now that she has that dress on. But I, who can see—

HEDDA [*at the glass door, impatient*]. Oh, you can't see anything.

TESMAN. It must be the mountain air in the Tyrol—

HEDDA [*curtly interrupting*]. I am exactly as I was when I started.

TESMAN. So you insist, but I'm quite certain you are not. Don't you agree with me, Auntie?

MISS TESMAN [*who has been gazing at her with folded hands*]. Hedda is lovely—lovely—lovely. [*Goes up to her, takes her head between both hands, draws it downward and kisses her hair.*] God bless and preserve Hedda Tesman—for George's sake.

HEDDA [*gently freeing herself*]. Oh! Let me go.

MISS TESMAN [*in quiet emotion*]. I shall not let a day pass without coming to see you.

TESMAN. No, you won't, will you, Auntie? Eh?

MISS TESMAN. Good-by—good-by! [*She goes out by the hall door.* TESMAN *accompanies her. The door remains half open.* TESMAN *can be heard repeating his message to Aunt Rina and his thanks for the slippers. In the meantime* HEDDA *walks about the room raising her arms and clenching her hands as if in desperation. Then she flings back the curtains from the glass door and stands there looking out. Presently* TESMAN *returns and closes the door behind him.*]

TESMAN [*picks up the slippers from the floor*]. What are you looking at, Hedda?

HEDDA [*once more calm and mistress of herself*]. I am only looking at the leaves. They are so yellow—so withered.

TESMAN [*wraps up the slippers and lays them on the table*]. Well, you see, we are well into September now.

HEDDA [*again restless*]. Yes, to think of it! Already in—in September.

TESMAN. Don't you think Aunt Julia's manner was strange, dear? Almost solemn? Can you imagine what was the matter with her? Eh?

HEDDA. I scarcely know her, you see. Is she often like that?

TESMAN. No, not as she was today.

HEDDA [*leaving the glass door*]. Do you think she was annoyed about the bonnet?

TESMAN. Oh, scarcely at all. Perhaps a little, just at the moment—

HEDDA. But what an idea, to pitch her bonnet about in the drawing room! No one does that sort of thing.

TESMAN. Well, you may be sure Aunt Julia won't do it again.

HEDDA. In any case, I shall manage to make my peace with her.

TESMAN. Yes, my dear, good Hedda, if you only would.

HEDDA. When you call this afternoon you might invite her to spend the evening here.

TESMAN. Yes, that I will. And there's one thing more you could do that would delight her heart.

HEDDA. What is it?

TESMAN. If you could only prevail on yourself to say *du* to her. For my sake, Hedda? Eh?

HEDDA. No, no, Tesman—you really mustn't ask that of me. I have told you so already. I shall try to call her "Aunt," and you must be satisfied with that.

TESMAN. Well, well. Only I think now that you belong to the family, you—

HEDDA. H'm—I can't in the least see why. [*She goes up toward the middle doorway.*]

TESMAN [*after a pause*]. Is there anything the matter with you, Hedda? Eh?

HEDDA. I'm only looking at my old piano. It doesn't go at all well with all the other things.

TESMAN. The first time I draw my salary we'll see about exchanging it.

HEDDA. No, no—no exchanging. I don't want to part

with it. Suppose we put it there in the inner room and then get another here in its place. When it's convenient, I mean.

TESMAN [*a little taken aback*]. Yes—of course we could do that.

HEDDA [*takes up the bouquet from the piano*]. These flowers were not here last night when we arrived.

TESMAN. Aunt Julia must have brought them for you.

HEDDA [*examining the bouquet*]. A visiting card. [*Takes it out and reads*] "Shall return later in the day." Can you guess whose card it is?

TESMAN. No. Whose? Eh?

HEDDA. The name is Mrs Elvsted.

TESMAN. Is it really? Sheriff Elvsted's wife? Miss Rysing that was.

HEDDA. Exactly. The girl with the irritating hair, that she was always showing off. An old flame of yours I've been told.

TESMAN [*laughing*]. Oh, that didn't last long, and it was before I knew you, Hedda. But fancy her being in town!

HEDDA. It's odd that she should call upon us. I have scarcely seen her since we left school.

TESMAN. I haven't seen her either for—heaven knows how long. I wonder how she can endure to live in such an out-of-the-way hole—eh?

HEDDA [*after a moment's thought says suddenly*]: Tell me, Tesman—isn't it somewhere near there that he —that—Eilert Lövborg is living?

TESMAN. Yes, he is somewhere in that part of the country.

[BERTA *enters by the hall door.*]

BERTA. That lady, ma'am, that brought some flowers a little while ago, is here again. [*Pointing.*] The flowers you have in your hand, ma'am.

HEDDA. Ah, is she? Well, please show her in.

[BERTA *opens the door for* MRS ELVSTED *and goes out herself.* MRS ELVSTED *is a woman of fragile figure,*

*with pretty, soft features. Her eyes are light blue,
large, round and somewhat prominent, with a
startled, inquiring expression. Her hair is remarkably light, almost flaxen, and unusually abundant
and wavy. She is a couple of years younger than*
HEDDA. *She wears a dark visiting dress, tasteful but
not quite in the latest fashion.*]

HEDDA [*receives her warmly*]. How do you do, my dear
    Mrs Elvsted? It's delightful to see you again.

MRS ELVSTED [*nervously struggling for self-control*]. Yes,
    it's a very long time since we met.

TESMAN [*gives her his hand*]. And we too—eh?

HEDDA. Thanks for your lovely flowers—

MRS ELVSTED. Oh, not at all. I would have come straight
    here yesterday afternoon, but I heard that you were
    away.

TESMAN. Have you just come to town? Eh?

MRS ELVSTED. I arrived yesterday, about midday. Oh, I
    was quite in despair when I heard that you were not
    at home.

HEDDA. In despair! How so?

TESMAN. Why, my dear Mrs Rysing—I mean Mrs Elv-
    sted—

HEDDA. I hope that you are not in any trouble?

MRS ELVSTED. Yes, I am. And I don't know another liv-
    ing creature here that I can turn to.

HEDDA [*laying the bouquet on the table*]. Come—let us
    sit here on the sofa.

MRS ELVSTED. Oh, I am too restless to sit down.

HEDDA. Oh no, you're not. Come here. [*She draws* MRS
    ELVSTED *down upon the sofa and sits at her side.*]

TESMAN. Well? What is it, Mrs Elvsted?

HEDDA. Has anything particular happened to you at
    home?

MRS ELVSTED. Yes—and no. Oh—I am so anxious that
    you should not misunderstand me.

HEDDA. Then your best plan is to tell us the whole
    story, Mrs Elvsted.

TESMAN. I suppose that's what you have come for—eh?

MRS ELVSTED. Yes, yes—of course it is. Well then, I must tell you—if you don't already know—that Eilert Lövborg is in town too.

HEDDA. Lövborg!

TESMAN. What! Has Eilert Lövborg come back? Fancy that, Hedda!

HEDDA. Well, well—I hear it.

MRS ELVSTED. He has been here a week already. Just fancy—a whole week! In this terrible town, alone! With so many temptations on all sides.

HEDDA. But my dear Mrs Elvsted—how does he concern you so much?

MRS ELVSTED [looks at her with a startled air and says rapidly]: He was the children's tutor.

HEDDA. Your children's?

MRS ELVSTED. My husband's. I have none.

HEDDA. Your stepchildren's, then?

MRS ELVSTED. Yes.

TESMAN [somewhat hesitantly]. Then was he—I don't know how to express it—was he—regular enough in his habits to be fit for the post? Eh?

MRS ELVSTED. For the last two years his conduct has been irreproachable.

TESMAN. Has it, indeed? Fancy that, Hedda!

HEDDA. I hear it.

MRS ELVSTED. Perfectly irreproachable, I assure you! In every respect. But all the same—now that I know he is here—in this great town—and with a large sum of money in his hands—I can't help being in mortal fear for him.

TESMAN. Why did he not remain where he was? With you and your husband? Eh?

MRS ELVSTED. After his book was published he was too restless and unsettled to remain with us.

TESMAN. Yes; by-the-bye, Aunt Julia told me he had published a new book.

MRS ELVSTED. Yes, a big book, dealing with the march

of civilization—in broad outline, as it were. It came out about a fortnight ago. And since it has sold so well and been so much read—and made such a sensation—

TESMAN. Has it, indeed? It must be something he has had lying by since his better days.

MRS ELVSTED. Long ago, you mean?

TESMAN. Yes.

MRS ELVSTED. No, he has written it all since he has been with us—within the last year.

TESMAN. Isn't that good news, Hedda? Think of that.

MRS ELVSTED. Ah yes, if only it would last!

HEDDA. Have you seen him here in town?

MRS ELVSTED. No, not yet. I have had the greatest difficulty in finding out his address. But this morning I discovered it at last.

HEDDA [*looks searchingly at her*]. Do you know, it seems to me a little odd of your husband—h'm—

MRS ELVSTED [*starting nervously*]. Of my husband! What?

HEDDA. That he should send you to town on such an errand—that he does not come himself and look after his friend.

MRS ELVSTED. Oh no, no—my husband has no time. And besides, I—I have some shopping to do.

HEDDA [*with a slight smile*]. Ah, that is a different matter.

MRS ELVSTED [*rising quickly and uneasily*]. And now I beg and implore you, Mr Tesman—receive Eilert Lövborg kindly if he comes to you! And that he is sure to do. You see, you were such great friends in the old days. And then you are interested in the same studies—the same branch of science—so far as I can understand.

TESMAN. We used to be, at any rate.

MRS ELVSTED. That is why I beg so earnestly that you—you too—will keep a sharp eye upon him. Oh, you will promise me that, Mr Tesman—won't you?

TESMAN. With the greatest of pleasure Mrs Rysing—

HEDDA. Elvsted.

TESMAN. I assure you that I shall do all I possibly can for Eilert. You may rely upon me.

MRS ELVSTED. Oh, how very, very kind of you! [*Presses his hands.*] Thanks, thanks, thanks! [*Frightened.*] You see, my husband is very fond of him!

HEDDA [*rising*]. You ought to write to him, Tesman. Perhaps he may not care to come to you of his own accord.

TESMAN. Well, perhaps it would be the right thing to do, Hedda. Eh?

HEDDA. And the sooner the better. Why not at once?

MRS ELVSTED [*imploringly*]. Oh, if you only would!

TESMAN. I'll write this moment. Have you his address, Mrs—Mrs Elvsted?

MRS ELVSTED. Yes. [*Takes a slip of paper from her pocket and hands it to him.*] Here it is.

TESMAN. Good, good. Then I'll go in— [*Looks about him.*] By-the-bye, my slippers? Oh, here. [*Takes the packet and is about to go.*]

HEDDA. Be sure to write him a cordial, friendly letter. And a good long one too.

TESMAN. Yes, I will.

MRS ELVSTED. But please, please don't say a word to show that I have suggested it.

TESMAN. No, how could you think I would? Eh? [*He goes out to the right through the inner room.*]

HEDDA [*goes up to* MRS ELVSTED, *smiles and says in a low voice*]: There. We have killed two birds with one stone.

MRS ELVSTED. What do you mean?

HEDDA. Could you not see that I wanted him to go?

MRS ELVSTED. Yes, to write the letter—

HEDDA. And that I might speak to you alone?

MRS ELVSTED [*confused*]. About the same thing?

HEDDA. Precisely.

MRS ELVSTED [*apprehensively*]. But there is nothing more, Mrs Tesman! Absolutely nothing!

HEDDA. Oh yes, but there is. There is a great deal more —I can see that. Sit here—and we'll have a cosy, confidential chat. [*She forces* MRS ELVSTED *to sit in the easy chair beside the stove and seats herself on one of the footstools.*]

MRS ELVSTED [*anxiously looking at her watch*]. But, my dear Mrs Tesman—I was really on the point of going.

HEDDA. Oh, you can't be in such a hurry. Well? Now tell me something about your life at home.

MRS ELVSTED. Oh, that is just what I care least to speak about.

HEDDA. But to me, dear—? Why, weren't we school fellows?

MRS ELVSTED. Yes, but you were in the class above me. Oh, how dreadfully afraid of you I was then!

HEDDA. Afraid of me?

MRS ELVSTED. *Yes,* dreadfully. For when we met on the stairs you used always to pull my hair.

HEDDA. Did I really?

MRS ELVSTED. Yes, and once you said you would burn it off my head.

HEDDA. Oh, that was all nonsense, of course.

MRS ELVSTED. Yes, but I was so silly in those days. And since then, too—we have drifted so far—far apart from each other. Our circles have been so entirely different.

HEDDA. Well then, we must try to drift together again. Now listen! At school we said *du* to each other and we called each other by our Christian names—

MRS ELVSTED. No, I am sure you must be mistaken.

HEDDA. No, not at all! I can remember quite distinctly. So now we are going to renew our old friendship. [*Draws the footstool closer to* MRS ELVSTED.] There now! [*Kisses her cheek.*] You must say *du* to me and call me Hedda.

MRS ELVSTED [*presses and pats her hands*]. Oh, how good and kind you are! I am not used to such kindness.

HEDDA. There, there, there! And I shall say *du* to you, as in the old days, and call you my dear Thora.

MRS ELVSTED. My name is Thea.

HEDDA. Why, of course! I meant Thea. [*Looks at her compassionately*.] So you are not accustomed to goodness and kindness, Thea? Not in your own home?

MRS ELVSTED. Oh, if I only had a home! But I haven't any; I have never had a home.

HEDDA [*looks at her for a moment*]. I almost suspected as much.

MRS ELVSTED [*gazing helplessly before her*]. Yes—yes—yes.

HEDDA. I don't quite remember—was it not as housekeeper that you first went to Mr Elvsted's?

MRS ELVSTED. I really went as governess. But his wife—his late wife—was an invalid and rarely left her room. So I had to look after the housekeeping as well.

HEDDA. And then—at last—you became mistress of the house.

MRS ELVSTED [*sadly*]. Yes, I did.

HEDDA. Let me see—about how long ago was that?

MRS ELVSTED. My marriage?

HEDDA. Yes.

MRS ELVSTED. Five years ago.

HEDDA. To be sure, it must be that.

MRS ELVSTED. Oh, those five years! Or at all events the last two or three of them! Oh, if you could only imagine—

HEDDA [*giving her a little slap on the hand*]. De? Fie, Thea!

MRS ELVSTED. Yes, yes, I will try— Well, if—you could only imagine and understand—

HEDDA [*lightly*]. Eilert Lövborg has been in your neighborhood about three years, hasn't he?

MRS ELVSTED [*looks at her doubtfully*]. Eilert Lövborg? Yes—he has.

HEDDA. Had you known him before, in town here?

MRS ELVSTED. Scarcely at all. I mean—I knew him by name, of course.

HEDDA. But you saw a good deal of him in the country?

MRS ELVSTED. Yes, he came to us every day. You see, he gave the children lessons; for in the long run I couldn't manage it all myself.

HEDDA. No, that's clear. And your husband—? I suppose he is often away from home?

MRS ELVSTED. Yes. Being sheriff, you know, he has to travel about a good deal in his district.

HEDDA [*leaning against the arm of the chair*]. Thea—my poor, sweet Thea—now you must tell me everything—exactly as it stands.

MRS ELVSTED. Well then, you must question me.

HEDDA. What sort of man is your husband, Thea? I mean—you know—in everyday life. Is he kind to you?

MRS ELVSTED [*evasively*]. I am sure he means well in everything.

HEDDA. I should think he must be altogether too old for you. There is at least twenty years' difference between you, is there not?

MRS ELVSTED [*irritably*]. Yes, that is true too. Everything about him is repellent to me! We have not a thought in common. We have no single point of sympathy—he and I.

HEDDA. But is he not fond of you all the same? In his own way?

MRS ELVSTED. Oh, I really don't know. I think he regards me simply as a useful property. And then it doesn't cost much to keep me. I am not expensive.

HEDDA. That is stupid of you.

MRS ELVSTED [*shakes her head*]. It cannot be otherwise —not with him. I don't think he really cares for anyone but himself—and perhaps a little for the children.

HEDDA. And for Eilert Lövborg, Thea.

MRS ELVSTED [*looking at her*]. For Eilert Lövborg? What put that into your head?

HEDDA. Well, my dear—I should say when he sends you after him all the way to town—[*Smiling almost imperceptibly.*] And besides, you said so yourself to Tesman.

MRS ELVSTED [*with a little nervous twitch*]. Did I? Yes, I suppose I did. [*Vehemently but not loudly.*] No—I may just as well make a clean breast of it at once! For it must all come out in any case.

HEDDA. Why, my dear Thea—

MRS ELVSTED. Well, to make a long story short: My husband did not know that I was coming.

HEDDA. What! Your husband didn't know it!

MRS ELVSTED. No, of course not. For that matter, he was away from home himself—he was traveling. Oh, I could bear it no longer, Hedda! I couldn't indeed—so utterly alone as I should have been in future.

HEDDA. Well? And then?

MRS ELVSTED. So I put together some of my things—what I needed most—as quietly as possible. And then I left the house.

HEDDA. Without a word?

MRS ELVSTED. Yes—and took the train straight to town.

HEDDA. Why, my dear, good Thea—to think of you daring to do it!

MRS ELVSTED [*rises and moves about the room*]. What else could I possibly do?

HEDDA. But what do you think your husband will say when you go home again?

MRS ELVSTED [*at the table, looks at her*]. Back to him?

HEDDA. Of course.

MRS ELVSTED. I shall never go back to him again.

HEDDA [*rising and going toward her*]. Then you have left your home—for good and all?

MRS ELVSTED. Yes. There was nothing else to be done.

HEDDA. But then—to take flight so openly.

MRS ELVSTED. Oh, it's impossible to keep things of that sort secret.

HEDDA. But what do you think people will say of you, Thea?

MRS ELVSTED. They may say what they like for aught *I* care. [*Seats herself wearily and sadly on the sofa.*] I have done nothing but what I had to do.

HEDDA [*after a short silence*]. And what are your plans now? What do you think of doing?

MRS ELVSTED. I don't know yet. I only know this, that I must live here, where Eilert Lövborg is—if I am to live at all.

HEDDA [*takes a chair from the table, seats herself beside her and strokes her hands*]. My dear Thea—how did this—this friendship—between you and Eilert Lövborg come about?

MRS ELVSTED. Oh, it grew up gradually. I gained a sort of influence over him.

HEDDA. Indeed?

MRS ELVSTED. He gave up his old habits. Not because I asked him to, for I never dared do that. But of course he saw how repulsive they were to me, and so he dropped them.

HEDDA [*concealing an involuntary smile of scorn*]. Then you have reclaimed him—as the saying goes—my little Thea.

MRS ELVSTED. So he says himself, at any rate. And he, on his side, has made a real human being of me—taught me to think and to understand so many things.

HEDDA. Did he give you lessons too, then?

MRS ELVSTED. No, not exactly lessons. But he talked to me—talked about such an infinity of things. And then came the lovely, happy time when I began to share in his work—when he allowed me to help him!

HEDDA. Oh, he did, did he?

MRS ELVSTED. Yes! He never wrote anything without my assistance.

HEDDA. You were two good comrades, in fact?

MRS ELVSTED [*eagerly*]. Comrades! Yes, fancy, Hedda— that is the very word he used! Oh, I ought to feel perfectly happy, and yet I cannot, for I don't know how long it will last.

HEDDA. Are you no surer of him than that?

MRS ELVSTED [*gloomily*]. A woman's shadow stands between Eilert Lövborg and me.

HEDDA [*looks at her anxiously*]. Who can that be?

MRS ELVSTED. I don't know. Someone he knew in his— in his past. Someone he has never been able wholly to forget.

HEDDA. What has he told you—about this?

MRS ELVSTED. He has only once—quite vaguely—alluded to it.

HEDDA. Well! And what did say?

MRS ELVSTED. He said that when they parted she threatened to shoot him with a pistol.

HEDDA [*with cool composure*]. Oh, nonsense! No one does that sort of thing here.

MRS ELVSTED. No. And that is why I think it must have been that red-haired singing woman whom he once—

HEDDA. Yes, very likely.

MRS ELVSTED. For I remember they used to say of her that she carried loaded firearms.

HEDDA. Oh—then of course it must have been she.

MRS ELVSTED [*wringing her hands*]. And now just fancy. Hedda—I hear that this singing woman—that she is in town again! Oh, I don't know what to do.

HEDDA [*glancing toward the inner room*]. Hush! Here comes Tesman. [*Rises and whispers*]: Thea—all this must remain between you and me.

MRS ELVSTED [*springing up*]. Oh yes, yes! for heaven's sake!

[GEORGE TESMAN, *with a letter in his hand, comes from the right through the inner room.*]

TESMAN. There now—the epistle is finished.

HEDDA. That's right. And now Mrs Elvsted is just going. Wait a moment—I'll go with you to the garden gate.

TESMAN. Do you think Berta could post the letter, Hedda dear?

HEDDA [*takes it*]. I will tell her to.

[BERTA *enters from the hall.*]

BERTA. Judge Brack wishes to know if Mrs Tesman will receive him.

HEDDA. Yes, ask Judge Brack to come in. And look here —put this letter in the post.

BERTA [*taking the letter*]. Yes, ma'am. [*She opens the door for* JUDGE BRACK *and goes out herself.* BRACK *is a man of forty-five, thickset but well built and elastic in his movements. His face is roundish with an aristocratic profile. His hair is short, still almost black and carefully dressed. His eyes are lively and sparkling, his eyebrows thick. His mustaches are also thick with short-cut ends. He wears a well-cut walking suit, a little too youthful for his age. He uses an eyeglass which he now and then lets drop.*]

BRACK [*with his hat in his hand, bowing*]. May one venture to call so early in the day?

HEDDA. Of course one may.

TESMAN [*presses his hand*]. You are welcome at any time. [*Introducing him.*] Judge Brack—Miss Rysing—

HEDDA. Oh!

BRACK [*bowing*]. Ah—delighted!

HEDDA [*looks at him and laughs*]. It's nice to have a look at you by daylight, Judge!

BRACK. Do you find me—altered?

HEDDA. A little younger, I think.

BRACK. Thank you so much.

TESMAN. But what do you think of Hedda—eh? Doesn't she look flourishing? She has actually—

HEDDA. Oh, do leave me alone. You haven't thanked Judge Brack for all the trouble he has taken—

BRACK. Oh, nonsense—it was a pleasure to me.

HEDDA. Yes, you are a friend indeed. But here stands Thea all impatience to be off—so au revoir, Judge. I shall be back again presently. [*Mutual salutations.* MRS ELVSTED *and* HEDDA *go out by the hall door.*]

BRACK. Well, is your wife tolerably satisfied?

TESMAN. Yes, we can't thank you sufficiently. Of course she talks of a little rearrangement here and there, and one or two things are still wanting. We shall have to buy some additional trifles.

BRACK. Indeed!

TESMAN. But we won't trouble you about these things. Hedda says she herself will look after what is wanting. Shan't we sit down? Eh?

BRACK. Thanks, for a moment. [*Seats himself beside the table.*] There is something I wanted to speak to you about, my dear Tesman.

TESMAN. Indeed? Ah, I understand! [*Seating himself.*] I suppose it's the serious part of the frolic that is coming now. Eh?

BRACK. Oh, the money question is not so very pressing; though, for that matter, I wish we had gone a little more economically to work.

TESMAN. But that would never have done, you know! Think of Hedda, my dear fellow! You, who know her so well— I couldn't possibly ask her to put up with a shabby style of living!

BRACK. No, no—that is just the difficulty.

TESMAN. And then—fortunately—it can't be long before I receive my appointment.

BRACK. Well, you see—such things are often apt to hang fire for a time.

TESMAN. Have you heard anything definite? Eh?

BRACK. Nothing exactly definite— [*Interrupting himself.*] But by-the-bye—I have one piece of news for you.

TESMAN. Well?

BRACK. Your old friend Eilert Lövborg has returned to town.

TESMAN. I know that already.

BRACK. Indeed! How did you learn it?

TESMAN. From the lady who went out with Hedda.

BRACK. Really? What was her name? I didn't quite catch it.

TESMAN. Mrs Elvsted.

BRACK. Aha—Sheriff Elvsted's wife? Of course—he has been living up in their regions.

TESMAN. And fancy—I'm delighted to hear that he is quite a reformed character!

BRACK. So they say.

TESMAN. And then he has published a new book—eh?

BRACK. Yes, indeed he has.

TESMAN. And I hear it has made some sensation!

BRACK. Quite an unusual sensation.

TESMAN. Fancy—isn't that good news! A man of such extraordinary talents—I felt so grieved to think that he had gone irretrievably to ruin.

BRACK. That was what everybody thought.

TESMAN. But I cannot imagine what he will take to now! How in the world will he be able to make his living? Eh?

[*During the last words* HEDDA *has entered by the hall door.*]

HEDDA [*to* BRACK, *laughing with a touch of scorn*]. Tesman is forever worrying about how people are to make their living.

TESMAN. Well, you see, dear—we were talking about poor Eilert Lövborg.

HEDDA [*glancing at him rapidly*]. Oh, indeed? [*Seats herself in the armchair beside the stove and asks indifferently*]: What is the matter with him?

TESMAN. Well—no doubt he has run through all his property long ago, and he can scarcely write a new book every year—eh? So I really can't see what is to become of him.

BRACK. Perhaps I can give you some information on that point.

TESMAN. Indeed!

BRACK. You must remember that his relations have a good deal of influence.

TESMAN. Oh, his relations, unfortunately, have entirely washed their hands of him.

BRACK. At one time they called him the hope of the family.

TESMAN. At one time, yes! But he has put an end to all that.

HEDDA. Who knows? [*With a slight smile.*] I hear they have reclaimed him up at Sheriff Elvsted's.

BRACK. And then this book that he has published—

TESMAN. Well, well, I hope to goodness they may find something for him to do. I have just written to him. I asked him to come and see us this evening, Hedda dear.

BRACK. But, my dear fellow, you are booked for my bachelors' party this evening. You promised on the pier last night.

HEDDA. Had you forgotten, Tesman?

TESMAN. Yes, I had utterly forgotten.

BRACK. But it doesn't matter, for you may be sure he won't come.

TESMAN. What makes you think that? Eh?

BRACK [*with a little hesitation, rising and resting his hands on the back of his chair*]. My dear Tesman—and you too, Mrs Tesman—I think I ought not to keep you in the dark about something—that—that—

TESMAN. That concerns Eilert?

BRACK. Both you and him.

TESMAN. Well, my dear judge, out with it.

BRACK. You must be prepared to find your appointment deferred longer than you desired or expected.

TESMAN [*jumping up uneasily*]. Is there some hitch about it? Eh?

BRACK. The nomination may perhaps be made conditional on the result of a competition—

TESMAN. Competition! Think of that, Hedda!

HEDDA [*leans farther back in the chair*]. Aha—aah!

TESMAN. But who can my competitor be? Surely not—?

BRACK. Yes, precisely—Eilert Lövborg.

TESMAN [*clasping his hands*]. No, no—it's quite inconceivable! Quite impossible! Eh?

BRACK. H'm—that is what it may come to, all the same.

TESMAN. Well, but, Judge Brack—it would show the most incredible lack of consideration for me. [*Gesticulates with his arms.*] For—just think—I'm a married man. We have been married on the strength of these prospects, Hedda and I, and run deep into debt and borrowed money from Aunt Julia too. Good heavens, they had as good as promised me the appointment. Eh?

BRACK. Well, well, well—no doubt you will get it in the end; only after a contest.

HEDDA [*immovable in her armchair*]. Fancy, Tesman, there will be a sort of sporting interest in that.

TESMAN. Why, my dearest Hedda, how can you be so indifferent about it?

HEDDA [*as before*]. I am not at all indifferent. I am most eager to see who wins.

BRACK. In any case, Mrs Tesman, it is best that you should know how matters stand. I mean—before you set about the little purchases I hear you are threatening.

HEDDA. This can make no difference.

BRACK. Indeed! Then I have no more to say. Good-by! [*To* TESMAN.] I shall look in on my way back from my afternoon walk and take you home with me.

TESMAN. Oh yes, yes—your news has quite upset me.

HEDDA [*reclining, holds out her hand*]. Good-by, Judge, and be sure you call in the afternoon.

BRACK. Many thanks. Good-by, good-by!

TESMAN [*accompanying him to the door*]. Good-by, my dear judge! You must really excuse me. [JUDGE BRACK *goes out by the hall door.*]

TESMAN [*crosses the room*]. Oh, Hedda—one should never rush into adventures. Eh?

HEDDA [*looks at him smilingly*]. Do you do that?

TESMAN. Yes, dear—there is no denying—it was adventurous to go and marry and set up house upon mere expectations.

HEDDA. Perhaps you are right there.

TESMAN. Well—at all events, we have our delightful home, Hedda! Fancy, the home we both dreamed of—the home we were in love with, I may almost say. Eh?

HEDDA [*rising slowly and wearily*]. It was part of our compact that we were to go into society—to keep open house.

TESMAN. Yes, if you only knew how I had been looking forward to it! Fancy—to see you as hostess—in a select circle? Eh? Well, well, well—for the present we shall have to get on without society, Hedda—only to invite Aunt Julia now and then. Oh, I intended you to lead such an utterly different life, dear!

HEDDA. Of course I cannot have my man in livery just yet.

TESMAN. Oh no, unfortunately. It would be out of the question for us to keep a footman, you know.

HEDDA. And the saddle horse I was to have had—

TESMAN [*aghast*]. The saddle horse!

HEDDA. I suppose I must not think of that now.

TESMAN. Good heavens, no! That's as clear as daylight.

HEDDA [*goes up the room*]. Well, I shall have one thing at least to kill time with in the meanwhile.

TESMAN [*beaming*]. Oh, thank heaven for that! What is it, Hedda? Eh?

HEDDA [*in the middle doorway, looks at him with covert scorn*]. My pistols, George.

TESMAN [*in alarm*]. Your pistols!

HEDDA [*with cold eyes*]. General Gabler's pistols. [*She goes out through the inner room to the left.*]

TESMAN [*rushes up to the middle doorway and calls after her*]. No, for heaven's sake, Hedda darling— don't touch those dangerous things! For my sake, Hedda! Eh?

ACT TWO

SCENE—*The room at the* TESMANS' *as in the first act, except that the piano has been removed and an elegant little writing table with bookshelves put in its place. A smaller table stands near the sofa on the left. Most of the bouquets have been taken away.* MRS ELVSTED'S *bouquet is upon the large table in front. It is afternoon.*

HEDDA, *dressed to receive callers, is alone in the room. She stands by the open glass door loading a revolver. The fellow to it lies in an open pistol case on the writing table.*

HEDDA [*looks down the garden and calls*]. So you are here again, Judge!

BRACK [*is heard calling from a distance*]. As you see, Mrs Tesman!

HEDDA [*raises the pistol and points*]. Now I'll shoot you, Judge Brack!

BRACK [*calling unseen*]. No, no, no! Don't stand aiming at me!

HEDDA. This is what comes of sneaking in by the back way. [*She fires.*]

BRACK [*nearer*]. Are you out of your senses!

HEDDA. Dear me—did I happen to hit you?

BRACK [*still outside*]. I wish you would let these pranks alone!

HEDDA. Come in then, Judge.

[BRACK, *dressed as though for a men's party, enters by
the glass door. He carries a light overcoat over his
arm.*]

BRACK. What the deuce—haven't you tired of that sport
yet? What are you shooting at?

HEDDA. Oh, I am only firing in the air.

BRACK [*gently takes the pistol out of her hand*]. Allow
me, madam! [*Looks at it.*] Ah—I know this pistol
well! [*Looks around.*] Where is the case? Ah, here it
is. [*Lays the pistol in it and shuts it.*] Now we won't
play at that game any more today.

HEDDA. Then what in heaven's name would you have
me do with myself?

BRACK. Have you had no visitors?

HEDDA [*closing the glass door*]. Not one. I suppose all
our set are still out of town.

BRACK. And is Tesman not at home either?

HEDDA [*at the writing table, putting the pistol case in
a drawer which she shuts*]. No. He rushed off to his
aunt's directly after lunch; he didn't expect you so
early.

BRACK. H'm—how stupid of me not to have thought of
that!

HEDDA [*turning her head to look at him*]. Why stupid?

BRACK. Because if I had thought of it I should have
come a little—earlier.

HEDDA [*crossing the room*]. Then you would have found
no one to receive you, for I have been in my room
changing my dress ever since lunch.

BRACK. And is there no sort of little chink that we
could hold a parley through?

HEDDA. You have forgotten to arrange one.

BRACK. That was another piece of stupidity.

HEDDA. Well, we must just settle down here—and wait.
Tesman is not likely to be back for some time yet.

BRACK. Never mind; I shall not be impatient.

[HEDDA *seats herself in the corner of the sofa.* BRACK *lays
his overcoat over the back of the nearest chair and*

*sits down but keeps his hat in his hand. A short si-
lence. They look at each other.*]

HEDDA. Well?

BRACK [*in the same tone*]. Well?

HEDDA. I spoke first.

BRACK [*bending a little forward*]. Come, let us have a
cosy little chat, Mrs Hedda.

HEDDA [*leaning further back in the sofa*]. Does it not
seem like a whole eternity since our last talk? Of
course I don't count those few words yesterday evening and this morning.

BRACK. You mean since our last confidential talk? Our
last tête-à-tête?

HEDDA. Well, yes—since you put it so.

BRACK. Not a day has passed but I have wished that
you were home again.

HEDDA. And I have done nothing but wish the same
thing.

BRACK. You? Really, Mrs Hedda? And I thought you
had been enjoying your tour so much!

HEDDA. Oh yes, you may be sure of that!

BRACK. But Tesman's letters spoke of nothing but happiness.

HEDDA. Oh, Tesman! You see, he thinks nothing so delightful as grubbing in libraries and making copies
of old parchments, or whatever you call them.

BRACK [*with a spice of malice*]. Well, that is his vocation in life—or part of it at any rate.

HEDDA. Yes, of course; and no doubt when it's your
vocation— But *I!* Oh, my dear Mr Brack, how mortally bored I have been.

BRACK [*sympathetically*]. Do you really say so? In
downright earnest?

HEDDA. Yes, you can surely understand it! To go for
six whole months without meeting a soul that knew
anything of our circle or could talk about the things
we are interested in.

BRACK. Yes, yes—I too should feel that a deprivation.

HEDDA. And then, what I found most intolerable of all—

BRACK. Well?

HEDDA. —was being everlastingly in the company of— one and the same person.

BRACK [*with a nod of assent*]. Morning, noon and night, yes—at all possible times and seasons.

HEDDA. I said "everlastingly."

BRACK. Just so. But I should have thought with our excellent Tesman one could—

HEDDA. Tesman is—a specialist, my dear judge.

BRACK. Undeniably.

HEDDA. And specialists are not at all amusing to travel with. Not in the long run at any rate.

BRACK. Not even—the specialist one happens to love?

HEDDA. Faugh—don't use that sickening word!

BRACK [*taken aback*]. What do you say, Mrs Hedda?

HEDDA [*half laughing, half irritated*]. You should just try it! To hear of nothing but the history of civilization morning, noon and night—

BRACK. Everlastingly.

HEDDA. Yes, yes, yes! And then all this about the domestic industry of the Middle Ages! That's the most disgusting part of it!

BRACK [*looks searchingly at her*]. But tell me—in that case how am I to understand your—? H'm—

HEDDA. My accepting George Tesman, you mean?

BRACK. Well, let us put it so.

HEDDA. Good heavens, do you see anything so wonderful in that?

BRACK. Yes and no—Mrs Hedda.

HEDDA. I had positively danced myself tired, my dear judge. My day was done. [*With a slight shudder.*] Oh no—I won't say that, nor think it either!

BRACK. You have assuredly no reason to.

HEDDA. Oh, reasons— [*Watching him closely.*] And George Tesman—after all, you must admit that he is correctness itself.

BRACK. His correctness and respectability are beyond all
   question.

HEDDA. And I don't see anything absolutely ridiculous
   about him. Do you?

BRACK. Ridiculous? N-no—I shouldn't exactly say so.

HEDDA. Well—and his powers of research, at all events,
   are untiring. I see no reason why he should not one
   day come to the front after all.

BRACK [looks at her hesitatingly]. I thought that you,
   like everyone else, expected him to attain the highest
   distinction.

HEDDA [with an expression of fatigue]. Yes, so I did.
   And then—since he was bent, at all hazards, on being
   allowed to provide for me—I really don't know why
   I should not have accepted his offer?

BRACK. No—if you look at it in that light.

HEDDA. It was more than my other adorers were prepared to do for me, my dear judge.

BRACK [laughing]. Well, I can't answer for all the rest;
   but as for myself, you know quite well that I have always entertained a—a certain respect for the marriage
   tie—for marriage as an institution, Mrs Hedda.

HEDDA [jestingly]. Oh, I assure you I have never cherished any hopes with respect to you.

BRACK. All I require is a pleasant and intimate interior,
   where I can make myself useful in every way and am
   free to come and go as—as a trusted friend—

HEDDA. Of the master of the house, do you mean?

BRACK [bowing]. Frankly—of the mistress first of all;
   but of course of the master, too, in the second place.
   Such a triangular friendship—if I may call it so—is
   really a great convenience for all parties, let me tell
   you.

HEDDA. Yes, I have many a time longed for someone to
   make a third on our travels. Oh—those railway-car-
   riage tête-à-têtes!

BRACK. Fortunately your wedding journey is over
   now.

HEDDA [*shaking her head*]. Not by a long—long way. I have only arrived at a station on the line.

BRACK. Well, then the passengers jump out and move about a little, Mrs Hedda.

HEDDA. I never jump out.

BRACK. Really?

HEDDA. No—because there is always someone standing by to—

BRACK [*laughing*]. To look at your ankles, do you mean?

HEDDA. Precisely.

BRACK. Well, but, dear me—

HEDDA [*with a gesture of repulsion*]. I won't have it. I would rather keep my seat where I happen to be—and continue the tête-à-tête.

BRACK. But suppose a third person were to jump in and join the couple.

HEDDA. Ah—that is quite another matter!

BRACK. A trusted, sympathetic friend—

HEDDA. —with a fund of conversation on all sorts of lively topics—

BRACK. —and not the least bit of a specialist!

HEDDA [*with an audible sigh*]. Yes, that would be a relief indeed.

BRACK [*hears the front door open and glances in that direction*]. The triangle is completed.

HEDDA [*half aloud*]. And on goes the train.

[GEORGE TESMAN, *in a gray walking suit with a soft felt hat enters from the hall. He has a number of unbound books under his arm and in his pockets.*]

TESMAN [*goes up to the table beside the corner settee*]. Ouf—what a load for a warm day—all these books. [*Lays them on the table.*] I'm positively perspiring, Hedda. Hallo—are you there already, my dear judge? Eh? Berta didn't tell me.

BRACK [*rising*]. I came in through the garden.

HEDDA. What books have you got there?

TESMAN [*stands looking them through*]. Some new

books on my special subjects—quite indispensable to me.

HEDDA. Your special subjects?

BRACK. Yes, books on his special subjects, Mrs Tesman. [BRACK *and* HEDDA *exchange a confidential smile.*]

HEDDA. Do you need still more books on your special subjects?

TESMAN. Yes, my dear Hedda, one can never have too many of them. Of course one must keep up with all that is written and published.

HEDDA. Yes, I suppose one must.

TESMAN [*searching among his books*]. And look here— I have got hold of Eilert Lövborg's new book too. [*Offering it to her.*] Perhaps you would like to glance through it, Hedda? Eh?

HEDDA. No, thank you. Or rather—afterwards perhaps.

TESMAN. I looked into it a little on the way home.

BRACK. What do you think of it—as a specialist?

TESMAN. I think it shows quite remarkable soundness of judgment. He never wrote like that before. [*Putting the books together.*] Now I shall take all these into my study. I'm longing to cut the leaves! And then I must change my clothes. [*To* BRACK.] I suppose we needn't start just yet? Eh?

BRACK. Oh, dear no—there is not the slightest hurry.

TESMAN. Well then, I will take my time. [*Is going with his books but stops in the doorway and turns.*] By-the-bye, Hedda—Aunt Julia is not coming this evening.

HEDDA. Not coming? Is it that affair of the bonnet that keeps her away?

TESMAN. Oh, not at all. How could you think such a thing of Aunt Julia? Just fancy! The fact is, Aunt Rina is very ill.

HEDDA. She always is.

TESMAN. Yes, but today she is much worse than usual, poor dear.

HEDDA. Oh, then it's only natural that her sister should

remain with her. I must bear my disappointment.

TESMAN. And you can't imagine, dear, how delighted
Aunt Julia seemed to be—because you had come
home looking so flourishing!

HEDDA [*half aloud, rising*]. Oh, those everlasting aunts!

TESMAN. What?

HEDDA [*going to the glass door*]. Nothing.

TESMAN. Oh, all right. [*He goes through the inner
room, out to the right.*] ·

BRACK. What bonnet were you talking about?

HEDDA. Oh, it was a little episode with Miss Tesman
this morning. She had lain down her bonnet on the
chair there—[*looks at him and smiles*]—and I pretended to think it was the servant's.

BRACK [*shaking his head*]. Now my dear Mrs Hedda,
how could you do such a thing? To that excellent
old lady too!

HEDDA [*nervously crossing the room*]. Well, you see—
these impulses come over me all of a sudden, and I
cannot resist them. [*Throws herself down in the easy
chair by the stove.*] Oh, I don't know how to explain it.

BRACK [*behind the easy chair*]. You are not really happy
—that is the bottom of it.

HEDDA [*looking straight before her*]. I know of no reason why I should be—happy. Perhaps you can give
me one?

BRACK. Well—amongst other things, because you have
got exactly the home you had set your heart on.

HEDDA [*looks up at him and laughs*]. Do you too believe
in that legend?

BRACK. Is there nothing in it, then?

HEDDA. Oh yes, there is something in it.

BRACK. Well?

HEDDA. There is this in it, that I made use of Tesman
to see me home from evening parties last summer—

BRACK. I, unfortunately, had to go quite a different
way.

HEDDA. That's true. I know you were going a different way last summer.

BRACK [*laughing*]. Oh! fie, Mrs Hedda! Well, then—you and Tesman—?

HEDDA. Well, we happened to pass here one evening; Tesman, poor fellow, was writhing in the agony of having to find conversation; so I took pity on the learned man—

BRACK [*smiles doubtfully*]. You took pity? H'm—

HEDDA. Yes, I really did. And so—to help him out of his torment—I happened to say, in pure thoughtlessness, that I should like to live in this villa.

BRACK. No more than that?

HEDDA. Not that evening.

BRACK. But afterward—

HEDDA. Yes, my thoughtlessness had consequences, my dear judge.

BRACK. Unfortunately that too often happens, Mrs Hedda.

HEDDA. Thanks! So you see it was this enthusiasm for Secretary Falk's villa that first constituted a bond of sympathy between George Tesman and me. From that came our engagement and our marriage and our wedding journey and all the rest of it. Well, well, my dear judge—as you make your bed so you must lie, I could almost say.

BRACK. This is exquisite! And you really cared not a rap about it all the time?

HEDDA. No, heaven knows I didn't.

BRACK. But now? Now that we have made it so home-like for you?

HEDDA. Uh—the rooms all seem to smell of lavender and dried love leaves. But perhaps it's Aunt Julia that has brought that scent with her.

BRACK [*laughing*]. No, I think it must be a legacy from the late Mrs Secretary Falk.

HEDDA. Yes, there is an odor of mortality about it. It reminds me of a bouquet—the day after the ball.

[*Clasps her hands behind her head, leans back in her chair and looks at him.*] Oh, my dear judge—you cannot imagine how horribly I shall bore myself here.

BRACK. Why should not you too find some sort of vocation in life, Mrs Hedda?

HEDDA. A vocation—that should attract me?

BRACK. If possible, of course.

HEDDA. Heaven knows what sort of a vocation that could be. I often wonder whether— [*Breaking off.*] But that would never do either.

BRACK. Who can tell? Let me hear what it is.

HEDDA. Whether I might not get Tesman to go into politics, I mean.

BRACK [*laughing*]. Tesman? No, really now, political life is not the thing for him—not at all in his line.

HEDDA. No, I daresay not. But if I could get him into it all the same?

BRACK. Why—what satisfaction could you find in that? If he is not fitted for that sort of thing, why should you want to drive him into it?

HEDDA. Because I am bored, I tell you! [*After a pause.*] So you think it quite out of the question that Tesman should ever get into the ministry?

BRACK. H'm—you see, my dear Mrs Hedda—to get into the ministry he would have to be a tolerably rich man.

HEDDA [*rising impatiently*]. Yes, there we have it! It is this genteel poverty I have managed to drop into! [*Crosses the room.*] That is what makes life so pitiable! So utterly ludicrous! For that's what it is.

BRACK. Now I should say the fault lay elsewhere.

HEDDA. Where, then?

BRACK. You have never gone through any really stimulating experience.

HEDDA. Anything serious, you mean?

BRACK. Yes, you may call it so. But now you may perhaps have one in store.

HEDDA [*tossing her head*]. Oh, you're thinking of the annoyances about this wretched professorship! But that must be Tesman's own affair. I assure you I shall not waste a thought upon it.

BRACK. No, no, I daresay not. But suppose now that what people call—in elegant language—a solemn responsibility were to come upon you? [*Smiling.*] A new responsibility, Mrs Hedda?

HEDDA [*angrily*]. Be quiet! Nothing of that sort will ever happen!

BRACK [*warily*]. We will speak of this again a year hence—at the very outside.

HEDDA [*curtly*]. I have no turn for anything of the sort, Judge Brack. No responsibilities for me!

BRACK. Are you so unlike the generality of women as to have no turn for duties which—

HEDDA [*beside the glass door*]. Oh, be quiet, I tell you! I often think there is only one thing in the world I have any turn for.

BRACK [*drawing near to her*]. And what is that, if I may ask?

HEDDA [*stands looking out*]. Boring myself to death. Now you know it. [*Turns, looks toward the inner room and laughs.*] Yes, as I thought! Here comes the professor.

BRACK [*softly, in a tone of warning*]. Come, come, come, Mrs Hedda!

[GEORGE TESMAN, *dressed for the party, with his gloves and hat in his hand, enters from the right through the inner room.*]

TESMAN. Hedda, has no message come from Eilert Lövborg? Eh?

HEDDA. No.

TESMAN. Then you'll see he'll be here presently.

BRACK. Do you really think he'll come?

TESMAN. Yes, I am almost sure of it. For what you were telling us this morning must have been a mere floating rumor.

BRACK. You think so?

TESMAN. At any rate, Aunt Julia said she did not believe for a moment that he would ever stand in my way again. Fancy that!

BRACK. Well then, that's all right.

TESMAN [*placing his hat and gloves on a chair on the right*]. Yes, but you must really let me wait for him as long as possible.

BRACK. We have plenty of time yet. None of my guests will arrive before seven or half-past.

TESMAN. Then meanwhile we can keep Hedda company and see what happens. Eh?

HEDDA [*placing* BRACK's *hat and overcoat upon the corner settee*]. And at the worst Mr Lövborg can remain here with me.

BRACK [*offering to take his things*]. Oh, allow me, Mrs Tesman! What do you mean by "at the worst"?

HEDDA. If he won't go with you and Tesman.

TESMAN [*looks dubiously at her*]. But, Hedda dear—do you think it would quite do for him to remain with you? Eh? Remember, Aunt Julia can't come.

HEDDA. No, but Mrs Elvsted is coming. We three can have a cup of tea together.

TESMAN. Oh yes, that will be all right.

BRACK [*smiling*]. And that would perhaps be the safest plan for him.

HEDDA. Why so?

BRACK. Well, you know, Mrs Tesman, how you used to gird at my little bachelor parties. You declared they were adapted only for men of the strictest principles.

HEDDA. But no doubt Mr Lövborg's principles are strict enough now. A converted sinner— [BERTA *appears at the hall door.*]

BERTA. There's a gentleman asking if you are at home, ma'am.

HEDDA. Well, show him in.

TESMAN [*softly*]. I'm sure it is he! Fancy that!

[EILERT LÖVBORG *enters from the hall. He is slim and lean, of the same age as* TESMAN *but looks older and somewhat worn out. His hair and beard are of a blackish brown, his face long and pale but with patches of color on the cheekbones. He is dressed in a well-cut black visiting suit, quite new. He has dark gloves and a silk hat. He stops near the door and makes a rapid bow, seeming somewhat embarrassed.*]

TESMAN [*goes up to him and shakes him warmly by the hand*]. Well, my dear Eilert—so at last we meet again!

LÖVBORG [*speaks in a subdued voice*]. Thanks for your letter, Tesman. [*Approaching* HEDDA.] Will you too shake hands with me, Mrs Tesman?

HEDDA [*taking his hand*]. I am glad to see you, Mr Löv- borg. [*With a motion of her hand.*] I don't know whether you two gentlemen—

LÖVBORG [*bowing slightly*]. Judge Brack, I think.

BRACK [*doing likewise*]. Oh yes—in the old days—

TESMAN [*to* LÖVBORG, *with his hands on his shoulders*]. And now you must make yourself entirely at home, Eilert! Mustn't he, Hedda? For I hear you are going to settle in town again. Eh?

LÖVBORG. Yes, I am.

TESMAN. Quite right, quite right. Let me tell you, I have got hold of your new book but I haven't had time to read it yet.

LÖVBORG. You may spare yourself the trouble.

TESMAN. Why so?

LÖVBORG. Because there is very little in it.

TESMAN. Just fancy—how can you say so?

BRACK. But it has been very much praised, I hear.

LÖVBORG. That was what I wanted; so I put nothing into the book but what everyone would agree with.

TESMAN. Well, but, my dear Eilert—

BRACK. Very wise of you.

LÖVBORG. For now I mean to win myself a position again—to make a fresh start.

TESMAN [*a little embarrassed*]. Ah, that is what you
wish to do? Eh?

LÖVBORG [*smiling, lays down his hat and draws a
packet, wrapped in paper, from his coat pocket*]. But
when this one appears, George Tesman, you will
have to read it. For this is the real book—the book
I have put my true self into.

TESMAN. Indeed? And what is it?

LÖVBORG. It is the continuation.

TESMAN. The continuation? Of what?

LÖVBORG. Of the book.

TESMAN. Of the new book?

LÖVBORG. Of course.

TESMAN. Why, my dear Eilert—does it not come down
to our own days?

LÖVBORG. Yes, it does; and this one deals with the future.

TESMAN. With the future! But, good heavens, we know
nothing of the future!

LÖVBORG. No, but there is a thing or two to be said
about it all the same. [*Opens the packet.*] Look
here—

TESMAN. Why, that's not your handwriting.

LÖVBORG. I dictated it. [*Turning over the pages.*] It falls
into two sections. The first deals with the civilizing
forces of the future. And here is the second—[*running through the pages toward the end*]—forecasting
the probable line of development.

TESMAN. How odd now! I should never have thought of
writing anything of that sort.

HEDDA [*at the glass door, drumming on the pane*]. H'm
—I daresay not.

LÖVBORG [*replacing the manuscript in its paper and
laying the packet on the table*]. I brought it thinking I might read you a little of it this evening.

TESMAN. That was very good of you, Eilert. But this
evening—? [*Looking at* BRACK.] I don't quite see how
we can manage it.

LÖVBORG. Well then, some other time. There is no hurry.

BRACK. I must tell you, Mr Lövborg—there is a little gathering at my house this evening—mainly in honor of Tesman, you know.

LÖVBORG [*looking for his hat*]. Oh—then I won't detain you.

BRACK. No, but listen—will you not do me the favor of joining us?

LÖVBORG [*curtly and decidedly*]. No, I can't—thank you very much.

BRACK. Oh, nonsense—do! We shall be quite a select little circle. And I assure you we shall have a "lively time," as Mrs Hed—as Mrs Tesman says.

LÖVBORG. I have no doubt of it. But nevertheless—

BRACK. And then you might bring your manuscript with you and read it to Tesman at my house. I could give you a room to yourselves.

TESMAN. Yes, think of that, Eilert—why shouldn't you? Eh?

HEDDA [*interposing*]. But, Tesman, if Mr Lövborg would really rather not! I am sure Mr Lövborg is much more inclined to remain here and have supper with me.

LÖVBORG [*looking at her*]. With you, Mrs Tesman?

HEDDA. And with Mrs Elvsted.

LÖVBORG. Ah! [*Lightly.*] I saw her for a moment this morning.

HEDDA. Did you? Well, she is coming this evening. So you see you are almost bound to remain, Mr Lövborg, or she will have no one to see her home.

LÖVBORG. That's true. Many thanks, Mrs Tesman—in that case I will remain.

HEDDA. Then I have one or two orders to give the servant. [*She goes to the hall door and rings.* BERTA *enters.* HEDDA *talks to her in a whisper and points toward the inner room.* BERTA *nods and goes out again.*]

TESMAN [*at the same time to* LÖVBORG]. Tell me, Eilert—
is it this new subject—the future—that you are going
to lecture about?

LÖVBORG. Yes.

TESMAN. They told me at the book seller's that you are
going to deliver a course of lectures this autumn.

LÖVBORG. That is my intention. I hope you won't take
it ill, Tesman.

TESMAN. Oh no, not in the least! But—

LÖVBORG. I can quite understand that it must be disagreeable to you.

TESMAN [*cast down*]. Oh, I can't expect you, out of consideration for me, to—

LÖVBORG. But I shall wait till you have received your
appointment.

TESMAN. Will you wait? Yes, but—are you not going to
compete with me? Eh?

LÖVBORG. No; it is only the moral victory I care for.

TESMAN. Why, bless me—then Aunt Julia was right
after all! Oh yes—I knew it! Hedda! Just fancy—
Eilert Lövborg is not going to stand in our way!

HEDDA [*curtly*]. Our way? Pray leave me out of the question. [*She goes up toward the inner room where*
BERTA *is placing a tray with decanters and glasses on
the table.* HEDDA *nods approval and comes forward
again.* BERTA *goes out.*]

TESMAN [*at the same time*]. And you, Judge Brack—
what do you say to this? Eh?

BRACK. Well, I say that a moral victory—h'm—may be
all very fine—

TESMAN. Yes, certainly. But all the same—

HEDDA [*looking at* TESMAN *with a cold smile*]. You stand
there looking as if you were thunderstruck.

TESMAN. Yes—so I am—I almost think—

BRACK. Don't you see, Mrs Tesman, a thunderstorm
has just passed over?

HEDDA [*pointing toward the inner room*]. Will you not
take a glass of cold punch, gentlemen?

BRACK [*looking at his watch*]. A stirrup cup? Yes, it wouldn't come amiss.

TESMAN. A capital idea, Hedda! Just the thing! Now that the weight has been taken off my mind—

HEDDA. Will you not join them, Mr Lövborg?

LÖVBORG [*with a gesture of refusal*]. No, thank you. Nothing for me.

BRACK. Why, bless me—cold punch is surely not poison.

LÖVBORG. Perhaps not for everyone.

HEDDA. I will keep Mr Lövborg company in the meantime.

TESMAN. Yes, yes, Hedda dear, do. [*He and* BRACK *go into the inner room, seat themselves, drink punch, smoke cigarettes and carry on a lively conversation during what follows.* EILERT LÖVBORG *remains beside the stove.* HEDDA *goes to the writing table.*]

HEDDA [*raising her voice a little*]. Do you care to look at some photographs, Mr Lövborg? You know Tesman and I made a tour in the Tyrol on our way home. [*She takes up an album and places it on the table beside the sofa, in the further corner of which she seats herself.* EILERT LÖVBORG *approaches, stops and looks at her. Then he takes a chair and seats himself at her left, with his back toward the inner room.*]

HEDDA [*opening the album*]. Do you see this range of mountains, Mr Lövborg? It's the Ortler group. Tesman has written the name underneath. Here it is: "The Ortler group near Meran."

LÖVBORG [*who has never taken his eyes off her, says softly and slowly*]: Hedda—Gabler!

HEDDA [*glancing hastily at him*]. Ah! Hush!

LÖVBORG [*repeats softly*]. Hedda Gabler!

HEDDA [*looking at the album*]. That was my name in the old days—when we two knew each other.

LÖVBORG. And I must teach myself never to say Hedda Gabler again—never, as long as I live.

HEDDA [*still turning over the pages*]. Yes, you must. And

I think you ought to practice in time. The sooner the better, I should say.

LÖVBORG [*in a tone of indignation*]. Hedda Gabler married? And married to—George Tesman!

HEDDA. Yes—so the world goes.

LÖVBORG. Oh, Hedda, Hedda—how could you throw yourself away!

HEDDA [*looks sharply at him*]. What? I can't allow this!

LÖVBORG. What do you mean? [TESMAN *comes into the room and goes toward the sofa.*]

HEDDA [*hears him coming and says in an indifferent tone*]: And this is a view from the Val d'Ampezzo, Mr Lövborg. Just look at these peaks! [*Looks affectionately up at* TESMAN.] What's the name of these curious peaks, dear?

TESMAN. Let me see. Oh, those are the Dolomites.

HEDDA. Yes, that's it! Those are the Dolomites, Mr Lövborg.

TESMAN. Hedda dear, I only wanted to ask whether I shouldn't bring you a little punch after all? For yourself at any rate—eh?

HEDDA. Yes, do, please; and perhaps a few biscuits.

TESMAN. No cigarettes?

HEDDA. No.

TESMAN. Very well. [*He goes into the inner room and out to the right.* BRACK *sits in the inner room and keeps an eye from time to time on* HEDDA *and* LÖVBORG.]

LÖVBORG [*softly, as before*]. Answer me, Hedda—how could you go and do this?

HEDDA [*apparently absorbed in the album*]. If you continue to say *du* to me I won't talk to you.

LÖVBORG. May I not say *du* when we are alone?

HEDDA. No. You may think it, but you mustn't say it.

LÖVBORG. Ah, I understand. It is an offense against George Tesman, whom you—love.

HEDDA [*glances at him and smiles*]. Love? What an idea!

LÖVBORG. You don't love him, then!

HEDDA. But I won't hear of any sort of unfaithfulness! Remember that.

LÖVBORG. Hedda—answer me one thing—

HEDDA. Hush!

[TESMAN *enters with a small tray from the inner room.*]

TESMAN. Here you are! Isn't this tempting? [*He puts the tray on the table.*]

HEDDA. Why do you bring it yourself?

TESMAN [*filling the glasses*]. Because I think it's such fun to wait upon you, Hedda.

HEDDA. But you have poured out two glasses. Mr Lövborg said he wouldn't have any.

TESMAN. No, but Mrs Elvsted will soon be here, won't she?

HEDDA. Yes, by-the-bye—Mrs Elvsted.

TESMAN. Had you forgotten her? Eh?

HEDDA. We were so absorbed in these photographs. [*Shows him a picture.*] Do you remember this little village?

TESMAN. Oh, it's that one just below the Brenner Pass. It was there we passed the night—

HEDDA. —and met that lively party of tourists.

TESMAN. Yes, that was the place. Fancy—if we could only have had you with us, Eilert! Eh? [*He returns to the inner room and sits beside* BRACK.]

LÖVBORG. Answer me this one thing, Hedda.

HEDDA. Well?

LÖVBORG. Was there no love in your friendship for me either? Not a spark—not a tinge of love in it?

HEDDA. I wonder if there was? To me it seems as though we were two good comrades—two thoroughly intimate friends. [*Smilingly.*] You especially were frankness itself.

LÖVBORG. It was you that made me so.

HEDDA. As I look back upon it all I think there was really something beautiful, something fascinating—something daring—in—in that secret intimacy—that comradeship which no living creature so much as dreamed of.

LÖVBORG. Yes, yes, Hedda! Was there not? When I used to come to your father's in the afternoon—and the general sat over at the window reading his papers—with his back toward us—

HEDDA. And we two on the corner sofa—

LÖVBORG. Always with the same illustrated paper before us—

HEDDA. For want of an album, yes.

LÖVBORG. Yes, Hedda, and when I made my confessions to you—told you about myself, things that at that time no one else knew! There I would sit and tell you of my escapades—my days and nights of devilment. Oh, Hedda—what was the power in you that forced me to confess these things?

HEDDA. Do you think it was any power in me?

LÖVBORG. How else can I explain it? And all those—those roundabout questions you used to put to me—

HEDDA. Which you understood so particularly well—

LÖVBORG. How could you sit and question me like that? Question me quite frankly—

HEDDA. In roundabout terms, please observe.

LÖVBORG. Yes, but frankly nevertheless. Cross-question me about—all that sort of thing?

HEDDA. And how could you answer, Mr Lövborg?

LÖVBORG. Yes, that is just what I can't understand—in looking back upon it. But tell me now, Hedda—was there not love at the bottom of our friendship? On your side did you not feel as though you might purge my stains away if I made you my confessor? Was it not so?

HEDDA. No, not quite.

LÖVBORG. What was your motive, then?

HEDDA. Do you think it quite incomprehensible that a young girl—when it can be done—without anyone knowing—

LÖVBORG. Well?

HEDDA. — should be glad to have a peep, now and then, into a world which—

LÖVBORG. Which—?

HEDDA. —which she is forbidden to know anything about?

LÖVBORG. So that was it?

HEDDA. Partly. Partly—I almost think.

LÖVBORG. Comradeship in the thirst for life. But why should not that, at any rate, have continued?

HEDDA. The fault was yours.

LÖVBORG. It was you that broke with me.

HEDDA. Yes, when our friendship threatened to develop into something more serious. Shame upon you, Eilert Lövborg! How could you think of wronging your—your frank comrade?

LÖVBORG [clenching his hands]. Oh, why did you not carry out your threat? Why did you not shoot me down?

HEDDA. Because I have such a dread of scandal.

LÖVBORG. Yes, Hedda, you are a coward at heart.

HEDDA. A terrible coward. [Changing her tone.] But it was a lucky thing for you. And now you have found ample consolation at the Elvsteds'.

LÖVBORG. I know what Thea has confided to you.

HEDDA. And perhaps you have confided to her something about us?

LÖVBORG. Not a word. She is too stupid to understand anything of that sort.

HEDDA. Stupid?

LÖVBORG. She is stupid about matters of that sort.

HEDDA. And I am cowardly. [Bends over toward him, without looking him in the face, and says more softly]: But now I will confide something to you.

LÖVBORG [eagerly]. Well?

HEDDA. The fact that I dared not shoot you down—

LÖVBORG. Yes!

HEDDA. —that was not my most arrant cowardice—that evening.

LÖVBORG [*looks at her a moment, understands and whispers passionately*]: Oh, Hedda! Hedda Gabler! Now I begin to see a hidden reason beneath our comradeship! You and I! After all, then, it was your craving for life—

HEDDA [*softly, with a sharp glance*]. Take care! Believe nothing of the sort!

[*Twilight has begun to fall. The hall door is opened from without by* BERTA.]

HEDDA [*closes the album with a bang and calls smilingly*]: Ah, at last! My darling Thea—come along!

[MRS ELVSTED *enters from the hall. She is in evening dress. The door is closed behind her.*]

HEDDA [*on the sofa, stretches out her arms toward her*]. My sweet Thea—you can't think how I have been longing for you!

[MRS ELVSTED, *in passing, exchanges slight salutations with the gentlemen in the inner room, then goes up to the table and gives* HEDDA *her hands.* EILERT LÖVBORG *has risen. He and* MRS ELVSTED *greet each other with a silent nod.*]

MRS ELVSTED. Ought I go in and talk to your husband for a moment?

HEDDA. Oh, not at all. Leave those two alone. They will soon be going.

MRS ELVSTED. Are they going out?

HEDDA. Yes, to a supper party.

MRS ELVSTED [*quickly, to* LÖVBORG]. Not you?

LÖVBORG. No.

HEDDA. Mr Lövborg remains with us.

MRS ELVSTED [*takes a chair and is about to seat herself at his side*]. Oh, how nice it is here!

HEDDA. No, thank you, my little Thea! Not there! You'll be good enough to come over here to me. I will sit between you.

MRS ELVSTED. Yes, just as you please. [*She goes round the table and seats herself on the sofa on* HEDDA'S *right.* LÖVBORG *reseats himself on his chair.*]

LÖVBORG [*after a short pause, to* HEDDA]. Is not she lovely to look at?

HEDDA [*lightly stroking her hair*]. Only to look at?

LÖVBORG. Yes. For we two—she and I—we are two real comrades. We have absolute faith in each other; so we can sit and talk with perfect frankness—

HEDDA. Not roundabout, Mr Lövborg?

LÖVBORG. Well—

MRS ELVSTED [*softly clinging close to* HEDDA.] Oh, how happy I am, Hedda; for, only think, he says I have inspired him too.

HEDDA [*looks at her with a smile*]. Ah! Does he say that, dear?

LÖVBORG. And then she is so brave, Mrs Tesman!

MRS ELVSTED. Good heavens—am I brave?

LÖVBORG. Exceedingly—where your comrade is concerned.

HEDDA. Ah yes—courage! If one only had that!

LÖVBORG. What then? What do you mean?

HEDDA. Then life would perhaps be livable after all. [*With a sudden change of tone.*] But now, my dearest Thea, you really must have a glass of cold punch.

MRS ELVSTED. No, thanks—I never take anything of that kind.

HEDDA. Well then, you, Mr Lövborg.

LÖVBORG. Nor I, thank you.

MRS ELVSTED. No, he doesn't either.

HEDDA [*looks fixedly at him*]. But if I say you shall?

LÖVBORG. It would be no use.

HEDDA [*laughing*]. Then I, poor creature, have no sort of power over you?

LÖVBORG. Not in that respect.

HEDDA. But seriously, I think you ought to—for your own sake.

MRS ELVSTED. Why, Hedda!

LÖVBORG. How so?

HEDDA. Or rather on account of other people.

LÖVBORG. Indeed?

HEDDA. Otherwise people might be apt to suspect that—in your heart of hearts—you did not feel quite secure —quite confident of yourself.

MRS ELVSTED [*softly*]. Oh! please, Hedda—

LÖVBORG. People may suspect what they like—for the present.

MRS ELVSTED [*joyfully*]. Yes, let them!

HEDDA. I saw it plainly in Judge Brack's face a moment ago.

LÖVBORG. What did you see?

HEDDA. His contemptuous smile when you dared not go with them into the inner room.

LÖVBORG. Dared not? Of course I preferred to stop here and talk to you.

MRS ELVSTED. What could be more natural, Hedda?

HEDDA. But the judge could not guess that. And I saw, too, the way he smiled and glanced at Tesman when you dared not accept his invitation to this wretched little supper party of his.

LÖVBORG. Dared not? Do you say I dared not?

HEDDA. I don't say so. But that was how Judge Brack understood it.

LÖVBORG. Well, let him.

HEDDA. Then you are not going with them?

LÖVBORG. I will stay here with you and Thea.

MRS ELVSTED. Yes, Hedda—how can you doubt that?

HEDDA [*smiles and nods approvingly to* LÖVBORG]. Firm as a rock! Faithful to your principles now and forever! Ah, that is how a man should be! [*Turns to* MRS ELVSTED *and caresses her.*] Well now, what did I tell you when you came to us this morning in such a state of distraction—

LÖVBORG [*surprised*]. Distraction!

MRS ELVSTED [*terrified*]. Hedda—oh, Hedda!

HEDDA. You can see for yourself, you haven't the slightest reason to be in such mortal terror— [*Interrupting herself.*] There! Now we can all three enjoy ourselves!

LÖVBORG [*who has given a start*]. Ah—what is all this, Mrs Tesman?

MRS ELVSTED. Oh, my God, Hedda! What are you saying? What are you doing?

HEDDA. Don't get excited! That horrid Judge Brack is sitting watching you.

LÖVBORG. So she was in mortal terror! On my account!

MRS ELVSTED [*softly and piteously*]. Oh, Hedda—now you have ruined everything!

LÖVBORG [*looks fixedly at her for a moment. His face is distorted*]. So that was my comrade's frank confidence in me?

MRS ELVSTED [*imploringly*]. Oh, my dearest friend—only let me tell you—

LÖVBORG [*takes one of the glasses of punch, raises it to his lips and says in a low, husky voice*]. Your health, Thea! [*He empties the glass, puts it down and takes the second.*]

MRS ELVSTED [*softly*]. Oh, Hedda, Hedda—how could you do this?

HEDDA. *I* do it? I? Are you crazy?

LÖVBORG. Here's to your health too, Mrs Tesman. Thanks for the truth. Hurrah for the truth! [*He empties the glass and is about to refill it.*]

HEDDA [*lays her hand on his arm*]. Come, come—no more for the present. Remember you are going out to supper.

MRS ELVSTED. No, no, no!

HEDDA. Hush! They are sitting watching you.

LÖVBORG [*putting down the glass*]. Now, Thea—tell me the truth—

MRS ELVSTED. Yes.

LÖVBORG. Did your husband know that you had come after me?

MRS ELVSTED [*wringing her hands*]. Oh, Hedda—do you hear what he is asking?

LÖVBORG. Was it arranged between you and him that you were to come to town and look after me? Perhaps it was the sheriff himself that urged you to come? Aha, my dear—no doubt he wanted my help in his office! Or was it at the card table that he missed me?

MRS ELVSTED [*softly, in agony*]. Oh, Lövborg, Lövborg!

LÖVBORG [*seizes a glass and is on the point of filling it*]. Here's a glass for the old sheriff too!

HEDDA [*preventing him*]. No more just now. Remember you have to read your manuscript to Tesman.

LÖVBORG [*calmly, putting down the glass*]. It was stupid of me, all this, Thea—to take it in this way, I mean. Don't be angry with me, my dear, dear comrade. You shall see—both you and the others—that if I was fallen once—now I have risen again! Thanks to you, Thea.

MRS ELVSTED [*radiant with joy*]. Oh, heaven be praised!

[BRACK *has in the meantime looked at his watch. He and* TESMAN *rise and come into the drawing room.*]

BRACK [*takes his hat and overcoat*]. Well, Mrs Tesman, our time has come.

HEDDA. I suppose it has.

LÖVBORG [*rising*]. Mine too, Judge Brack.

MRS ELVSTED [*softly and imploringly*]. Oh, Lövborg, don't do it!

HEDDA [*pinching her arm*]. They can hear you!

MRS ELVSTED [*with a suppressed shriek*]. Ow!

LÖVBORG [*to* BRACK]. You were good enough to invite me.

BRACK. Well, are you coming after all?

LÖVBORG. Yes, many thanks.

BRACK. I'm delighted.

LÖVBORG [*to* TESMAN, *putting the parcel of MS in his pocket*]. I should like to show you one or two things before I send it to the printers.

TESMAN. Fancy—that will be delightful. But, Hedda dear, how is Mrs Elvsted to get home? Eh?

HEDDA. Oh, that can be managed somehow.

LÖVBORG [*looking toward the ladies*]. Mrs Elvsted? Of course I'll come again and fetch her. [*Approaching.*] At ten or thereabouts, Mrs Tesman? Will that do?

HEDDA. Certainly. That will do capitally.

TESMAN. Well then, that's all right. But you must not expect me so early, Hedda.

HEDDA. Oh, you may stop as long—as long as ever you please.

MRS ELVSTED [*trying to conceal her anxiety*]. Well then, Mr Lövborg—I shall remain here until you come.

LÖVBORG [*with his hat in his hands*]. Pray do, Mrs Elvsted.

BRACK. And now off goes the excursion train, gentlemen! I hope we shall have a lively time, as a certain fair lady puts it.

HEDDA. Ah, if only the fair lady could be present unseen!

BRACK. Why unseen?

HEDDA. In order to hear a little of your liveliness at first hand, Judge Brack.

BRACK [*laughingly*]. I should not advise the fair lady to try it.

TESMAN [*also laughing*]. Come, you're a nice one, Hedda! Fancy that!

BRACK. Well, good-by, good-by, ladies.

LÖVBORG [*bowing*]. About ten o'clock then.

[BRACK, LÖVBORG *and* TESMAN *go out by the hall door. At the same time* BERTA *enters from the inner room with a lighted lamp which she places on the dining-room table; she goes out by the way she came.*]

MRS ELVSTED [*who has risen and is wandering restlessly about the room*]. Hedda—Hedda—what will come of all this?

HEDDA. At ten o'clock—he will be here. I can see him already—with vine leaves in his hair—flushed and fearless—

MRS ELVSTED. Oh, I hope he may.

HEDDA. And then, you see—then he will have regained control over himself. Then he will be a free man for all his days.

MRS ELVSTED. Oh God!—If he would only come as you see him now!

HEDDA. He will come as I see him—so and not otherwise! [*Rises and approaches* THEA.] You may doubt him as long as you please; I believe in him. And now we will try—

MRS ELVSTED. You have some hidden motive in this, Hedda!

HEDDA. Yes, I have. I want for once in my life to have power to mold a human destiny.

MRS ELVSTED. Have you not the power?

HEDDA. I have not—and have never had it.

MRS ELVSTED. Not your husband's?

HEDDA. Do you think that is worth the trouble? Oh, if you could only understand how poor I am. And fate has made you so rich! [*Clasps her passionately in her arms.*] I think I must burn your hair off after all.

MRS ELVSTED. Let me go! Let me go! I am afraid of you, Hedda!

BERTA [*in the middle doorway*]. Tea is laid in the dining room, ma'am.

HEDDA. Very well. We are coming.

MRS ELVSTED. No, no, no! I would rather go home alone! At once!

HEDDA. Nonsense! First you shall have a cup of tea, you little stupid. And then—at ten o'clock—Eilert Lövborg will be here—with vine leaves in his hair. [*She drags* MRS ELVSTED *almost by force toward the middle doorway.*]

ACT THREE

SCENE—*The room at the* TESMANS'. *The curtains are drawn over the middle doorway and also over the glass door. The lamp, half turned down and with a shade over it, is burning on the table. In the stove, the door of which stands open, there has been a fire which is now nearly burnt out.*

MRS ELVSTED, *wrapped in a large shawl and with her feet upon a footrest, sits close to the stove, sunk back in the armchair.* HEDDA, *fully dressed, lies sleeping upon the sofa with a sofa blanket over her.*

MRS ELVSTED [*after a pause suddenly sits up in her chair and listens eagerly. Then she sinks back again wearily, moaning to herself*]. Not yet! Oh God—oh God—not yet!

[BERTA *slips in by the hall door. She has a letter in her hand.*]

MRS ELVSTED [*turns and whispers eagerly*]. Well—has anyone come?

BERTA [*softly*]. Yes, a girl has brought this letter.

MRS ELVSTED [*quickly, holding out her hand*]. A letter! Give it to me!

BERTA. No, it's for Doctor Tesman, ma'am.

MRS ELVSTED. Oh, indeed.

BERTA. It was Miss Tesman's servant that brought it. I'll lay it here on the table.

MRS ELVSTED. Yes, do.

BERTA [*laying down the letter*]. I think I had better put out the lamp. It's smoking.

MRS ELVSTED. Yes, put it out. It must soon be daylight now.

BERTA [*putting out the lamp*]. It is daylight already, ma'am.

MRS ELVSTED. Yes, broad day! And no one come back yet!

BERTA. Lord bless you, ma'am—I guessed how it would be.

MRS ELVSTED. You guessed.

BERTA. Yes, when I saw that a certain person had come back to town—and that he went off with them. For we've heard enough about that gentlemen before now.

MRS ELVSTED. Don't speak so loud. You will waken Mrs Tesman.

BERTA [*looks toward the sofa and sighs*]. No, no—let her sleep, poor thing. Shan't I put some wood on the fire?

MRS ELVSTED. Thanks, not for me.

BERTA. Oh, very well. [*She goes softly out by the hall door.*]

HEDDA [*is awakened by the shutting of the door and looks up*]. What's that?

MRS ELVSTED. It was only the servant.

HEDDA [*looking about her*]. Oh, we're here! Yes, now I remember. [*Sits erect upon the sofa, stretches herself and rubs her eyes.*] What o'clock is it, Thea?

MRS ELVSTED [*looks at her watch*]. It's past seven.

HEDDA. When did Tesman come home?

MRS ELVSTED. He has not come.

HEDDA. Not come home yet?

MRS ELVSTED [*rising*]. No one has come.

HEDDA. Think of our watching and waiting here till four in the morning—

MRS ELVSTED [*wringing her hands*]. And how I watched and waited for him!

HEDDA [*yawns and says with her hand before her mouth*]: Well, well—we might have spared ourselves the trouble.

MRS ELVSTED. Did you get a little sleep?

HEDDA. Oh yes, I believe I have slept pretty well. Have you not?

MRS ELVSTED. Not for a moment. I couldn't, Hedda!—not to save my life.

HEDDA [*rises and goes toward her*]. There—there—there! There's nothing to be so alarmed about. I understand quite well what has happened.

MRS ELVSTED. Well, what do you think? Won't you tell me?

HEDDA. Why, of course it has been a very late affair at Judge Brack's—

MRS ELVSTED. Yes, yes, that is clear enough. But all the same—

HEDDA. And then, you see, Tesman hasn't cared to come home and ring us up in the middle of the night. [*Laughing.*] Perhaps he wasn't inclined to show himself either—immediately after a jollification.

MRS ELVSTED. But in that case—where can he have gone?

HEDDA. Of course he has gone to his aunt's and slept there. They have his old room ready for him.

MRS ELVSTED. No, he can't be with them, for a letter has just come for him from Miss Tesman. There it lies.

HEDDA. Indeed? [*Looks at the address.*] Why, yes, it's addressed in Aunt Julia's own hand. Well then, he has remained at Judge Brack's. And as for Eilert Lövborg—he is sitting, with vine leaves in his hair, reading his manuscript.

MRS ELVSTED. Oh, Hedda, you are just saying things you don't believe a bit.

HEDDA. You really are a little blockhead, Thea.

MRS ELVSTED. Oh yes, I suppose I am.

HEDDA. And how mortally tired you look.

MRS ELVSTED. Yes, I am mortally tired.

HEDDA. Well then, you must do as I tell you. You must

go into my room and lie down for a little while.

MRS ELVSTED. Oh no, no—I shouldn't be able to sleep.

HEDDA. I am sure you would.

MRS ELVSTED. Well, but your husband is certain to come soon now, and then I want to know at once.

HEDDA. I shall take care to let you know when he comes.

MRS ELVSTED. Do you promise me, Hedda?

HEDDA. Yes, rely upon me. Just you go in and have a sleep in the meantime.

MRS ELVSTED. Thanks; then I'll try to. [*She goes off through the inner room.*]

[HEDDA *goes up to the glass door and draws back the curtains. The broad daylight streams into the room. Then she takes a little hand glass from the writing table, looks at herself in it and arranges her hair. Next she goes to the hall door and presses the bell button.* BERTA *presently appears at the hall door.*]

BERTA. Did you want anything, ma'am?

HEDDA. Yes; you must put some more wood in the stove. I am shivering.

BERTA. Bless me—I'll make up the fire at once. [*She rakes the embers together and lays a piece of wood upon them, then stops and listens.*] That was a ring at the front door, ma'am.

HEDDA. Then go to the door. I will look after the fire.

BERTA. It'll soon burn up. [*She goes out by the hall door.*]

[HEDDA *kneels on the footrest and lays some more pieces of wood in the stove. After a short pause* GEORGE TESMAN *enters from the hall. He looks tired and rather serious. He steals on tiptoe toward the middle doorway and is about to slip through the curtains.*]

HEDDA [*at the stove, without looking up*]. Good morning.

TESMAN [*turns*]. Hedda! [*Approaching her.*] Good heavens—are you up so early? Eh?

HEDDA. Yes, I am up very early this morning.

TESMAN. And I never doubted you were still sound asleep! Fancy that, Hedda!

HEDDA. Don't speak so loud. Mrs Elvsted is resting in my room.

TESMAN. Has Mrs Elvsted been here all night?

HEDDA. Yes, since no one came to fetch her.

TESMAN. Ah, to be sure.

HEDDA [*closes the door of the stove and rises*]. Well, did you enjoy yourself at Judge Brack's?

TESMAN. Have you been anxious about me? Eh?

HEDDA. No, I should never think of being anxious. But I asked if you had enjoyed yourself.

TESMAN. Oh yes—for once in a way. Especially the beginning of the evening, for then Eilert read me part of his book. We arrived more than an hour too early —fancy that! And Brack had all sorts of arrangements to make—so Eilert read to me.

HEDDA [*seating herself by the table on the right*]. Well? Tell me, then—

TESMAN [*sitting on a footstool near the stove*]. Oh! Hedda, you can't conceive what a book that is going to be! I believe it is one of the most remarkable things that has ever been written. Fancy that!

HEDDA. Yes, yes; I don't care about that—

TESMAN. I must make a confession to you, Hedda. When he had finished reading—a horrid feeling came over me.

HEDDA. A horrid feeling?

TESMAN. I felt jealous of Eilert for having had it in him to write such a book. Only think, Hedda!

HEDDA. Yes, yes, I am thinking!

TESMAN. And then how pitiful to think that he—with all his gifts—should be irreclaimable after all.

HEDDA. I suppose you mean that he has more courage than the rest?

TESMAN. No, not at all—I mean that he is incapable of taking his pleasures in moderation.

HEDDA. And what came of it all—in the end?

TESMAN. Well, to tell the truth, I think it might best be described as an orgy, Hedda.

HEDDA. Had he vine leaves in his hair?

TESMAN. Vine leaves? No, I saw nothing of the sort. But he made a long, rambling speech in honor of the woman who had inspired him in his work—that was the phrase he used.

HEDDA. Did he name her?

TESMAN. No, he didn't; but I can't help thinking he meant Mrs Elvsted. You may be sure he did.

HEDDA. Well—where did you part from him?

TESMAN. On the way to town. We broke up—the last of us at any rate—all together, and Brack came with us to get a breath of fresh air. And then, you see, we agreed to take Eilert home; for he had had far more than was good for him.

HEDDA. I daresay.

TESMAN. But now comes the strange part of it, Hedda; or, I should rather say, the melancholy part of it. I declare I am almost ashamed—on Eilert's account—to tell you—

HEDDA. Oh, go on.

TESMAN. Well, as we were getting near town, you see, I happened to drop a little behind the others. Only for a minute or two—fancy that!

HEDDA. Yes, yes, yes, but—?

TESMAN. And then, as I hurried after them—what do you think I found by the wayside? Eh?

HEDDA. Oh, how should I know!

TESMAN. You mustn't speak of it to a soul, Hedda! Do you hear! Promise me, for Eilert's sake. [*Draws a parcel, wrapped in paper, from his coat pocket.*] Fancy, dear—I found this.

HEDDA. Is not that the parcel he had with him yesterday?

TESMAN. Yes, it is the whole of his precious, irreplaceable manuscript! And he had gone and lost it and knew nothing about it. Only fancy, Hedda. So deplorably—

HEDDA. But why did you not give him back the parcel at once?

TESMAN. I didn't dare to—in the state he was then in—

HEDDA. Did you not tell any of the others that you had found it?

TESMAN. Oh, far from it! You can surely understand that for Eilert's sake I wouldn't do that.

HEDDA. So no one knows that Eilert Lövborg's manuscript is in your possession?

TESMAN. No. And no one must know it.

HEDDA. Then what did you say to him afterward?

TESMAN. I didn't talk to him again at all, for when we got in among the streets he and two or three of the others gave us the slip and disappeared. Fancy that!

HEDDA. Indeed! They must have taken him home then.

TESMAN. Yes, so it would appear. And Brack, too, left us.

HEDDA. And what have you been doing with yourself since?

TESMAN. Well, I and some of the others went home with one of the party, a jolly fellow, and took our morning coffee with him; or perhaps I should rather call it our night coffee—eh? But now, when I have rested a little and given Eilert, poor fellow, time to have his sleep out, I must take this back to him.

HEDDA [holds out her hand for the packet]. No—don't give it to him! Not in such a hurry, I mean. Let me read it first.

TESMAN. No, my dearest Hedda, I mustn't, I really mustn't.

HEDDA. You must not?

TESMAN. No—for you can imagine what a state of despair he will be in when he awakens and misses the manuscript. He has no copy of it, you must know! He told me so.

HEDDA [looking searchingly at him]. Can such a thing not be reproduced? Written over again?

TESMAN. No, I don't think that would be possible. For the inspiration, you see—

HEDDA. Yes, yes—I suppose it depends on that. [*Lightly.*] But by-the-bye—here is a letter for you.

TESMAN. Fancy!

HEDDA [*handing it to him*]. It came early this morning.

TESMAN. It's from Aunt Julia! What can it be? [*He lays the packet on the other footstool, opens the letter, runs his eye through it and jumps up.*] Oh, Hedda— she says that poor Aunt Rina is dying!

HEDDA. Well, we were prepared for that.

TESMAN. And that if I want to see her again I must make haste. I'll run in to them at once.

HEDDA [*suppressing a smile.*] Will you run?

TESMAN. Oh, dearest Hedda—if you could only make up your mind to come with me! Just think!

HEDDA [*rises and says wearily, repelling the idea*]: No, no, don't ask me. I will not look upon sickness and death. I loathe all sorts of ugliness.

TESMAN. Well, well then— [*Bustling around.*] My hat— my overcoat? Oh, in the hall—I do hope I mayn't come too late, Hedda! Eh?

HEDDA. Oh, if you run—

BERTA. Judge Brack is at the door and wishes to know if he may come in.

TESMAN. At this time! No, I can't possibly see him.

HEDDA. But I can. [*To* BERTA.] Ask Judge Brack to come in. [BERTA *goes out.*]

HEDDA [*quickly whispering*]. The parcel, Tesman! [*She snatches it up from the stool.*]

TESMAN. Yes, give it to me!

HEDDA. No, no, I will keep it till you come back. [*She goes to the writing table and places it in the book- case.* TESMAN *stands in a flurry of haste and cannot get his gloves on.*]

[JUDGE BRACK *enters from the hall.*]

HEDDA [*nodding to him*]. You are an early bird, I must say.

BRACK. Yes, don't you think so? [*To* TESMAN.] Are you on the move too?

TESMAN. Yes, I must rush off to my aunts'. Fancy—the invalid one is lying at death's door, poor creature.

BRACK. Dear me, is she, indeed? Then on no account let me detain you. At such a critical moment—

TESMAN. Yes, I must really rush— Good-by! Good-by! [*He hastens out by the hall door.*]

HEDDA [*approaching*]. You seem to have made a particularly lively night of it at your rooms, Judge Brack.

BRACK. I assure you I have not had my clothes off, Mrs Hedda.

HEDDA. Not you either?

BRACK. No, as you may see. But what has Tesman been telling you of the night's adventures?

HEDDA. Oh, some tiresome story. Only that they went and had coffee somewhere or other.

BRACK. I have heard about that coffee party already. Eilert Lövborg was not with them, I fancy?

HEDDA. No, they had taken him home before that.

BRACK. Tesman too?

HEDDA. No, but some of the others, he said.

BRACK [*smiling*]. George Tesman is really an ingenuous creature, Mrs Hedda.

HEDDA. Yes, heaven knows he is. Then is there something behind all this?

BRACK. Yes, perhaps there may be.

HEDDA. Well then, sit down, my dear judge, and tell your story in comfort. [*She seats herself to the left of the table.* BRACK *sits near her, at the long side of the table.*]

HEDDA. Now then?

BRACK. I had special reasons for keeping track of my guests—or rather of some of my guests—last night.

HEDDA. Of Eilert Lövborg among the rest, perhaps?

BRACK. Frankly, yes.

HEDDA. Now you make me really curious.

BRACK. Do you know where he and one or two of the others finished the night, Mrs Hedda?

HEDDA. If it is not quite unmentionable, tell me.

BRACK. Oh no, it's not at all unmentionable. Well, they put in an appearance at a particularly animated soiree.

HEDDA. Of the lively kind?

BRACK. Of the very liveliest.

HEDDA. Tell me more of this, Judge Brack.

BRACK. Lövborg, as well as the others, had been invited in advance. I knew all about it. But he had declined the invitation; for now, as you know, he has become a new man.

HEDDA. Up at the Elvsteds', yes. But he went after all, then?

BRACK. Well, you see, Mrs Hedda—unhappily the spirit moved him at my rooms last evening—

HEDDA. Yes, I hear he found inspiration.

BRACK. Pretty violent inspiration. Well, I fancy that altered his purpose; for we menfolk are unfortunately not always so firm in our principles as we ought to be.

HEDDA. Oh, I am sure you are an exception, Judge Brack. But as to Lövborg?

BRACK. To make a long story short—he landed at last in Mademoiselle Diana's rooms.

HEDDA. Mademoiselle Diana's?

BRACK. It was Mademoiselle Diana that was giving the soiree to a select circle of her admirers and her lady friends.

HEDDA. Is she a red-haired woman?

BRACK. Precisely.

HEDDA. A sort of a—singer?

BRACK. Oh yes—in her leisure moments. And, moreover, a mighty huntress—of men—Mrs Hedda. You have no doubt heard of her. Eilert Lövborg was one of her most enthusiastic protectors—in the days of his glory.

HEDDA. And how did all this end?

BRACK. Far from amicably, it appears. After a most tender meeting they seem to have come to blows—

HEDDA. Lövborg and she?

BRACK. Yes. He accused her or her friends of having robbed him. He declared that his pocketbook had disappeared—and other things as well. In short he seems to have made a furious disturbance.

HEDDA. And what came of it all?

BRACK. It came to a general scrimmage in which the ladies as well as the gentlemen took part. Fortunately the police at last appeared on the scene.

HEDDA. The police too?

BRACK. Yes. I fancy it will prove a costly frolic for Eilert Lövborg, crazy being that he is.

HEDDA. How so?

BRACK. He seems to have made a violent resistance—to have hit one of the constables on the head and torn the coat off his back. So they had to march him off to the police station with the rest.

HEDDA. How have you learnt all this?

BRACK. From the police themselves.

HEDDA [*gazing straight before her*]. So that is what happened. Then he had no vine leaves in his hair?

BRACK. Vine leaves, Mrs Hedda?

HEDDA [*changing her tone*]. But tell me now, Judge— what is your real reason for tracking out Eilert Lövborg's movements so carefully?

BRACK. In the first place, it could not be entirely indifferent to me if it should appear in the police court that he came straight from my house.

HEDDA. Will the matter come into court then?

BRACK. Of course. However, I should scarcely have troubled so much about that. But I thought that as a friend of the family it was my duty to supply you and Tesman with a full account of his nocturnal exploits.

HEDDA. Why so, Judge Brack?

BRACK. Why, because I have a shrewd suspicion that he intends to use you as a sort of blind.

HEDDA. Oh, how can you think such a thing!

BRACK. Good heavens, Mrs Hedda—we have eyes in our head. Mark my words! This Mrs Elvsted will be in no hurry to leave town again.

HEDDA. Well, even if there should be anything between them, I suppose there are plenty of other places where they could meet.

BRACK. Not a single home. Henceforth, as before, every respectable house will be closed against Eilert Lövborg.

HEDDA. And so ought mine to be, you mean?

BRACK. Yes. I confess it would be more than painful to me if this personage were to be made free of your house. How superfluous, how intrusive he would be if he were to force his way into—

HEDDA. —into the triangle?

BRACK. Precisely. It would simply mean that I should find myself homeless.

HEDDA [*looks at him with a smile*]. So you want to be the one cock in the basket—that is your aim.

BRACK [*nods slowly and lowers his voice*]. Yes, that is my aim. And for that I will fight—with every weapon I can command.

HEDDA [*her smile vanishing*]. I see you are a dangerous person—when it comes to the point.

BRACK. Do you think so?

HEDDA. I am beginning to think so. And I am exceedingly glad to think—that you have no sort of hold over me.

BRACK [*laughing equivocally*]. Well, well, Mrs Hedda—perhaps you are right there. If I had, who knows what I might be capable of?

HEDDA. Come, come now, Judge Brack. That sounds almost like a threat.

BRACK [*rising*]. Oh, not at all! The triangle, you know, ought, if possible, to be spontaneously constructed.

HEDDA. There I agree with you.

BRACK. Well, now I have said all I had to say, and I had better be getting back to town. Good-by, Mrs Hedda. [*He goes toward the glass door.*]

HEDDA [*rising*]. Are you going through the garden?

BRACK. Yes, it's a short cut for me.

HEDDA. And then it is a back way too.

BRACK. Quite so. I have no objection to back ways. They may be piquant enough at times.

HEDDA. When there is ball practice going on you mean?

BRACK [*in the doorway, laughing to her*]. Oh, people don't shoot their tame poultry, I fancy.

HEDDA [*also laughing*]. Oh no, when there is only one cock in the basket— [*They exchange laughing nods of farewell. He goes. She closes the door behind him.*]

[HEDDA, *who has become quite serious, stands for a moment looking out. Presently she goes and peeps through the curtain over the middle doorway. Then she goes to the writing table, takes* LÖVBORG's *packet out of the bookcase and is on the point of looking through its contents.* BERTA *is heard speaking loudly in the hall.* HEDDA *turns and listens. Then she hastily locks up the packet in the drawer and lays the key on the inkstand.*]

[EILERT LÖVBORG, *with his greatcoat on and his hat in his hand, tears open the hall door. He looks somewhat confused and irritated.*]

LÖVBORG [*looking toward the hall*]. And I tell you I must and will come in! There! [*He closes the door, turns and sees* HEDDA, *at once regains his self-control and bows.*]

HEDDA [*at the writing table*]. Well, Mr Lövborg, this is rather a late hour to call for Thea.

LÖVBORG. You mean rather an early hour to call on you. Pray pardon me.

HEDDA. How do you know that she is still here?

LÖVBORG. They told me at her lodgings that she had been out all night.

HEDDA [*going to the oval table*]. Did you notice anything about the people of the house when they said
that? ˎ

LÖVBORG [*looks inquiringly at her*]. Notice anything
about them?

HEDDA. I mean, did they seem to think it odd?

LÖVBORG [*suddenly understanding*]. Oh yes, of course!
I am dragging her down with me! However, I didn't
notice anything. I suppose Tesman is not up yet?

HEDDA. No—I think not.

LÖVBORG. When did he come home?

HEDDA. Very late.

LÖVBORG. Did he tell you anything?

HEDDA. Yes, I gathered that you had had an exceedingly
jolly evening at Judge Brack's.

LÖVBORG. Nothing more?

HEDDA. I don't think so. However, I was so dreadfully
sleepy—

[MRS ELVSTED *enters through the curtains of the middle
doorway.*]

MRS ELVSTED [*going toward him*]. Ah, Lövborg! At last!

LÖVBORG. Yes, at last. And too late!

MRS ELVSTED [*looks anxiously at him*]. What is too late?

LÖVBORG. Everything is too late now. It is all over with
me.

MRS ELVSTED. Oh no, no—don't say that!

LÖVBORG. You will say the same when you hear—

MRS ELVSTED. I won't hear anything!

HEDDA. Perhaps you would prefer to talk to her alone!
If so, I will leave you.

LÖVBORG. No, stay—you too. I beg you to stay.

MRS ELVSTED. Yes, but I won't hear anything, I tell you.

LÖVBORG. It is not last night's adventures that I want to
talk about.

MRS ELVSTED. What is it then?

LÖVBORG. I want to say that now our ways must part.

MRS ELVSTED. Part!

HEDDA [*involuntarily*]. I knew it!

LÖVBORG. You can be of no more service to me, Thea.

MRS ELVSTED. How can you stand there and say that! No more service to you! Am I not to help you now, as before? Are we not to go on working together?

LÖVBORG. Henceforward I shall do no work.

MRS ELVSTED [*despairingly*]. Then what am I to do with my life?

LÖVBORG. You must try to live your life as if you had never known me.

MRS ELVSTED. But you know I cannot do that!

LÖVBORG. Try if you cannot, Thea. You must go home again.

MRS ELVSTED [*in vehement protest*]. Never in this world! Where you are, there will I be also! I will not let myself be driven away like this! I will remain here! I will be with you when the book appears.

HEDDA [*half aloud, in suspense*]. Ah yes—the book!

LÖVBORG [*looks at her*]. My book and Thea's, for that is what it is.

MRS ELVSTED. Yes, I feel that it is. And that is why I have a right to be with you when it appears! I will see with my own eyes how respect and honor pour in upon you afresh. And the happiness—the happiness—oh, I must share it with you!

LÖVBORG. Thea—our book will never appear.

HEDDA. Ah!

MRS ELVSTED. Never appear!

LÖVBORG. Can never appear.

MRS ELVSTED [*in agonized foreboding*]. Lövborg—what have you done with the manuscript?

HEDDA [*looks anxiously at him*]. Yes, the manuscript?

MRS ELVSTED. Where is it?

LÖVBORG. Oh! Thea—don't ask me about it!

MRS ELVSTED. Yes, yes, I will know. I demand to be told at once.

LÖVBORG. The manuscript— Well then— I have torn the manuscript into a thousand pieces.

MRS ELVSTED [*shrieks*]. Oh no, no!

HEDDA [*involuntarily*]. But that's not—

LÖVBORG [*looks at her*]. Not true, you think?

HEDDA [*collecting herself*]. Oh well, of course—since you say so. But it sounded so improbable.

LÖVBORG. It is true, all the same.

MRS ELVSTED [*wringing her hands*]. Oh God!—oh God! Hedda—torn his own work to pieces!

LÖVBORG. I have torn my own life to pieces. So why should I not tear my lifework too?

MRS ELVSTED. And you did this last night?

LÖVBORG. Yes, I tell you! Tore it into a thousand pieces and scattered them on the fiord—far out. There there is cool sea water at any rate—let them drift upon it—drift with the current and the wind. And then presently they will sink—deeper and deeper—as I shall, Thea.

MRS ELVSTED. Do you know, Lövborg, that what you have done with the book—I shall think of it to my dying day as though you had killed a little child.

LÖVBORG. Yes, you are right. It is a sort of child murder.

MRS ELVSTED. How could you then! Did not the child belong to me too?

HEDDA [*almost inaudibly*]. Ah, the child—

MRS ELVSTED [*breathing heavily*]. It is all over then. Well, well, now I will go, Hedda.

HEDDA. But you are not going away from town?

MRS ELVSTED. Oh, I don't know what I shall do. I see nothing but darkness before me. [*She goes out by the hall door.*]

HEDDA [*stands waiting for a moment*]. So you are not going to see her home, Mr Lövborg?

LÖVBORG. I? Through the streets? Would you have people see her walking with me?

HEDDA. Of course I don't know what else may have happened last night. But is it so utterly irretrievable?

LÖVBORG. It will not end with last night—I know that perfectly well. And the thing is that now I have no taste for that sort of life either. I won't begin it anew. She has broken my courage and my power of braving life out.

HEDDA [*looking straight before her*]. So that pretty little fool has had her fingers in a man's destiny. [*Looks at him.*] But all the same, how could you treat her so heartlessly?

LÖVBORG. Oh, don't say that it was heartless!

HEDDA. To go and destroy what has filled her whole soul for months and years! You do not call that heartless!

LÖVBORG. To you I can tell the truth, Hedda.

HEDDA. The truth?

LÖVBORG. First promise me—give me your word—that what I now confide to you Thea shall never know.

HEDDA. I give you my word.

LÖVBORG. Good. Then let me tell you that what I said just now was untrue.

HEDDA. About the manuscript?

LÖVBORG. Yes. I have not torn it to pieces—nor thrown it into the fiord.

HEDDA. No, n— But—where is it then?

LÖVBORG. I have destroyed it none the less—utterly destroyed it, Hedda! Thea said that what I had done seemed to her like a child murder.

HEDDA. Yes, so she said.

LÖVBORG. But to kill this child—that is not the worst thing a father can do to it.

HEDDA. Not the worst?

LÖVBORG. No. I wanted to spare Thea from hearing the worst.

HEDDA. Then what is the worst?

LÖVBORG. Suppose now, Hedda, that a man—in the small hours of the morning—came home to his child's mother after a night of riot and debauchery and said: "Listen—I have been here and there—in this place and in that. And I have taken our child with me—to this place and to that. And I have lost the child—utterly lost it. The devil knows into

what hands it may have fallen—who may have had
their clutches on it."

HEDDA. Well—but when all is said and done, you know
—that was only a book.

LÖVBORG. Thea's soul was in that book.

HEDDA. Yes, so I understand.

LÖVBORG. And you can understand, too, that for her
and me together no future is possible.

HEDDA. What path do you mean to take then?

LÖVBORG. None. I will only try to make an end of it
all—the sooner the better.

HEDDA. I don't understand. [*A step nearer to him.*] Eilert Lövborg—listen to me. Will you not try to—to
do it beautifully?

LÖVBORG. Beautifully? [*Smiling.*] With vine leaves in
my hair, as you used to dream in the old days?

HEDDA. No, no. I have lost my faith in the vine leaves.
But beautifully, nevertheless! For once in a way!
Good-by! You must go now—and do not come here
any more.

LÖVBORG. Good-by, Mrs Tesman. And give George Tesman my love. [*He is on the point of going.*]

HEDDA. No, wait! I must give you a memento to take
with you. [*She goes to the writing table and opens
the drawer and the pistol case, then returns to* LÖV-
BORG *with one of the pistols.*]

LÖVBORG [*looks at her*]. This? Is this the memento?

HEDDA [*nodding slowly*]. Do you recognize it? It was
aimed at you once.

LÖVBORG. You should have used it then.

HEDDA. Take it—and do you use it now.

LÖVBORG [*puts the pistol in his breast pocket*]. Thanks!

HEDDA. And beautifully, Eilert Lövborg. Promise me
that!

LÖVBORG. Good-by, Hedda Gabler. [*He goes out by the
hall door.*]

[HEDDA *listens for a moment at the door. Then she goes
up to the writing table, takes out the packet of man-*

uscript, *peeps under the cover, draws a few of the sheets half out and looks at them. Next she goes over and seats herself in the armchair beside the stove, with the packet in her lap. Presently she opens the stove door and then the packet.*]

HEDDA [*throws one of the quires into the fire and whispers to herself*]. Now I am burning your child, Thea! Burning it, curlylocks! [*Throwing one or two more quires into the stove.*] Your child and Eilert Lövborg's. [*Throws the rest in.*] I am burning—I am burning your child.

ACT FOUR

SCENE—*The same rooms at the* TESMANS'. *It is evening. The drawing room is in darkness. The back room is lighted by the hanging lamp over the table. The curtains over the glass door are drawn close.*

HEDDA, *dressed in black, walks to and fro in the dark room. Then she goes into the back room and disappears for a moment to the left. She is heard to strike a few chords on the piano. Presently she comes in sight again and returns to the drawing room.*

BERTA *enters from the right, through the inner room, with a lighted lamp, which she places on the table in front of the corner settee in the drawing room. Her eyes are red with weeping, and she has black ribbons in her cap. She goes quietly and circumspectly out to the right.*

HEDDA *goes up to the glass door, lifts the curtain a little aside and looks out into the darkness.*

Shortly afterward MISS TESMAN, *in mourning, with a bonnet and veil on, comes in from the hall.* HEDDA *goes toward her and holds out her hand.*

MISS TESMAN. Yes, Hedda, here I am, in mourning and forlorn; for now my poor sister has at last found peace.

HEDDA. I have heard the news already, as you see. Tesman sent me a card.

MISS TESMAN. Yes, he promised me he would. But nevertheless I thought that to Hedda—here in the house of life—I ought myself to bring the tidings of death.

HEDDA. That was very kind of you.

MISS TESMAN. Ah, Rina ought not to have left us just now. This is not the time for Hedda's house to be a house of mourning.

HEDDA [changing the subject]. She died quite peacefully, did she not, Miss Tesman?

MISS TESMAN. Oh, her end was so calm, so beautiful. And then she had the unspeakable happiness of seeing George once more—and bidding him good-by. Has he come home yet?

HEDDA. No. He wrote that he might be detained. But won't you sit down?

MISS TESMAN. No, thank you, my dear, dear Hedda. I should like to, but I have so much to do. I must prepare my dear one for her rest as well as I can. She shall go to her grave looking her best.

HEDDA. Can I not help you in any way?

MISS TESMAN. Oh, you must not think of it! Hedda Tesman must have no hand in such mournful work. Nor let her thoughts dwell on it either—not at this time.

HEDDA. One is not always mistress of one's thoughts.

MISS TESMAN [continuing]. Ah yes, it is the way of the world. At home we shall be sewing a shroud, and here there will soon be sewing too, I suppose—but of another sort, thank God!

[GEORGE TESMAN enters by the hall door.]

HEDDA. Ah, you have come at last!

TESMAN. You here, Aunt Julia? With Hedda? Fancy that!

MISS TESMAN. I was just going, my dear boy. Well, have you done all you promised?

TESMAN. No; I'm really afraid I have forgotten half of it. I must come to you again tomorrow. Today my brain is all in a whirl. I can't keep my thoughts together.

MISS TESMAN. Why, my dear George, you mustn't take it in this way.

TESMAN. Mustn't? How do you mean?

MISS TESMAN. Even in your sorrow you must rejoice, as I do—rejoice that she is at rest.

TESMAN. Oh yes, yes—you are thinking of Aunt Rina.

HEDDA. You will feel lonely now, Miss Tesman.

MISS TESMAN. Just at first, yes. But that will not last very long, I hope. I daresay I shall soon find an occupant for poor Rina's little room.

TESMAN. Indeed? Who do you think will take it? Eh?

MISS TESMAN. Oh, there's always some poor invalid or other in want of nursing, unfortunately.

HEDDA. Would you really take such a burden upon you again?

MISS TESMAN. A burden! Heaven forgive you, child—it has been no burden to me.

HEDDA. But suppose you had a total stranger on your hands—

MISS TESMAN. Oh, one soon makes friends with sick folk, and it's such an absolute necessity for me to have someone to live for. Well, heaven be praised, there may soon be something in this house, too, to keep an old aunt busy.

HEDDA. Oh, don't trouble about anything here.

TESMAN. Yes, just fancy what a nice time we three might have together if—

HEDDA. If—?

TESMAN [*uneasily*]. Oh, nothing. It will all come right. Let us hope so—eh?

MISS TESMAN. Well, well, I daresay you two want to talk to each other. [*Smiling.*] And perhaps Hedda may have something to tell you too, George. Good-by! I must go home to Rina. [*Turning at the door.*] How strange it is to think that now Rina is with me and with my poor brother as well!

TESMAN. Yes, fancy that, Aunt Julia! Eh?

[MISS TESMAN *goes out by the hall door.*]

HEDDA [*follows* TESMAN *coldly and searchingly with her eyes*]. I almost believe your aunt Rina's death affects you more than it does your aunt Julia.

TESMAN. Oh, it's not that alone. It's Eilert I am so terribly uneasy about.

HEDDA [*quickly*]. Is there anything new about him?

TESMAN. I looked in at his rooms this afternoon, intending to tell him the manuscript was in safe keeping.

HEDDA. Well, did you not find him?

TESMAN. No. He wasn't at home. But afterward I met Mrs Elvsted, and she told me that he had been here early this morning.

HEDDA. Yes, directly after you had gone.

TESMAN. And he said that he had torn his manuscript to pieces—eh?

HEDDA. Yes, so he declared.

TESMAN. Why, good heavens, he must have been completely out of his mind! And I suppose you thought it best not to give it back to him, Hedda?

HEDDA. No, he did not get it.

TESMAN. But of course you told him that we had it?

HEDDA. No. [*Quickly.*] Did you tell Mrs Elvsted?

TESMAN. No; I thought I had better not. But you ought to have told him. Fancy if, in desperation, he should go and do himself some injury! Let me have the manuscript, Hedda. I will take it to him at once. Where is it?

HEDDA [*cold and immovable, leaning on the armchair*]. I have not got it.

TESMAN. Have not got it? What in the world do you mean?

HEDDA. I have burned it—every line of it.

TESMAN [*with a violent movement of terror*]. Burned! Burned Eilert's manuscript!

HEDDA. Don't scream so. The servant might hear you.

TESMAN. Burned! Why, good God! No, no, no! It's impossible!

HEDDA. It is so, nevertheless.

TESMAN. Do you know what you have done, Hedda? It's
unlawful appropriation of lost property. Fancy that!
Just ask Judge Brack, and he'll tell you what it is.

HEDDA. I advise you not to speak of it—either to Judge
Brack or to anyone else.

TESMAN. But how could you do anything so unheard
of? What put it into your head? What possessed you?
Answer me that—eh?

HEDDA [*suppressing an almost imperceptible smile*]. I
did it for your sake, George.

TESMAN. For my sake!

HEDDA. This morning, when you told me about what he
had read to you—

TESMAN. Yes, yes—what then?

HEDDA. You acknowledged that you envied him his
work.

TESMAN. Oh, of course I didn't mean that literally.

HEDDA. No matter—I could not bear the idea that anyone should throw you into the shade.

TESMAN [*in an outburst of mingled doubt and joy*].
Hedda! Oh, is this true? But—but—I never knew you
to show your love like that before. Fancy that!

HEDDA. Well, I may as well tell you that—just at this
time— [*Impatiently breaking off.*] No, no; you can
ask Aunt Julia. She will tell you fast enough.

TESMAN. Oh, I almost think I understand you, Hedda!
[*Clasps his hands together.*] Great heavens! Do you
really mean it! Eh?

HEDDA. Don't shout so. The servant might hear.

TESMAN [*laughing in irrepressible glee*]. The servant!
Why, how absurd you are, Hedda. It's only my old
Berta. Why, I'll tell Berta myself.

HEDDA [*clenching her hands together in desperation*].
Oh, it is killing me—it is killing me, all this!

TESMAN. What is, Hedda? Eh?

HEDDA [*coldly, controlling herself*]. All this—absurdity—
George.

TESMAN. Absurdity! Do you see anything absurd in my
being overjoyed at the news? But after all—perhaps I
had better not say anything to Berta.

HEDDA. Oh—why not that too?

TESMAN. No, no, not yet! But I must certainly tell Aunt
Julia. And then that you have begun to call me
George too! Fancy that! Oh, Aunt Julia will be so
happy—so happy!

HEDDA. When she hears that I have burned Eilert Lövborg's manuscript—for your sake?

TESMAN. No, by-the-bye—that affair of the manuscript—
of course nobody must know about that. But that
you love me so much, Hedda—Aunt Julia must really
share my joy in that! I wonder, now, whether this
sort of thing is usual in young wives? Eh?

HEDDA. I think you had better ask Aunt Julia that question too.

TESMAN. I will indeed, some time or other. [*Looks uneasy and downcast again.*] And yet the manuscript—
the manuscript! Good God! It is terrible to think
what will become of poor Eilert now.

[MRS ELVSTED, *dressed as in the first act, with hat and
cloak, enters by the hall door.*]

MRS ELVSTED [*greets them hurriedly and says in evident
agitation*]: Oh, dear Hedda, forgive my coming
again.

HEDDA. What is the matter with you, Thea?

TESMAN. Something about Eilert Lövborg again—eh?

MRS ELVSTED. Yes! I am dreadfully afraid some misfortune has happened to him.

HEDDA [*seizes her arm*]. Ah—do you think so?

TESMAN. Why, good lord—what makes you think that,
Mrs Elvsted?

MRS ELVSTED. I heard them talking of him at my boardinghouse—just as I came in. Oh, the most incredible rumors are afloat about him today.

TESMAN. Yes, fancy, so I heard too! And I can bear witness that he went straight home to bed last night. Fancy that!

HEDDA. Well, what did they say at the boardinghouse?

MRS ELVSTED. Oh, I couldn't make out anything clearly. Either they knew nothing definite or else— They stopped talking when they saw me, and I did not dare to ask.

TESMAN [*moving about uneasily*]. We must hope—we must hope that you misunderstood them, Mrs Elvsted.

MRS ELVSTED. No, no; I am sure it was of him they were talking. And I heard something about the hospital or—

TESMAN. The hospital?

HEDDA. No—surely that cannot be!

MRS ELVSTED. Oh, I was in such mortal terror! I went to his lodgings and asked for him there.

HEDDA. You could make up your mind to that, Thea!

MRS ELVSTED. What else could I do? I really could bear the suspense no longer.

TESMAN. But you didn't find him either—eh?

MRS ELVSTED. No. And the people knew nothing about him. He hadn't been home since yesterday afternoon, they said.

TESMAN. Yesterday! Fancy, how could they say that?

MRS ELVSTED. Oh, I am sure something terrible must have happened to him.

TESMAN. Hedda dear—how would it be if I were to go and make inquiries?

HEDDA. No, no—don't you mix yourself up in this affair.

[JUDGE BRACK, *with his hat in his hand, enters by the hall door, which* BERTA *opens and closes behind him. He looks grave and bows in silence*.]

TESMAN. Oh, is that you, my dear judge? Eh?

BRACK. Yes. It was imperative I should see you this evening.

TESMAN. I can see you have heard the news about Aunt Rina.

BRACK. Yes, that among other things.

TESMAN. Isn't it sad—eh?

BRACK. Well, my dear Tesman, that depends on how you look at it.

TESMAN [*looks doubtfully at him*]. Has anything else happened?

BRACK. Yes.

HEDDA [*in suspense*]. Anything sad, Judge Brack?

BRACK. That, too, depends on how you look at it, Mrs Tesman.

MRS ELVSTED [*unable to restrain her anxiety*]. Oh! It is something about Eilert Lövborg!

BRACK [*with a glance at her*]. What makes you think that, madam? Perhaps you have already heard something?

MRS ELVSTED [*in confusion*]. No, nothing at all, but—

TESMAN. Oh, for heaven's sake, tell us!

BRACK [*shrugging his shoulders*]. Well, I regret to say Eilert Lövborg has been taken to the hospital. He is lying at the point of death.

MRS ELVSTED [*shrieks*]. Oh God! Oh God!

TESMAN. To the hospital! And at the point of death!

HEDDA [*involuntarily*]. So soon then—

MRS ELVSTED [*wailing*]. And we parted in anger, Hedda!

HEDDA [*whispers*]. Thea—Thea—be careful!

MRS ELVSTED [*not heeding her*]. I must go to him! I must see him alive!

BRACK. It is useless, madam. No one will be admitted.

MRS ELVSTED. Oh, at least tell me what has happened to him. What is it?

TESMAN. You don't mean to say that he has himself— Eh?

HEDDA. Yes, I am sure he has.

TESMAN. Hedda, how can you—?

BRACK [*keeping his eyes fixed upon her*]. Unfortunately you have guessed quite correctly, Mrs Tesman.

MRS ELVSTED. Oh, how horrible!

TESMAN. Himself, then! Fancy that!

HEDDA. Shot himself!

BRACK. Rightly guessed again, Mrs Tesman.

MRS ELVSTED [*with an effort at self-control*]. When did it happen, Mr Brack?

BRACK. This afternoon between three and four.

TESMAN. But, good lord, where did he do it? Eh?

BRACK [*with some hesitation*]. Where? Well—I suppose at his lodgings.

MRS ELVSTED. No, that cannot be; for I was there between six and seven.

BRACK. Well then, somewhere else. I don't know exactly. I only know that he was found. He had shot himself—in the breast.

MRS ELVSTED. Oh, how terrible! That he should die like that!

HEDDA [*to* BRACK]. Was it in the breast?

BRACK. Yes—as I told you.

HEDDA. Not in the temple?

BRACK. In the breast, Mrs Tesman.

HEDDA. Well, well—the breast is a good place too.

BRACK. How do you mean, Mrs Tesman?

HEDDA [*evasively*]. Oh, nothing—nothing.

TESMAN. And the wound is dangerous, you say—eh?

BRACK. Absolutely mortal. The end has probably come by this time.

MRS ELVSTED. Yes, yes, I feel it. The end! The end! Oh, Hedda!

TESMAN. But tell me, how have you learned all this?

BRACK [*curtly*]. Through one of the police. A man I had some business with.

HEDDA [*in a clear voice*]. At last a deed worth doing!

TESMAN [*terrified*]. Good heavens, Hedda! What are you saying?

HEDDA. I say there is beauty in this.

BRACK. H'm, Mrs Tesman—

TESMAN. Beauty! Fancy that!

MRS ELVSTED. Oh, Hedda, how can you talk of beauty in such an act!

HEDDA. Eilert Lövborg has himself made up his account with life. He has had the courage to do—the one right thing.

MRS ELVSTED. No, you must never think that was how it happened! It must have been in delirium that he did it.

TESMAN. In despair!

HEDDA. That he did not. I am certain of that.

MRS ELVSTED. Yes, yes! In delirium! Just as when he tore up our manuscript.

BRACK [starting]. The manuscript? He has torn that up?

MRS ELVSTED. Yes, last night.

TESMAN [whispers softly]. Oh, Hedda, we shall never get over this.

BRACK. H'm, very extraordinary.

TESMAN [moving about the room]. To think of Eilert going out of the world in this way! And not leaving behind him the book that would have immortalized his name—

MRS ELVSTED. Oh, if only it could be put together again!

TESMAN. Yes, if it only could! I don't know what I would not give—

MRS ELVSTED. Perhaps it can, Mr Tesman.

TESMAN. What do you mean?

MRS ELVSTED [searches in the pocket of her dress]. Look here. I have kept all the loose notes he used to dictate from.

HEDDA [a step forward]. Ah!

TESMAN. You have kept them, Mrs Elvsted! Eh?

MRS ELVSTED. Yes, I have them here. I put them in my pocket when I left home. Here they still are.

TESMAN. Oh, do let me see them!

MRS ELVSTED [*hands him a bundle of papers*]. But they are in such disorder—all mixed up.

TESMAN. Fancy if we could make something out of them after all! Perhaps if we two put our heads together—

MRS ELVSTED. Oh yes, at least let us try.

TESMAN. We will manage it! We must! I will dedicate my life to this task.

HEDDA. You, George? Your life?

TESMAN. Yes, or rather all the time I can spare. My own collections must wait in the meantime. Hedda—you understand, eh? I owe this to Eilert's memory.

HEDDA. Perhaps.

TESMAN. And so, my dear Mrs Elvsted, we will give our whole minds to it. There is no use in brooding over what can't be undone—eh? We must try to control our grief as much as possible, and—

MRS ELVSTED. Yes, yes, Mr Tesman, I will do the best I can.

TESMAN. Well then, come here. I can't rest until we have looked through the notes. Where shall we sit? Here? No, in there, in the back room. Excuse me, my dear judge. Come with me, Mrs Elvsted.

MRS ELVSTED. Oh, if only it were possible! [TESMAN and MRS ELVSTED *go into the back room. She takes off her hat and cloak. They both sit at the table under the hanging lamp and are soon deep in an eager examination of the papers.* HEDDA *crosses to the stove and sits in the armchair. Presently* BRACK *goes up to her.*]

HEDDA [*in a low voice*]. Oh, what sense of freedom it gives me, this act of Eilert Lövborg's.

BRACK. Freedom, Mrs Hedda? Well, of course, it is a release for him—

HEDDA. I mean for me. It gives me a sense of freedom to know that a deed of deliberate courage is still possible in this world—a deed of spontaneous beauty.

BRACK [*smiling*]. H'm—my dear Mrs Hedda—

HEDDA. Oh, I know what you are going to say. For you are a kind of specialist too, like—you know!

BRACK [*looking hard at her*]. Eilert Lövborg was more to you than perhaps you are willing to admit to yourself. Am I wrong?

HEDDA. I don't answer such questions. I only know Eilert Lövborg has had the courage to live his life after his own fashion. And then—the last great act, with its beauty! Ah! That he should have the will and the strength to turn away from the banquet of life—so early.

BRACK. I am sorry, Mrs Hedda, but I fear I must dispel an amiable illusion.

HEDDA. Illusion?

BRACK. Which could not have lasted long in any case.

HEDDA. What do you mean?

BRACK. Eilert Lövborg did not shoot himself voluntarily.

HEDDA. Not voluntarily?

BRACK. No. The thing did not happen exactly as I told it.

HEDDA [*in suspense*]. Have you concealed something? What is it?

BRACK. For poor Mrs Elvsted's sake I idealized the facts a little.

HEDDA. What are the facts?

BRACK. First, that he is already dead.

HEDDA. At the hospital?

BRACK. Yes—without regaining consciousness.

HEDDA. What more have you concealed?

BRACK. This—the event did not happen at his lodgings.

HEDDA. Oh, that can make no difference.

BRACK. Perhaps it may. For I must tell you—Eilert Lövborg was found shot in—in Mademoiselle Diana's boudoir.

HEDDA [*makes a motion as if to rise but sinks back again*]. That is impossible, Judge Brack! He cannot have been there again today.

BRACK. He was there this afternoon. He went there, he said, to demand the return of something which they had taken from him. Talked wildly about a lost child—

HEDDA. Ah—so that was why—

BRACK. I thought probably he meant his manuscript, but now I hear he destroyed that himself. So I suppose it must have been his pocketbook.

HEDDA. Yes, no doubt. And there—there he was found?

BRACK. Yes, there. With a pistol in his breast pocket, discharged. The ball had lodged in a vital part.

HEDDA. In the breast—yes.

BRACK. No—in the bowels.

HEDDA [*looks up at him with an expression of loathing*]. That too! Oh, what curse is it that makes everything I touch turn ludicrous and mean?

BRACK. There is one point more, Mrs Hedda—another disagreeable feature in the affair.

HEDDA. And what is that?

BRACK. The pistol he carried—

HEDDA [*breathless*]. Well? What of it?

BRACK. He must have stolen it.

HEDDA [*leaps up*]. Stolen it! That is not true! He did not steal it!

BRACK. No other explanation is possible. He must have stolen it— Hush!

[TESMAN *and* MRS ELVSTED *have risen from the table in the back room and come into the drawing room.*]

TESMAN [*with the papers in both his hands*]. Hedda dear, it is almost impossible to see under that lamp. Think of that!

HEDDA. Yes, I am thinking.

TESMAN. Would you mind our sitting at your writing table—eh?

HEDDA. If you like. [*Quickly.*] No, wait! Let me clear it first.

TESMAN. Oh, you needn't trouble, Hedda. There is plenty of room.

HEDDA. No, no; let me clear it, I say! I will take these

things in and put them on the piano. There! [*She has drawn out an object, covered with sheet music, from under the bookcase, places several other pieces of music upon it and carries the whole into the inner room to the left.* TESMAN *lays the scraps of paper on the writing table and moves the lamp there from the corner table.* HEDDA *returns.*]

HEDDA [*behind* MRS ELVSTED'S *chair, gently ruffling her hair*]. Well, my sweet Thea, how goes it with Eilert Lövborg's monument?

MRS ELVSTED [*looks dispiritedly up at her*]. Oh, it will be terribly hard to put in order.

TESMAN. We must manage it. I am determined. And arranging other people's papers is just the work for me.

[HEDDA *goes over to the stove and seats herself on one of the footstools.* BRACK *stands over her, leaning on the armchair.*]

HEDDA [*whispers*]. What did you say about the pistol?

BRACK [*softly*]. That he must have stolen it.

HEDDA. Why stolen it?

BRACK. Because every other explanation ought to be impossible, Mrs Hedda.

HEDDA. Indeed?

BRACK [*glances at her*]. Of course Eilert Lövborg was here this morning. Was he not?

HEDDA. Yes.

BRACK. Were you alone with him?

HEDDA. Part of the time.

BRACK. Did you not leave the room whilst he was here?

HEDDA. No.

BRACK. Try to recollect. Were you not out of the room a moment?

HEDDA. Yes, perhaps just a moment—out in the hall.

BRACK. And where was your pistol case during that time?

HEDDA. I had it locked up in—

BRACK. Well, Mrs Hedda?

HEDDA. The case stood there on the writing table.

BRACK. Have you looked since to see whether both the pistols are there?

HEDDA. No.

BRACK. Well, you need not. I saw the pistol found in Lövborg's pocket, and I knew it at once as the one I had seen yesterday—and before too.

HEDDA. Have you it with you?

BRACK. No, the police have it.

HEDDA. What will the police do with it?

BRACK. Search till they find the owner.

HEDDA. Do you think they will succeed?

BRACK [*bends over her and whispers*]. No, Hedda Gabler—not so long as I say nothing.

HEDDA [*looks frightened at him*]. And if you do not say nothing—what then?

BRACK [*shrugs his shoulders*]. There is always the possibility that the pistol was stolen.

HEDDA [*firmly*]. Death rather than that.

BRACK [*smiling*]. People say such things—but they don't do them.

HEDDA [*without replying*]. And supposing the pistol was stolen and the owner is discovered? What then?

BRACK. Well, Hedda—then comes the scandal.

HEDDA. The scandal!

BRACK. Yes, the scandal—of which you are mortally afraid. You will, of course, be brought before the court—both you and Mademoiselle Diana. She will have to explain how the thing happened—whether it was an accidental shot or murder. Did the pistol go off as he was trying to take it out of his pocket to threaten her with? Or did she tear the pistol out of his hand, shoot him and push it back into his pocket? That would be quite like her, for she is an able-bodied young person, this same Mademoiselle Diana.

HEDDA. But *I* have nothing to do with all this repulsive business.

BRACK. No. But you will have to answer the question: Why did you give Eilert Lövborg the pistol? And what conclusions will people draw from the fact that you did give it to him?

HEDDA [*lets her head sink*]. That is true. I did not think of that.

BRACK. Well, fortunately there is no danger so long as I say nothing.

HEDDA [*looks up at him*]. So I am in your power, Judge Brack. You have me at your beck and call from this time forward.

BRACK [*whispers softly*]. Dearest Hedda—believe me—I shall not abuse my advantage.

HEDDA. I am in your power none the less. Subject to your will and your demands. A slave, a slave then! [*Rises impetuously.*] No, I cannot endure the thought of that! Never!

BRACK [*looks half mockingly at her*]. People generally get used to the inevitable.

HEDDA [*returns his look*]. Yes, perhaps. [*She crosses to the writing table. Suppressing an involuntary smile, she imitates* TESMAN's *intonations.*] Well? Are you getting on, George? Eh?

TESMAN. Heaven knows, dear. In any case it will be the work of months.

HEDDA [*as before*]. Fancy that! [*Passes her hands softly through* MRS ELVSTED's *hair.*] Doesn't it seem strange to you, Thea? Here are you sitting with Tesman—just as you used to sit with Eilert Lövborg?

MRS ELVSTED. Ah, if I could only inspire your husband in the same way.

HEDDA. Oh, that will come too—in time.

TESMAN. Yes, do you know, Hedda—I really think I begin to feel something of the sort. But won't you go and sit with Brack again?

HEDDA. Is there nothing I can do to help you two?

TESMAN. No, nothing in the world. [*Turning his head.*]

I trust to you to keep Hedda company, my dear
Brack.

BRACK [*with a glance at* HEDDA]. With the very greatest
of pleasure.

HEDDA. Thanks. But I am tired this evening. I will go
in and lie down a little on the sofa.

TESMAN. Yes, do, dear—eh?

[HEDDA *goes into the back room and draws the curtains.
A short pause. Suddenly she is heard playing a wild
dance on the piano.*]

MRS ELVSTED [*starts from her chair*]. Oh—what is that?

TESMAN [*runs to the doorway*]. Why, my dearest Hedda
—don't play dance music tonight! Just think of Aunt
Rina! And of Eilert too!

HEDDA [*puts her head out between the curtains*]. And
of Aunt Julia. And of all the rest of them. After this
I will be quiet. [*Closes the curtains again.*]

TESMAN [*at the writing table*]. It's not good for her to
see us at this distressing work. I'll tell you what, Mrs
Elvsted—you shall take the empty room at Aunt
Julia's, and then I will come over in the evenings
and we can sit and work there—eh?

HEDDA [*in the inner room*]. I hear what you are saying,
Tesman. But how am *I* to get through the evenings
out here?

TESMAN [*turning over the papers*]. Oh, I daresay Judge
Brack will be so kind as to look in now and then,
even though I am out.

BRACK [*in the armchair, calls out gaily*]. Every blessed
evening, with all the pleasure in life, Mrs Tesman!
We shall get on capitally together, we two!

HEDDA [*speaking loud and clear*]. Yes, don't you flatter
yourself we will, Judge Brack? Now that you are the
one cock in the basket— [*A shot is heard within.* TES-
MAN, MRS ELVSTED *and* BRACK *leap to their feet.*]

TESMAN. Oh, now she is playing with those pistols
again. [*He throws back the curtains and runs in, followed by* MRS ELVSTED. HEDDA *lies stretched on the*

sofa, lifeless. Confusion and cries. BERTA *enters in alarm from the right.*]

TESMAN [*shrieks to* BRACK]. Shot herself! Shot herself in the temple! Fancy that!

BRACK [*half fainting in the armchair*]. Good God!— people don't do such things.

A DOLL'S HOUSE

PERSONS OF THE PLAY

TORVALD HELMER
NORA, *his wife*
DR RANK
MRS LINDE
NILS KROGSTAD
HELMER'S THREE YOUNG CHILDREN
ANNE, *their nurse*
A HOUSEMAID
A PORTER

The action takes place in Helmer's house.

ACT ONE

SCENE—*A room furnished comfortably and tastefully but not extravagantly. At the back a door to the right leads to the entrance hall; another to the left leads to* HELMER'S *study. Between the doors stands a piano. In the middle of the left-hand wall is a door and beyond a window. Near the window are a round table, armchairs and a small sofa. In the right-hand wall, at the farther end, another door: and on the same side, nearer the footlights, a stove, two easy chairs and a rocking chair; between the stove and the door a small table. Engravings on the walls; a cabinet with china and other small objects; a small bookcase with well-bound books. The floors are carpeted, and a fire burns in the stove. It is winter.*

A bell rings in the hall; shortly afterward the door is heard to open. Enter NORA, *humming a tune and in high spirits. She is in outdoor dress and carries a number of parcels; these she lays on the table to the right. She leaves the outer door open after her, and through it is seen a* PORTER *who is carrying a Christmas tree and a basket, which he gives to the* MAID *who has opened the door.*

NORA. Hide the Christmas tree carefully, Helen. Be sure the children do not see it till this evening, when it is dressed. [*To the* PORTER, *taking out her purse.*] How much?

PORTER. Sixpence.

NORA. There is a shilling. No, keep the change. [*The*
PORTER *thanks her and goes out.* NORA *shuts the door.*
She is laughing to herself as she takes off her hat and
coat. She takes a packet of macaroons from her
pocket and eats one or two, then goes cautiously to
her husband's door and listens.] Yes, he is in. [*Still*
humming, she goes to the table on the right.]

HELMER [*calls out from his room*]. Is that my little lark
twittering out there?

NORA [*busy opening some of the parcels*]. Yes, it is!

HELMER. Is it my little squirrel bustling about?

NORA. Yes!

HELMER. When did my squirrel come home?

NORA. Just now. [*Puts the bag of macaroons into her*
pocket and wipes her mouth.] Come in here, Torvald, and see what I have bought.

HELMER. Don't disturb me. [*A little later he opens the*
door and looks into the room, pen in hand.] Bought,
did you say? All these things? Has my little spend-
thrift been wasting money again?

NORA. Yes, but, Torvald, this year we really can let ourselves go a little. This is the first Christmas that we
have not needed to economize.

HELMER. Still, you know, we can't spend money reck-
lessly.

NORA. Yes, Torvald, we may be a wee bit more reckless
now, mayn't we? Just a tiny wee bit! You are going to
have a big salary and earn lots and lots of money.

HELMER. Yes, after the new year; but then it will be a
whole quarter before the salary is due.

NORA. Pooh! We can borrow till then.

HELMER. Nora! [*Goes up to her and takes her playfully*
by the ear.] The same little featherhead! Suppose,
now, that I borrowed fifty pounds today and you
spent it all in the Christmas week and then on New
Year's Eve a slate fell on my head and killed me
and—

NORA [*putting her hands over his mouth*]. Oh! don't say such horrid things.

HELMER. Still, suppose that happened,—what then?

NORA. If that were to happen, I don't suppose I should care whether I owed money or not.

HELMER. Yes, but what about the people who had lent it?

NORA. They? Who would bother about them? I should not know who they were.

HELMER. That is like a woman! But seriously, Nora, you know what I think about that. No debt, no borrowing. There can be no freedom or beauty about a home life that depends on borrowing and debt. We two have kept bravely on the straight road so far, and we will go on the same way for the short time longer that there need be any struggle.

NORA [*moving toward the stove*]. As you please, Torvald.

HELMER [*following her*]. Come, come, my little skylark must not droop her wings. What is this! Is my little squirrel out of temper? [*Taking out his purse.*] Nora, what do you think I have got here?

NORA [*turning round quickly*]. Money!

HELMER. There you are. [*Gives her some money.*] Do you think I don't know what a lot is wanted for housekeeping at Christmas time?

NORA [*counting*]. Ten shillings—a pound—two pounds! Thank you, thank you, Torvald; that will keep me going for a long time.

HELMER. Indeed it must.

NORA. Yes, yes, it will. But come here and let me show you what I have bought. And all so cheap! Look, here is a new suit for Ivar and a sword, and a horse and a trumpet for Bob, and a doll and dolly's bedstead for Emmy—they are very plain, but anyway she will soon break them in pieces. And here are dress lengths and handkerchiefs for the maids; old Anne ought really to have something better.

HELMER. And what is in this parcel?

NORA [*crying out*]. No, no! You mustn't see that till this evening.

HELMER. Very well. But now tell me, you extravagant little person, what would you like for yourself?

NORA. For myself? Oh, I am sure I don't want anything.

HELMER. Yes, but you must. Tell me something reasonable that you would particularly like to have.

NORA. No, I really can't think of anything—unless, Torvald—

HELMER. Well?

NORA [*playing with his coat buttons and without raising her eyes to his*]. If you really want to give me something, you might—you might—

HELMER. Well, out with it!

NORA [*speaking quickly*]. You might give me money, Torvald. Only just as much as you can afford; and then one of these days I will buy something with it.

HELMER. But, Nora—

NORA. Oh, do! dear Torvald; please, please do! Then I will wrap it up in beautiful gilt paper and hang it on the Christmas tree. Wouldn't that be fun?

HELMER. What are little people called that are always wasting money?

NORA. Spendthrifts—I know. Let us do as I suggest, Torvald, and then I shall have time to think what I am most in want of. That is a very sensible plan, isn't it?

HELMER [*smiling*]. Indeed it is—that is to say, if you were really to save out of the money I give you and then really buy something for yourself. But if you spend it all on the housekeeping and any number of unnecessary things, then I merely have to pay up again.

NORA. Oh, but, Torvald—

HELMER. You can't deny it, my dear little Nora. [*Puts his arm around her waist.*] It's a sweet little spendthrift, but she uses up a deal of money. One would hardly believe how expensive such little persons are!

NORA. It's a shame to say that. I do really save all I can.

HELMER [*laughing*]. That's very true—all you can. But you can't save anything!

NORA [*smiling quietly and happily*]. You haven't any idea how many expenses we skylarks and squirrels have, Torvald.

HELMER. You are an odd little soul. Very like your father. You always find some new way of wheedling money out of me, and as soon as you have got it it seems to melt in your hands. You never know where it has gone. Still, one must take you as you are. It is in the blood; for indeed it is true that you can inherit these things, Nora.

NORA. Ah, I wish I had inherited many of Papa's qualities.

HELMER. And I would not wish you to be anything but just what you are, my sweet little skylark. But, do you know, it strikes me that you are looking rather—what shall I say?—rather uneasy today.

NORA. Do I?

HELMER. You do, really. Look straight at me.

NORA [*looks at him*]. Well?

HELMER [*wagging his finger at her*]. Hasn't Miss Sweet Tooth been breaking rules in town today?

NORA. No; what makes you think that?

HELMER. Hasn't she paid a visit to the confectioner's?

NORA. No, I assure you, Torvald—

HELMER. Not been nibbling sweets?

NORA. No, certainly not.

HELMER. Not even taken a bite at a macaroon or two?

NORA. No, Torvald, I assure you, really—

HELMER. There, there, of course I was only joking.

NORA [*going to the table on the right*]. I should not think of going against your wishes.

HELMER. No, I am sure of that; besides, you gave me your word. [*Going up to her.*] Keep your little Christmas secrets to yourself, my darling. They will all be

revealed tonight when the Christmas tree is lit, no
doubt.

NORA. Did you remember to invite Doctor Rank?

HELMER. No. But there is no need; as a matter of course
he will come to dinner with us. However, I will ask
him when he comes in this morning. I have ordered
some good wine. Nora, you can't think how I am
looking forward to this evening.

NORA. So am I! And how the children will enjoy themselves, Torvald!

HELMER. It is splendid to feel that one has a perfectly
safe appointment and a big enough income. It's delightful to think of, isn't it?

NORA. It's wonderful!

HELMER. Do you remember last Christmas? For a full
three weeks beforehand you shut yourself up every
evening till long after midnight, making ornaments
for the Christmas tree and all the other fine things
that were to be a surprise to us. It was the dullest
three weeks I ever spent!

NORA. I didn't find it dull.

HELMER [*smiling*]. But there was precious little result,
Nora.

NORA. Oh, you shouldn't tease me about that again.
How could I help the cat's going in and tearing
everything to pieces?

HELMER. Of course you couldn't, poor little girl. You
had the best of intentions to please us all, and that's
the main thing. But it is a good thing that our hard
times are over.

NORA. Yes, it is really wonderful.

HELMER. This time I needn't sit here and be dull all
alone and you needn't ruin your dear eyes and your
pretty little hands—

NORA [*clapping her hands*]. No, Torvald, I needn't any
longer, need I! It's wonderfully lovely to hear you say
so! [*Taking his arm.*] Now I will tell you how I have

been thinking we ought to arrange things, Torvald. As soon as Christmas is over— [*A bell rings in the hall.*] There's the bell. [*She tidies the room a little.*] There's someone at the door. What a nuisance!

HELMER. If it is a caller, remember I am not at home.

MAID [*in the doorway*]. A lady to see you, ma'am—a stranger.

NORA. Ask her to come in.

MAID [*to* HELMER]. The doctor came at the same time, sir.

HELMER. Did he go straight into my room?

MAID. Yes sir.

[HELMER *goes into his room. The* MAID *ushers in* MRS LINDE, *who is in traveling dress, and shuts the door.*]

MRS LINDE [*in a dejected and timid voice*]. How do you do, Nora?

NORA [*doubtfully*]. How do you do—

MRS LINDE. You don't recognize me, I suppose.

NORA. No, I don't know—yes, to be sure, I seem to— [*Suddenly.*] Yes! Christine! Is it really you?

MRS LINDE. Yes, it is I.

NORA. Christine! To think of my not recognizing you! And yet how could I? [*In a gentle voice.*] How you have altered, Christine!

MRS LINDE. Yes, I have indeed. In nine, ten long years—

NORA. Is it so long since we met? I suppose it is. The last eight years have been a happy time for me, I can tell you. And so now you have come into the town and have taken this long journey in winter—that was plucky of you.

MRS LINDE. I arrived by steamer this morning.

NORA. To have some fun at Christmas time, of course. How delightful! We will have such fun together! But take off your things. You are not cold, I hope. [*Helps her.*] Now we will sit down by the stove and be cozy. No, take this armchair; I will sit here in the rocking chair. [*Takes her hands.*] Now you look like

your old self again; it was only the first moment—
You are a little paler, Christine, and perhaps a little
thinner.

MRS LINDE. And much, much older, Nora.

NORA. Perhaps a little older; very, very little; certainly
not much. [*Stops suddenly and speaks seriously.*]
What a thoughtless creature I am, chattering away
like this. My poor, dear Christine, do forgive me.

MRS LINDE. What do you mean, Nora?

NORA [*gently*]. Poor Christine, you are a widow.

MRS LINDE. Yes; it is three years ago now.

NORA. Yes, I knew; I saw it in the papers. I assure you,
Christine, I meant ever so often to write to you at
the time, but I always put it off and something always prevented me.

MRS LINDE. I quite understand, dear.

NORA. It was very bad of me, Christine. Poor thing, how
you must have suffered. And he left you nothing?

MRS LINDE. No.

NORA. And no children?

MRS LINDE. No.

NORA. Nothing at all, then?

MRS LINDE. Not even any sorrow or grief to live upon.

NORA [*looking incredulously at her*]. But, Christine, is
that possible?

MRS LINDE [*smiles sadly and strokes her hair*]. It sometimes happens, Nora.

NORA. So you are quite alone. How dreadfully sad that
must be. I have three lovely children. You can't see
them just now, for they are out with their nurse. But
now you must tell me all about it.

MRS LINDE. No, no; I want to hear about you.

NORA. No, you must begin. I mustn't be selfish today;
today I must only think of your affairs. But there is
one thing I must tell you. Do you know we have just
had a great piece of good luck?

MRS LINDE. No, what is it?

NORA. Just fancy, my husband has been made manager of the bank!

MRS LINDE. Your husband? What good luck!

NORA. Yes, tremendous! A barrister's profession is such an uncertain thing, especially if he won't undertake unsavory cases; and naturally Torvald has never been willing to do that, and I quite agree with him. You may imagine how pleased we are! He is to take up his work in the bank at the new year, and then he will have a big salary and lots of commissions. For the future we can live quite differently—we can do just as we like. I feel so relieved and so happy, Christine! It will be splendid to have heaps of money and not need to have any anxiety, won't it?

MRS LINDE. Yes, anyhow I think it would be delightful to have what one needs.

NORA. No, not only what one needs but heaps and heaps of money.

MRS LINDE [smiling]. Nora, Nora, haven't you learned sense yet? In our schooldays you were a great spend-thrift.

NORA [laughing]. Yes, that is what Torvald says now. [Wags her finger at her.] But "Nora, Nora" is not so silly as you think. We have not been in a position for me to waste money. We have both had to work.

MRS LINDE. You too?

NORA. Yes; odds and ends, needlework, crochet work, embroidery and that kind of thing. [Dropping her voice.] And other things as well. You know Torvald left his office when we were married? There was no prospect of promotion there, and he had to try and earn more than before. But during the first year he overworked himself dreadfully. You see, he had to make money every way he could; and he worked early and late; but he couldn't stand it and fell dreadfully ill, and the doctors said it was necessary for him to go south.

MRS LINDE. You spent a whole year in Italy, didn't you?

NORA. Yes. It was no easy matter to get away, I can tell you. It was just after Ivar was born, but naturally we had to go. It was a wonderfully beautiful journey, and it saved Torvald's life. But it cost a tremendous lot of money, Christine.

MRS LINDE. So I should think.

NORA. It cost about two hundred and fifty pounds. That's a lot, isn't it?

MRS LINDE. Yes, and in emergencies like that it is lucky to have the money.

NORA. I ought to tell you that we had it from Papa.

MRS LINDE. Oh, I see. It was just about that time that he died, wasn't it?

NORA. Yes; and, just think of it, I couldn't go and nurse him. I was expecting little Ivar's birth every day and I had my poor sick Torvald to look after. My dear, kind father—I never saw him again, Christine. That was the saddest time I have known since our marriage.

MRS LINDE. I know how fond you were of him. And then you went off to Italy?

NORA. Yes; you see, we had money then, and the doctors insisted on our going, so we started a month later.

MRS LINDE. And your husband came back quite well?

NORA. As sound as a bell!

MRS LINDE. But—the doctor?

NORA. What doctor?

MRS LINDE. I thought your maid said the gentleman who arrived here just as I did was the doctor.

NORA. Yes, that was Doctor Rank but he doesn't come here professionally. He is our greatest friend and comes in at least once every day. No, Torvald has not had an hour's illness since then, and our children are strong and healthy and so am I. [*Jumps up and claps her hands.*] Christine! Christine! It's good to be alive and happy! But how horrid of me; I am talking of nothing but my own affairs. [*Sits on a stool near her*

and rests her arms on her knees.] You mustn't be angry with me. Tell me, is it really true that you did
not love your husband? Why did you marry him?

MRS LINDE. My mother was alive then and was bedrid-
den and helpless, and I had to provide for my two
younger brothers; so I did not think I was justified
in refusing his offer.

NORA. No, perhaps you were quite right. He was rich
at that time, then?

MRS LINDE. I believe he was quite well off. But his business was a precarious one, and when he died it all
went to pieces and there was nothing left.

NORA. And then?

MRS LINDE. Well, I had to turn my hand to anything I
could find—first a small shop, then a small school and
so on. The last three years have seemed like one long
working day, with no rest. Now it is at an end, Nora.
My poor mother needs me no more, for she is gone;
and the boys do not need me either; they have got
situations and can shift for themselves.

NORA. What a relief you must feel it.

MRS LINDE. No indeed; I only feel my life unspeakably
empty. No one to live for any more. [*Gets up restlessly.*] That was why I could not stand the life in my
little backwater any longer. I hope it may be easier
here to find something which will busy me and oc-
cupy my thoughts. If only I could have the good luck
to get some regular work—office work of some kind—

NORA. But, Christine, that is so frightfully tiring, and
you look tired out now. You had far better go away
to some watering place.

MRS LINDE [*walking to the window*]. I have no father to
give me money for a journey, Nora.

NORA [*rising*]. Oh, don't be angry with me.

MRS LINDE [*going up to her*]. It is you that must not be
angry with me, dear. The worst of a position like
mine is that it makes one so bitter. No one to work
for and yet obliged to be always on the lookout for

chances. One must live, and so one becomes selfish. When you told me of the happy turn your fortunes have taken—you will hardly believe it—I was delighted not so much on your account as on my own.

NORA. How do you mean? Oh, I understand. You mean that perhaps Torvald could get you something to do.

MRS LINDE. Yes, that was what I was thinking of.

NORA. He must, Christine. Just leave it to me; I will broach the subject very cleverly—I will think of something that will please him very much. It will make me so happy to be of some use to you.

MRS LINDE. How kind you are, Nora, to be so anxious to help me! It is doubly kind in you, for you know so little of the burdens and troubles of life.

NORA. I? I know so little of them?

MRS LINDE [*smiling*]. My dear! Small household cares and that sort of thing! You are a child, Nora.

NORA [*tosses her head and crosses the stage*]. You ought not to be so superior.

MRS LINDE. No?

NORA. You are just like the others. They all think that I am incapable of anything really serious—

MRS LINDE. Come, come.

NORA. —that I have gone through nothing in this world of cares.

MRS LINDE. But, my dear Nora, you have just told me all your troubles.

NORA. Pooh!—those were trifles. [*Lowering her voice.*] I have not told you the important thing.

MRS LINDE. The important thing? What do you mean?

NORA. You look down upon me altogether, Christine—but you ought not to. You are proud, aren't you, of having worked so hard and so long for your mother?

MRS LINDE. Indeed, I don't look down on anyone. But it is true that I am both proud and glad to think that I was privileged to make the end of my mother's life almost free from care.

NORA. And you are proud to think of what you have done for your brothers.

MRS LINDE. I think I have the right to be.

NORA. I think so too. But now listen to this; I too have something to be proud and glad of.

MRS LINDE. I have no doubt you have. But what do you refer to?

NORA. Speak low. Suppose Torvald were to hear! He mustn't on any account—no one in the world must know, Christine, except you.

MRS LINDE. But what is it?

NORA. Come here. [*Pulls her down on the sofa beside her.*] Now I will show you that I too have something to be proud and glad of. It was I who saved Torvald's life.

MRS LINDE. "Saved"? How?

NORA. I told you about our trip to Italy. Torvald would never have recovered if he had not gone there.

MRS LINDE. Yes, but your father gave you the necessary funds.

NORA [*smiling*]. Yes, that is what Torvald and the others think, but—

MRS LINDE. But—

NORA. Papa didn't give us a shilling. It was I who procured the money.

MRS LINDE. You? All that large sum?

NORA. Two hundred and fifty pounds. What do you think of that?

MRS LINDE. But, Nora, how could you possibly do it? Did you win a prize in the lottery?

NORA [*contemptuously*]. In the lottery? There would have been no credit in that.

MRS LINDE. But where did you get it from, then?

NORA [*humming and smiling with an air of mystery*]. Hm, hm! Aha!

MRS LINDE. Because you couldn't have borrowed it.

NORA. Couldn't I? Why not?

MRS LINDE. No, a wife cannot borrow without her husband's consent.

NORA [*tossing her head*]. Oh, if it is a wife who has any head for business—a wife who has the wit to be a little bit clever—

MRS LINDE. I don't understand it at all, Nora.

NORA. There is no need you should. I never said I had borrowed the money. I may have got it some other way. [*Lies back on the sofa.*] Perhaps I got it from some other admirers. When anyone is as attractive as I am—

MRS LINDE. You are a mad creature.

NORA. Now you know you're full of curiosity, Christine.

MRS LINDE. Listen to me, Nora dear. Haven't you been a little bit imprudent?

NORA [*sits up straight*]. Is it imprudent to save your husband's life?

MRS LINDE. It seems to me imprudent, without his knowledge, to—

NORA. But it was absolutely necessary that he should not know! My goodness, can't you understand that? It was necessary he should have no idea what a dangerous condition he was in. It was to me that the doctors came and said that his life was in danger and that the only thing to save him was to live in the south. Do you suppose I didn't try, first of all, to get what I wanted as if it were for myself? I told him how much I should love to travel abroad like other young wives; I tried tears and entreaties with him; I told him that he ought to remember the condition I was in and that he ought to be kind and indulgent to me; I even hinted that he might raise a loan. That nearly made him angry, Christine. He said I was thoughtless and that it was his duty as my husband not to indulge me in my whims and caprices—as I believe he called them. Very well, I thought, you must be saved—and that was how I came to devise a way out of the difficulty.

MRS LINDE. And did your husband never get to know from your father that the money had not come from him?

NORA. No, never. Papa died just at that time. I had meant to let him into the secret and beg him never to reveal it. But he was so ill then—alas, there never was any need to tell him.

MRS LINDE. And since then have you never told your secret to your husband?

NORA. Good heavens, no! How could you think so? A man who has such strong opinions about these things! And besides, how painful and humiliating it would be for Torvald, with his manly independence, to know that he owed me anything! It would upset our mutual relations altogether; our beautiful happy home would no longer be what it is now.

MRS LINDE. Do you mean never to tell him about it?

NORA [*meditatively and with a half-smile*]. Yes—some-day, perhaps, after many years, when I am no longer as nice looking as I am now. Don't laugh at me! I mean, of course, when Torvald is no longer as de-voted to me as he is now; when my dancing and dressing-up and reciting have palled on him; then it may be a good thing to have something in reserve— [*Breaking off.*] What nonsense! That time will never come. Now what do you think of my great secret, Christine? Do you still think I am of no use? I can tell you too, that this affair has caused me a lot of worry. It has been by no means easy for me to meet my engagements punctually. I may tell you that there is something that is called, in business, quarterly in-terest and another thing called payment in install-ments, and it is always so dreadfully difficult to man-age them. I have had to save a little here and there, where I could, you understand. I have not been able to put aside much from my housekeeping money, for Torvald must have a good table. I couldn't let my children be shabbily dressed; I have felt obliged to

use up all he gave me for them, the sweet little darlings!

MRS LINDE. So it has all had to come out of your own
necessaries of life, poor Nora?

NORA. Of course. Besides, I was the one responsible for
it. Whenever Torvald has given me money for new
dresses and such things I have never spent more than
half of it; I have always bought the simplest and
cheapest things. Thank heaven any clothes look well
on me, and so Torvald has never noticed it. But it
was often very hard on me, Christine—because it is
delightful to be really well dressed, isn't it?

MRS LINDE. Quite so.

NORA. Well, then I have found other ways of earning
money. Last winter I was lucky enough to get a lot
of copying to do, so I locked myself up and sat writing every evening until quite late at night. Many a
time I was desperately tired, but all the same it was
a tremendous pleasure to sit there working and earning money. It was like being a man.

MRS LINDE. How much have you been able to pay off in
that way?

NORA. I can't tell you exactly. You see, it is very difficult
to keep an account of a business matter of that kind.
I only know that I have paid every penny that I
could scrape together. Many a time I was at my wits'
end. [*Smiles.*] Then I used to sit here and imagine
that a rich old gentleman had fallen in love with
me—

MRS LINDE. What! Who was it?

NORA. Be quiet!—that he had died and that when his
will was opened it contained, written in big letters,
the instruction: "The lovely Mrs Nora Helmer is to
have all I possess paid over to her at once in cash."

MRS LINDE. But, my dear Nora—who could the man be?

NORA. Good gracious, can't you understand? There was
no old gentleman at all; it was only something that
I used to sit here and imagine, when I couldn't think

of any way of procuring money. But it's all the same now; the tiresome old person can stay where he is as far as I am concerned; I don't care about him or his will either, for I am free from care now. [*Jumps up.*] My goodness, it's delightful to think of, Christine! Free from care! To be able to be free from care, quite free from care; to be able to play and romp with the children; to be able to keep the house beautifully and have everything just as Torvald likes it! And, think of it, soon the spring will come and the big blue sky! Perhaps we shall be able to take a little trip—perhaps I shall see the sea again! Oh, it's a wonderful thing to be alive and be happy. [*A bell is heard in the hall.*]

MRS LINDE [*rising*]. There is the bell; perhaps I had better go.

NORA. No, don't go; no one will come in here; it is sure to be for Torvald.

SERVANT [*at the hall door*]. Excuse me, ma'am—there is a gentleman to see the master, and as the doctor is with him—

NORA. Who is it?

KROGSTAD [*at the door*]. It is I, Mrs Helmer. [MRS LINDE *starts, trembles and turns to the window.*]

NORA [*takes a step toward him and speaks in a strained, low voice*]. You? What is it? What do you want to see my husband about?

KROGSTAD. Bank business—in a way. I have a small post in the bank, and I hear your husband is to be our chief now.

NORA. Then it is—

KROGSTAD. Nothing but dry business matters, Mrs Helmer; absolutely nothing else.

NORA. Be so good as to go into the study then. [*She bows indifferently to him and shuts the door into the hall, then comes back and makes up the fire in the stove.*]

MRS LINDE. Nora—who was that man?

NORA. A lawyer of the name of Krogstad.

MRS LINDE. Then it really was he.

NORA. Do you know the man?

MRS LINDE. I used to—many years ago. At one time he
was a solicitor's clerk in our town.

NORA. Yes, he was.

MRS LINDE. He is greatly altered.

NORA. He made a very unhappy marriage.

MRS LINDE. He is a widower now, isn't he?

NORA. With several children. There now, it is burning
up. [*Shuts the door of the stove and moves the rocking chair aside.*]

MRS LINDE. They say he carries on various kinds of
business.

NORA. Really! Perhaps he does; I don't know anything
about it. But don't let us think of business; it is so
tiresome.

DR RANK [*comes out of* HELMER'S *study. Before he shuts
the door he calls to him*]. No, my dear fellow, I won't
disturb you; I would rather go in to your wife for a
little while. [*Shuts the door and sees* MRS LINDE.] I
beg your pardon; I am afraid I am disturbing you
too.

NORA. No, not at all. [*Introducing him.*] Doctor Rank,
Mrs Linde.

RANK. I have often heard Mrs Linde's name mentioned
here. I think I passed you on the stairs when I arrived, Mrs Linde?

MRS LINDE. Yes, I go up very slowly; I can't manage
stairs well.

RANK. Ah! Some slight internal weakness?

MRS LINDE. No, the fact is I have been overworking myself.

RANK. Nothing more than that? Then I suppose you
have come to town to amuse yourself with our enter-
tertainments?

MRS LINDE. I have come to look for work.

RANK. Is that a good cure for overwork?

MRS LINDE. One must live, Doctor Rank.

RANK. Yes, the general opinion seems to be that it is necessary.

NORA. Look here, Doctor Rank—you know you want to live.

RANK. Certainly. However wretched I may feel, I want to prolong the agony as long as possible. All my patients are like that. And so are those who are morally diseased; one of them, and a bad case too, is at this very moment with Helmer—

MRS LINDE [*sadly*]. Ah!

NORA. Whom do you mean?

RANK. A lawyer of the name of Krogstad, a fellow you don't know at all. He suffers from a diseased moral character, Mrs Helmer, but even he began talking of its being highly important that he should live.

NORA. Did he? What did he want to speak to Torvald about?

RANK. I have no idea; I only heard that it was something about the bank.

NORA. I didn't know this—what's his name?—Krogstad had anything to do with the bank.

RANK. Yes, he has some sort of appointment there. [*To* MRS LINDE.] I don't know whether you find also in your part of the world that there are certain people who go zealously snuffing about to smell out moral corruption and, as soon as they have found some, put the person concerned into some lucrative position where they can keep their eye on him. Healthy natures are left out in the cold.

MRS LINDE. Still I think the sick are those who most need taking care of.

RANK [*shrugging his shoulders*]. Yes, there you are. That is the sentiment that is turning society into a sick house.

[NORA, *who has been absorbed in her thoughts, breaks*

out into smothered laughter and claps her hands.]

RANK. Why do you laugh at that? Have you any notion what society really is?

NORA. What do I care about tiresome society? I am laughing at something quite different, something extremely amusing. Tell me, Doctor Rank, are all the people who are employed in the bank dependent on Torvald now?

RANK. Is that what you find so extremely amusing?

NORA [*smiling and humming*]. That's my affair! [*Walking about the room.*] It's perfectly glorious to think that we have—that Torvald has so much power over so many people. [*Takes the packet from her pocket.*] Doctor Rank, what do you say to a macaroon?

RANK. What, macaroons? I thought they were forbidden here.

NORA. Yes, but these are some Christine gave me.

MRS LINDE. What! I?

NORA. Oh well, don't be alarmed! You couldn't know that Torvald had forbidden them. I must tell you that he is afraid they will spoil my teeth. But, bah! —once in a way— That's so, isn't it, Doctor Rank? By your leave! [*Puts a macaroon into his mouth.*] You must have one too, Christine. And I shall have one, just a little one—or at most two. [*Walking about.*] I am tremendously happy. There is just one thing in the world now that I should dearly love to do.

RANK. Well, what is that?

NORA. It's something I should dearly love to say if Torvald could hear me.

RANK. Well, why can't you say it?

NORA. No, I daren't; it's so shocking.

MRS LINDE. Shocking?

RANK. Well, I should not advise you to say it. Still, with us you might. What is it you would so much like to say if Torvald could hear you?

NORA. I should just love to say— Well, I'm damned!

RANK. Are you mad?

MRS LINDE. Nora dear!

RANK. Say it, here he is!

NORA [*hiding the packet*]. Hush! Hush! Hush!

[HELMER *comes out of his room with his coat over his his arm and his hat in his hand.*]

NORA. Well, Torvald dear, have you got rid of him?

HELMER. Yes, he has just gone.

NORA. Let me introduce you—this is Christine, who has come to town.

HELMER. Christine? Excuse me, but I don't know—

NORA. Mrs Linde, dear; Christine Linde.

HELMER. Of course. A school friend of my wife's, I presume?

MRS LINDE. Yes, we have known each other since then.

NORA. And just think, she has taken a long journey in order to see you.

HELMER. What do you mean?

MRS LINDE. No, really, I—

NORA. Christine is tremendously clever at bookkeeping, and she is frightfully anxious to work under some clever man, so as to perfect herself—

HELMER. Very sensible, Mrs Linde.

NORA. And when she heard you had been appointed manager of the bank—the news was telegraphed, you know—she traveled here as quick as she could. Torvald, I am sure you will be able to do something for Christine, for my sake, won't you?

HELMER. Well, it is not altogether impossible. I presume you are a widow, Mrs Linde?

MRS LINDE. Yes.

HELMER. And have had some experience of bookkeeping?

MRS LINDE. Yes, a fair amount.

HELMER. Ah well, it's very likely I may be able to find something for you.

NORA [*clapping her hands*]. What did I tell you?

HELMER. You have just come at a fortunate moment, Mrs Linde.

MRS LINDE. How am I to thank you?

HELMER. There is no need. [*Puts on his coat.*] But to-day you must excuse me—

RANK. Wait a minute; I will come with you. [*Brings his fur coat from the hall and warms it at the fire.*]

NORA. Don't be long away, Torvald, dear.

HELMER. About an hour, not more.

NORA. Are you going too, Christine?

MRS LINDE [*putting on her cloak*]. Yes, I must go and look for a room.

HELMER. Oh well, then, we can walk down the street together.

NORA [*helping her*]. What a pity it is we are so short of space here; I am afraid it is impossible for us—

MRS LINDE. Please don't think of it! Good-by, Nora dear, and many thanks.

NORA. Good-by for the present. Of course you will come back this evening. And you too, Doctor Rank. What do you say? If you are well enough? Oh, you must be! Wrap yourself up well. [*They go to the door all talking together. Children's voices are heard on the staircase.*]

NORA. There they are. There they are! [*She runs to open the door. The* NURSE *comes in with the children.*] Come in! Come in! [*Stoops and kisses them.*] Oh, you sweet blessings! Look at them, Christine! Aren't they darlings?

RANK. Don't let us stand here in the draught.

HELMER. Come along, Mrs Linde; the place will only be bearable for a mother now!

[RANK, HELMER *and* MRS LINDE *go downstairs. The* NURSE *comes forward with the children;* NORA *shuts the hall door.*]

NORA. How fresh and well you look! Such red cheeks!— like apples and roses. [*The children all talk at once while she speaks to them.*] Have you had great fun? That's splendid! What, you pulled both Emmy and Bob along on the sledge? Both at once? That *was*

good. You are a clever boy, Ivar. Let me take her for
a little, Anne. My sweet little baby doll! [*Takes the
baby from the* MAID *and dances it up and down.*] Yes,
yes, Mother will dance with Bob too. What! Have
you been snowballing? I wish I had been there too!
No, no, I will take their things off, Anne; please let
me do it, it is such fun. Go in now, you look half
frozen. There is some hot coffee for you on the stove.

[*The* NURSE *goes into the room on the left.* NORA *takes
off the children's things and throws them about
while they all talk to her at once.*]

NORA. *Really!* Did a big dog run after you? But it didn't
bite you? No, dogs don't bite nice little dolly children. You mustn't look at the parcels, Ivar. What are
they? Ah, I daresay you would like to know. No, no—
it's something nasty! Come, let us have a game! What
shall we play at? Hide and seek? Yes, we'll play hide
and seek. Bob shall hide first. Must I hide? Very well,
I'll hide first. [*She and the children laugh and shout
and romp in and out of the room; at last* NORA *hides
under the table; the children rush in and look for
her but do not see her; they hear her smothered
laughter, run to the table, lift up the cloth and find
her. Shouts of laughter. She crawls forward and pre-
tends to frighten them. Fresh laughter. Meanwhile
there has been a knock at the hall door but none of
them has noticed it. The door is half opened and*
KROGSTAD *appears. He waits a little; the game goes
on.*]

KROGSTAD. Excuse me, Mrs Helmer.

NORA [*with a stifled cry turns round and gets up onto
her knees*]. Ah! What do you want?

KROGSTAD. Excuse me, the outer door was ajar; I suppose someone forgot to shut it.

NORA [*rising*]. My husband is out, Mr Krogstad.

KROGSTAD. I know that.

NORA. What do you want here then?

KROGSTAD. A word with you.

NORA. With me? [*To the children, gently.*] Go in to
Nurse. What? No, the strange man won't do Mother
any harm. When he has gone we will have another
game. [*She takes the children into the room on the
left and shuts the door after them.*] You want to
speak to me?

KROGSTAD. Yes, I do.

NORA. Today? It is not the first of the month yet.

KROGSTAD. No, it is Christmas Eve, and it will depend
on yourself what sort of a Christmas you will spend.

NORA. What do you want? Today it is absolutely impossible for me—

KROGSTAD. We won't talk about that till later on. This
is something different. I presume you can give me a
moment?

NORA. Yes—yes, I can—although—

KROGSTAD. Good. I was in Olsen's Restaurant and saw
your husband going down the street—

NORA. Yes?

KROGSTAD. With a lady.

NORA. What then?

KROGSTAD. May I make so bold as to ask if it was a Mrs
Linde?

NORA. It was.

KROGSTAD. Just arrived in town?

NORA. Yes, today.

KROGSTAD. She is a great friend of yours, isn't she?

NORA. She is. But I don't see—

KROGSTAD. I knew her too, once upon a time.

NORA. I am aware of that.

KROGSTAD. Are you? So you know all about it; I thought
as much. Then I can ask you, without beating about
the bush—is Mrs Linde to have an appointment in
the bank?

NORA. What right have you to question me, Mr Krogstad? You, one of my husband's subordinates! But
since you ask, you shall know. Yes, Mrs Linde *is* to

have an appointment. And it was I who pleaded her cause, Mr Krogstad, let me tell you that.

KROGSTAD. I was right in what I thought then.

NORA [*walking up and down the stage*]. Sometimes one has a tiny little bit of influence, I should hope. Because one is a woman it does not necessarily follow that— When anyone is in a subordinate position, Mr Krogstad, they should really be careful to avoid offending anyone who—who—

KROGSTAD. Who has influence?

NORA. Exactly.

KROGSTAD [*changing his tone*]. Mrs Helmer, you will be so good as to use your influence on my behalf.

NORA. What? What do you mean?

KROGSTAD. You will be so kind as to see that I am allowed to keep my subordinate position in the bank.

NORA. What do you mean by that? Who proposes to take your post away from you?

KROGSTAD. Oh, there is no necessity to keep up the pretence of ignorance. I can quite understand that your friend is not very anxious to expose herself to the chance of rubbing shoulders with me, and I quite understand, too, whom I have to thank for being turned off.

NORA. But I assure you—

KROGSTAD. Very likely; but, to come to the point, the time has come when I should advise you to use your influence to prevent that.

NORA. But, Mr Krogstad, I *have* no influence.

KROGSTAD. Haven't you? I thought you said yourself just now—

NORA. Naturally I did not mean you to put that construction on it. I! What should make you think I have any influence of that kind with my husband?

KROGSTAD. Oh, I have known your husband from our student days. I don't suppose he is any more unassailable than other husbands.

NORA. If you speak slightingly of my husband, I shall turn you out of the house.

KROGSTAD. You are bold, Mrs Helmer.

NORA. I am not afraid of you any longer. As soon as the New Year comes I shall in a very short time be free of the whole thing.

KROGSTAD [*controlling himself*]. Listen to me, Mrs Helmer. If necessary, I am prepared to fight for my small post in the bank as if I were fighting for my life.

NORA. So it seems.

KROGSTAD. It is not only for the sake of the money; indeed, that weighs least with me in the matter. There is another reason—well, I may as well tell you. My position is this. I daresay you know, like everybody else, that once, many years ago, I was guilty of an indiscretion.

NORA. I think I have heard something of the kind.

KROGSTAD. The matter never came into court, but every way seemed to be closed to me after that. So I took to the business that you know of. I had to do something; and, honestly, I don't think I've been one of the worst. But now I must cut myself free from all that. My sons are growing up; for their sake I must try and win back as much respect as I can in the town. This post in the bank was like the first step up for me—and now your husband is going to kick me downstairs again into the mud.

NORA. But you must believe me, Mr Krogstad; it is not in my power to help you at all.

KROGSTAD. Then it is because you haven't the will, but I have means to compel you.

NORA. You don't mean that you will tell my husband that I owe you money?

KROGSTAD. Hm! Suppose I were to tell him?

NORA. It would be perfectly infamous of you. [*Sobbing.*] To think of his learning my secret, which has been my joy and pride, in such an ugly, clumsy way—that he should learn it from you! And it would put me in a horribly disagreeable position.

KROGSTAD. Only disagreeable?

NORA [*impetuously*]. Well, do it then!—and it will be the worse for you. My husband will see for himself what a blackguard you are, and you certainly won't keep your post then.

KROGSTAD. I asked you if it was only a disagreeable scene at home that you were afraid of?

NORA. If my husband does get to know of it, of course he will at once pay you what is still owing, and we shall have nothing more to do with you.

KROGSTAD [*coming a step nearer*]. Listen to me, Mrs Helmer. Either you have a very bad memory or you know very little of business. I shall be obliged to remind you of a few details.

NORA. What do you mean?

KROGSTAD. When your husband was ill you came to me to borrow two hundred and fifty pounds.

NORA. I didn't know anyone else to go to.

KROGSTAD. I promised to get you that amount—

NORA. Yes, and you did so.

KROGSTAD. I promised to get you that amount on certain conditions. Your mind was so taken up with your husband's illness and you were so anxious to get the money for your journey that you seem to have paid no attention to the conditions of our bargain. Therefore it will not be amiss if I remind you of them. Now I promised to get the money on the security of a bond which I drew up.

NORA. Yes, and which I signed.

KROGSTAD. Good. But below your signature there were a few lines constituting your father a surety for the money; those lines your father should have signed.

NORA. Should? He did sign them.

KROGSTAD. I had left the date blank; that is to say your father should himself have inserted the date on which he signed the paper. Do you remember that?

NORA. Yes, I think I remember.

KROGSTAD. Then I gave you the bond to send by post to your father. Is that not so?

NORA. Yes.

KROGSTAD. And you naturally did so at once, because five or six days afterward you brought me the bond with your father's signature. And then I gave you the money.

NORA. Well, haven't I been paying it off regularly?

KROGSTAD. Fairly so, yes. But—to come back to the matter in hand—that must have been a very trying time for you, Mrs Helmer?

NORA. It was, indeed.

KROGSTAD. Your father was very ill, wasn't he?

NORA. He was very near his end.

KROGSTAD. And died soon afterward?

NORA. Yes.

KROGSTAD. Tell me, Mrs Helmer, can you by any chance remember what day your father died?—on what day of the month, I mean.

NORA. Papa died on the twenty-ninth of September.

KROGSTAD. That is correct; I have ascertained it for myself. And, as that is so, there is a discrepancy [*taking a paper from his pocket*] which I cannot account for.

NORA. What discrepancy? I don't know—

KROGSTAD. The discrepancy consists, Mrs Helmer, in the fact that your father signed this bond three days after his death.

NORA. What do you mean? I don't understand.

KROGSTAD. Your father died on the twenty-ninth of September. But look here; your father has dated his signature the second of October. It is a discrepancy, isn't it? [NORA *is silent.*] Can you explain it to me? [NORA *is still silent.*] It is a remarkable thing, too, that the words "second of October," as well as the year, are not written in your father's handwriting but in one that I think I know. Well, of course it can be explained; your father may have forgotten to date his signature and someone else may have dated it haphazard before they knew of his death. There is no harm in that. It all depends on the signature of the name, and *that* is genuine, I suppose, Mrs Helmer? It was your father himself who signed his name here?

NORA [*after a short pause, throws her head up and looks defiantly at him*]. No, it was not. It was I that wrote Papa's name.

KROGSTAD. Are you aware that is a dangerous confession?

NORA. In what way? You shall have your money soon.

KROGSTAD. Let me ask you a question: why did you not send the paper to your father?

NORA. It was impossible; Papa was so ill. If I had asked him for his signature, I should have had to tell him what the money was to be used for; and when he was so ill himself I couldn't tell him that my husband's life was in danger—it was impossible.

KROGSTAD. It would have been better for you if you had given up your trip abroad.

NORA. No, that was impossible. That trip was to save my husband's life; I couldn't give that up.

KROGSTAD. But did it never occur to you that you were committing a fraud on me?

NORA. I couldn't take that into account; I didn't trouble myself about you at all. I couldn't bear you because you put so many heartless difficulties in my way although you knew what a dangerous condition my husband was in.

KROGSTAD. Mrs Helmer, you evidently do not realize clearly what it is that you have been guilty of. But I can assure you that my one false step, which lost me all my reputation, was nothing more or nothing worse than what you have done.

NORA. You? Do you ask me to believe that you were brave enough to run a risk to save your wife's life?

KROGSTAD. The law cares nothing about motives.

NORA. Then it must be a very foolish law.

KROGSTAD. Foolish or not, it is the law by which you will be judged if I produce this paper in court.

NORA. I don't believe it. Is a daughter not to be allowed to spare her dying father anxiety and care? Is a wife not to be allowed to save her husband's life? I don't know much about law, but I am certain that there must be laws permitting such things as that. Have you no knowledge of such laws—you who are a lawyer? You must be a very poor lawyer, Mr Krogstad.

KROGSTAD. Maybe. But matters of business—such business as you and I have had together—do you think I don't understand that? Very well. Do as you please. But let me tell you this—if I lose my position a second time, you shall lose yours with me. [*He bows and goes out through the hall.*]

NORA [*appears buried in thought for a short time, then tosses her head*]. Nonsense! Trying to frighten me like that! I am not so silly as he thinks. [*Begins to busy herself putting the children's things in order.*] And yet— No, it's impossible! I did it for love's sake.

THE CHILDREN [*in the doorway on the left*]. Mother, the stranger man has gone out through the gate.

NORA. Yes, dears, I know. But don't tell anyone about the stranger man. Do you hear? Not even Papa.

CHILDREN. No, Mother; but will you come and play again?

NORA. No, no—not now.

CHILDREN. But, Mother, you promised us.

NORA. Yes, but I can't now. Run away in; I have such a lot to do. Run away in, my sweet little darlings. [*She gets them into the room by degrees and shuts the door on them, then sits down on the sofa, takes up a piece of needlework and sews a few stitches but soon stops.*] No! [*Throws down the work, gets up, goes to the hall door and calls out.*] Helen! bring the tree in. [*Goes to the table on the left, opens a drawer and stops again.*] No, no! It is quite impossible!

MAID [*coming in with the tree*]. Where shall I put it, ma'am?

NORA. Here, in the middle of the floor.

MAID. Shall I get you anything else?

NORA. No, thank you. I have all I want.

[*Exit* MAID.]

NORA [*begins dressing the tree*]. A candle here—and flowers here— The horrible man! It's all nonsense— there's nothing wrong. The tree shall be splendid! I will do everything I can think of to please you, Torvald! I will sing for you, dance for you—[HELMER *comes in with some papers under his arm.*] Oh, are you back already?

HELMER. Yes. Has anyone been here?

NORA. Here? No.

HELMER. That is strange. I saw Krogstad going out the gate.

NORA. Did you? Oh yes, I forgot, Krogstad was here for a moment.

HELMER. Nora, I can see from your manner that he has been here begging you to say a good word for him.

NORA. Yes.

HELMER. And you were to appear to do it of your own accord; you were to conceal from me the fact of his having been here; didn't he beg that of you too?

NORA. Yes, Torvald, but—

HELMER. Nora, Nora, and you would be a party to that sort of thing? To have any talk with a man like that and give him any sort of promise? And to tell me a lie into the bargain?

NORA. A lie?

HELMER. Didn't you tell me no one had been here? [*Shakes his finger at her.*] My little songbird must never do that again. A songbird must have a clean beak to chirp with—no false notes! [*Puts his arm around her waist.*] That is so, isn't it? Yes, I am sure it is. [*Lets her go.*] We will say no more about it. [*Sits down by the stove.*] How warm and snug it is here! [*Turns over his papers.*]

NORA [*after a short pause during which she busies herself with the Christmas tree*]. Torvald!

HELMER. Yes.

NORA. I am looking forward tremendously to the fancy-dress ball at the Stenborgs' the day after tomorrow.

HELMER. And I am tremendously curious to see what you are going to surprise me with.

NORA. It was very silly of me to want to do that.

HELMER. What do you mean?

NORA. I can't hit upon anything that will do; everything I think of seems so silly and insignificant.

HELMER. Does my little Nora acknowledge that at last?

NORA [*standing behind his chair with her arms on the back of it*]. Are you very busy, Torvald?

HELMER. Well—

NORA. What are all those papers?

HELMER. Bank business.

NORA. Already?

HELMER. I have got authority from the retiring manager to undertake the necessary changes in the staff and in the rearrangement of the work, and I must make use of the Christmas week for that, so as to have everything in order for the new year.

NORA. Then that was why this poor Krogstad—

HELMER. Hm!

NORA [*leans against the back of his chair and strokes his hair*]. If you hadn't been so busy, I should have asked you a tremendously big favor, Torvald.

HELMER. What is that? Tell me.

NORA. There is no one has such good taste as you. And I do so want to look nice at the fancy-dress ball. Torvald, couldn't you take me in hand and decide what I shall go as and what sort of a dress I shall wear?

HELMER. Aha! So my obstinate little woman is obliged to get someone to come to her rescue?

NORA. Yes, Torvald, I can't get along a bit without your help.

HELMER. Very well, I will think it over; we shall manage to hit upon something.

NORA. That is nice of you. [*Goes to the Christmas tree. A short pause.*] How pretty the red flowers look! But tell me, was it really something very bad that this Krogstad was guilty of?

HELMER. He forged someone's name. Have you any idea what that means?

NORA. Isn't it possible that he was driven to do it by necessity?

HELMER. Yes; or, as in so many cases, by imprudence. I am not so heartless as to condemn a man altogether because of a single false step of that kind.

NORA. No, you wouldn't, would you, Torvald?

HELMER. Many a man has been able to retrieve his character if he has openly confessed his fault and taken his punishment.

NORA. Punishment?

HELMER. But Krogstad did nothing of that sort; he got himself out of it by a cunning trick, and that is why he has gone under altogether.

NORA. But do you think it would—

HELMER. Just think how a guilty man like that has to lie and play the hypocrite with everyone, how he has to wear a mask in the presence of those near and dear to him, even before his own wife and children. And about the children—that is the most terrible part of it all, Nora.

NORA. How?

HELMER. Because such an atmosphere of lies infects and poisons the whole life of a home. Each breath the children take in such a house is full of the germs of evil.

NORA [*coming nearer him*]. Are you sure of that?

HELMER. My dear, I have often seen it in the course of my life as a lawyer. Almost everyone who has gone to the bad early in life has had a deceitful mother.

NORA. Why do you only say—mother?

HELMER. It seems most commonly to be the mother's influence, though naturally a bad father's would have the same result. Every lawyer is familiar with the fact. This Krogstad, now, has been persistently poisoning his own children with lies and dissimulation; that is why I say he has lost àll moral character. [*Holds out his hands to her*]. That is why my sweet little Nora must promise me not to plead his cause. Give me your hand on it. Come, come, what is this? Give me your hand. There now, that's settled. I assure you it would be quite impossible for me to work with him; I literally feel physically ill when I am in the company of such people.

NORA [*takes her hand out of his and goes to the opposite side of the Christmas tree*]. How hot it is in here, and I have such a lot to do.

HELMER [*getting up and putting his papers in order*]. Yes, and I must try and read through some of these before dinner, and I must think about your costume too. And it is just possible I may have something ready in gold paper to hang up on the tree. [*Puts his hand on her head.*] My precious little singing bird! [*He goes into his room and shuts the door after him.*]

NORA [*after a pause, whispers*]: No, no—it isn't true. It's impossible; it must be impossible.

[*The* NURSE *opens the door on the left.*]

NURSE. The little ones are begging so hard to be allowed to come in to Mamma.

NORA. No, no, no! Don't let them come in to me! You stay with them, Anne.

NURSE. Very well, ma'am. [*Shuts the door.*]

NORA [*pale with terror*]. Deprave my little children? Poison my home? [*A short pause. Then she tosses her head.*] It's not true. It can't possibly be true.

ACT TWO

THE SAME SCENE—*The Christmas tree is in the corner by
the piano, stripped of its ornaments and with burned-
down candle ends on its disheveled branches.* NORA'S
*cloak and hat are lying on the sofa. She is alone in the
room, walking about uneasily. She stops by the sofa
and takes up her cloak.*

NORA [*drops the cloak*]. Someone is coming now. [*Goes
to the door and listens.*] No—it is no one. Of course
no one will come today, Christmas Day—nor tomorrow either. But perhaps— [*Opens the door and looks
out.*] No, nothing in the letter box; it is quite empty.
[*Comes forward.*] What rubbish! Of course he can't
be in earnest about it. Such a thing couldn't happen; it is impossible—I have three little children.

[*Enter the* NURSE *from the room on the left, carrying a
big cardboard box.*]

NURSE. At last I have found the box with the fancy
dress.

NORA. Thanks; put it on the table.

NURSE [*in doing so*]. But it is very much in want of
mending.

NORA. I should like to tear it into a hundred thousand
pieces.

NURSE. What an idea! It can easily be put in order—
just a little patience.

NORA. Yes, I will go and get Mrs Linde to come and
help me with it.

NURSE. What, out again? In this horrible weather? You will catch cold, ma'am, and make yourself ill.

NORA. Well, worse than that might happen. How are the children?

NURSE. The poor little souls are playing with their Christmas presents, but—

NORA. Do they ask much for me?

NURSE. You see, they are so accustomed to having their mamma with them.

NORA. Yes—but, Nurse, I shall not be able to be so much with them now as I was before.

NURSE. Oh well, young children easily get accustomed to anything.

NORA. Do you think so? Do you think they would forget their mother if she went away altogether?

NURSE. Good heavens!—went away altogether?

NORA. Nurse, I want you to tell me something I have often wondered about—how could you have the heart to put your own child out among strangers?

NURSE. I was obliged to if I wanted to be little Nora's nurse.

NORA. Yes, but how could you be willing to do it?

NURSE. What, when I was going to get such a good place by it? A poor girl who has got into trouble should be glad to. Besides, that wicked man didn't do a single thing for me.

NORA. But I suppose your daughter has quite forgotten you.

NURSE. No, indeed she hasn't. She wrote to me when she was confirmed and when she was married.

NORA [*putting her arms round her neck*]. Dear old Anne, you were a good mother to me when I was little.

NURSE. Little Nora, poor dear, had no other mother but me.

NORA. And if my little ones had no other mother, I am sure you would— What nonsense I am talking!

[*Opens the box.*] Go in to them. Now I must— You will see tomorrow how charming I shall look.

NURSE. I am sure there will be no one at the ball so charming as you, ma'am. [*Goes into the room on the left.*]

NORA [*begins to unpack the box but soon pushes it away from her*]. If only I dared go out. If only no one would come. If only I could be sure nothing would happen here in the meantime. Stuff and nonsense! No one will come. Only I mustn't think about it. I will brush my muff. What lovely, lovely gloves! Out of my thoughts, out of my thoughts! One, two, three, four, five, six— [*Screams.*] Ah! there is someone coming. [*Makes a movement toward the door but stands irresolute.*]

[*Enter* MRS LINDE *from the hall, where she has taken off her cloak and hat.*]

NORA. Oh, it's you, Christine. There is no one else out there, is there? How good of you to come!

MRS LINDE. I heard you were up asking for me.

NORA. Yes, I was passing by. As a matter of fact, it is something you could help me with. Let us sit down here on the sofa. Look here. Tomorrow evening there is to be a fancy-dress ball at the Stenborgs', who live above us, and Torvald wants me to go as a Neapolitan fishergirl and dance the tarantella that I learnt at Capri.

MRS LINDE. I see; you are going to keep up the character.

NORA. Yes, Torvald wants me to. Look, here is the dress; Torvald had it made for me there, but now it is all so torn, and I haven't any idea—

MRS LINDE. We will easily put that right. It is only some of the trimming come unsewn here and there. Needle and thread? Now then, that's all we want.

MRS LINDE [*sewing*]. So you are going to be dressed up tomorrow, Nora. I will tell you what—I shall come in for a moment and see you in your fine feathers. But I have completely forgotten to thank you for a delightful evening yesterday.

NORA [*gets up and crosses the stage*]. Well, I don't think yesterday was as pleasant as usual. You ought to have come down to town a little earlier, Christine. Certainly Torvald does understand how to make a house dainty and attractive.

MRS LINDE. And so do you, it seems to me; you are not your father's daughter for nothing. But tell me, is Doctor Rank always as depressed as he was yesterday?

NORA. No; yesterday it was very noticeable. I must tell you that he suffers from a very dangerous disease. He has consumption of the spine, poor creature. His father was a horrible man who committed all sorts of excesses, and that is why his son was sickly from childhood, do you understand?

MRS LINDE [*dropping her sewing*]. But, my dearest Nora, how do you know anything about such things?

NORA [*walking about*]. Pooh! When you have three children you get visits now and then from—from married women who know something of medical matters, and they talk about one thing and another.

MRS LINDE [*goes on sewing. A short silence*]. Does Doctor Rank come here every day?

NORA. Every day regularly. He is Torvald's most intimate friend and a friend of mine too. He is just like one of the family.

MRS LINDE. But tell me this—is he perfectly sincere? I mean, isn't he the kind of man that is very anxious to make himself agreeable?

NORA. Not in the least. What makes you think that?

MRS LINDE. When you introduced him to me yesterday he declared he had often heard my name mentioned in this house, but afterward I noticed that your husband hadn't the slightest idea who I was. So how could Doctor Rank—

NORA. That is quite right, Christine. Torvald is so absurdly fond of me that he wants me absolutely to himself, as he says. At first he used to seem almost jealous if I mentioned any of the dear folks at home, so naturally I gave up doing so. But I often talk about such things with Doctor Rank because he likes hearing about them.

MRS LINDE. Listen to me, Nora. You are still very like a child in many things, and I am older than you in many ways and have a little more experience. Let me tell you this—you ought to make an end of it with Doctor Rank.

NORA. What ought I to make an end of?

MRS LINDE. Of two things, I think. Yesterday you talked some nonsense about a rich admirer who was to leave you money—

NORA. An admirer who doesn't exist, unfortunately! But what then?

MRS LINDE. Is Doctor Rank a man of means?

NORA. Yes, he is.

MRS LINDE. And has no one to provide for?

NORA. No, no one; but—

MRS LINDE. And comes here every day?

NORA. Yes, I told you so.

MRS LINDE. But how can this well-bred man be so tactless?

NORA. I don't understand you at all.

MRS LINDE. Don't prevaricate, Nora. Do you suppose I don't guess who lent you the two hundred and fifty pounds?

NORA. Are you out of your senses? How can you think of such a thing! A friend of ours, who comes here every day! Do you realize what a horribly painful position that would be?

MRS LINDE. Then it really isn't he?

NORA. No, certainly not. It would never have entered into my head for a moment. Besides, he had no money to lend then; he came into his money afterward.

MRS LINDE. Well, I think that was lucky for you, my dear Nora.

NORA. No, it would never have come into my head to ask Doctor Rank. Although I am quite sure that if I had asked him—

MRS LINDE. But of course you won't.

NORA. Of course not. I have no reason to think it could possibly be necessary. But I am quite sure that if I told Doctor Rank—

MRS LINDE. Behind your husband's back?

NORA. I must make an end of it with the other one, and that will be behind his back too. I *must* make an end of it with him.

MRS LINDE. Yes, that is what I told you yesterday, but—

NORA [*walking up and down*]. A man can put a thing like that straight much easier than a woman.

MRS LINDE. One's husband, yes.

NORA. Nonsense! [*Standing still.*] When you pay off a debt you get your bond back, don't you?

MRS LINDE. Yes, as a matter of course.

NORA. And can tear it into a hundred thousand pieces and burn it up—the nasty dirty paper!

MRS LINDE [*looks hard at her, lays down her sewing and gets up slowly*]. Nora, you are concealing something from me.

NORA. Do I look as if I were?

MRS LINDE. Something has happened to you since yesterday morning. Nora, what is it?

NORA [*going nearer to her*]. Christine! [*Listens.*] Hush! There's Torvald come home. Do you mind going in to the children for the present? Torvald can't bear to see dressmaking going on. Let Anne help you.

MRS LINDE [*gathering some of the things together*]. Cer-

006

tainly—but I am not going away from here till we
have had it out with one another. [*She goes into the
room on the left as* HELMER *comes in from the hall.*]

NORA [*going up to* HELMER]. I have wanted you so
much, Torvald dear.

HELMER. Was that the dressmaker?

NORA. No, it was Christine; she is helping me to put
my dress in order. You will see I shall look quite
smart.

HELMER. Wasn't that a happy thought of mine, now?

NORA. Splendid! But don't you think it is nice of me,
too, to do as you wish?

HELMER. Nice?—because you do as your husband
wishes? Well, well, you little rogue, I am sure you
did not mean it in that way. But I am not going
to disturb you; you will want to be trying on your
dress, I expect.

NORA. I suppose you are going to work.

HELMER. Yes. [*Shows her a bundle of papers.*] Look at
that. I have just been in to the bank. [*Turns to go
into his room.*]

NORA. Torvald.

HELMER. Yes.

NORA. If your little squirrel were to ask you for something very, very prettily—

HELMER. What then?

NORA. Would you do it?

HELMER. I should like to hear what it is first.

NORA. Your squirrel would run about and do all her
tricks if you would be nice and do what she wants.

HELMER. Speak plainly.

NORA. Your skylark would chirp, chirp about in every
room, with her song rising and falling—

HELMER. Well, my skylark does that anyhow.

NORA. I would play the fairy and dance for you in the
moonlight, Torvald.

HELMER. Nora—you surely don't mean that request you
made of me this morning?

NORA [*going near him*]. Yes, Torvald, I beg you so earnestly—

HELMER. Have you really the courage to open up that question again?

NORA. Yes, dear, you *must* do as I ask; you *must* let Krogstad keep his post in the bank.

HELMER. My dear Nora, it is his post that I have arranged Mrs Linde shall have.

NORA. Yes, you have been awfully kind about that, but you could just as well dismiss some other clerk instead of Krogstad.

HELMER. This is simply incredible obstinacy! Because you chose to give him a thoughtless promise that you would speak for him I am expected to—

NORA. That isn't the reason, Torvald. It is for your own sake. This fellow writes in the most scurrilous newspapers; you have told me so yourself. He can do you an unspeakable amount of harm. I am frightened to death of him.

HELMER. Ah, I understand; it is recollections of the past that scare you.

NORA. What do you mean?

HELMER. Naturally you are thinking of your father.

NORA. Yes—yes, of course. Just recall to your mind what these malicious creatures wrote in the papers about Papa and how horribly they slandered him. I believe they would have procured his dismissal if the Department had not sent you over to inquire into it and if you had not been so kindly disposed and helpful to him.

HELMER. My little Nora, there is an important difference between your father and me. Your father's reputation as a public official was not above suspicion. Mine is, and I hope it will continue to be so as long as I hold my office.

NORA. You never can tell what mischief these men may contrive. We ought to be so well off, so snug and happy here in our peaceful home, and have no cares—you and I and the children, Torvald! That is why I beg you so earnestly—

HELMER. And it is just by interceding for him that you make it impossible for me to keep him. It is already known at the bank that I mean to dismiss Krogstad. Is it to get about now that the new manager has changed his mind at his wife's bidding?

NORA. And what if it did?

HELMER. Of course!—if only this obstinate little person can get her way! Do you suppose I am going to make myself ridiculous before my whole staff, to let people think I am a man to be swayed by all sorts of outside influence? I should very soon feel the consequences of it, I can tell you! And besides, there is one thing that makes it quite impossible for me to have Krogstad in the bank as long as I am manager.

NORA. Whatever is that?

HELMER. His moral failings I might perhaps have overlooked if necessary—

NORA. Yes, you could—couldn't you?

HELMER. And I hear he is a good worker too. But I knew him when we were boys. It was one of those rash friendships that so often prove an incubus in afterlife. I may as well tell you plainly, we were once on very intimate terms with one another. But this tactless fellow lays no restraint on himself when other people are present. On the contrary, he thinks it gives him the right to adopt a familiar tone with me, and every minute it is "I say, Helmer, old fellow!" and that sort of thing. I assure you it is extremely painful for me. He would make my position in the bank intolerable.

NORA. Torvald, I don't believe you mean that.

HELMER. Don't you? Why not?

NORA. Because it is such a narrow-minded way of looking at things.

HELMER. What are you saying? Narrow-minded? Do you think I am narrow-minded?

NORA. No, just the opposite, dear—and it is exactly for that reason—

HELMER. It's the same thing. You say my point of view is narrow-minded, so I must be so too. Narrow-minded! Very well—I must put an end to this. [*Goes to the hall door and calls.*] Helen!

NORA. What are you going to do?

HELMER [*looking among his papers*]. Settle it. [*Enter* MAID.] Look here; take this letter and go downstairs with it at once. Find a messenger and tell him to deliver it and be quick. The address is on it, and here is the money.

MAID. Very well, sir. [*Exit with the letter.*]

HELMER [*putting his papers together*]. Now then, little Miss Obstinate.

NORA [*breathlessly*]. Torvald—what was that letter?

HELMFR. Krogstad's dismissal.

NORA. Call her back, Torvald! There is still time. Oh, Torvald, call her back! Do it for my sake—for your own sake—for the children's sake! Do you hear me, Torvald? Call her back! You don't know what that letter can bring upon us.

HELMER. It's too late.

NORA. Yes, it's too late.

HELMER. My dear Nora, I can forgive the anxiety you are in, although really it is an insult to me. It is, indeed. Isn't it an insult to think that I should be afraid of a starving quill driver's vengeance? But I forgive you nevertheless, because it is such eloquent witness to your great love for me. [*Takes her in his arms.*] And that is as it should be, my own darling Nora. Come what will, you may be sure I shall have both courage and strength if they be needed. You will see I am man enough to take everything upon myself.

NORA [*in a horror-stricken voice*]. What do you mean by that?

HELMER. Everything, I say.

NORA [*recovering herself*]. You will never have to do that.

HELMER. That's right. Well, we will share it, Nora, as man and wife should. That is how it shall be. [*Caressing her.*] Are you content now? There! there!—not these frightened dove's eyes! The whole thing is only the wildest fancy! Now you must go and play through the tarantella and practice with your tambourine. I shall go into the inner office and shut the door, and I shall hear nothing; you can make as much noise as you please. [*Turns back at the door.*] And when Rank comes tell him where he will find me. [*Nods to her, takes his papers and goes into his room and shuts the door after him.*]

NORA [*bewildered with anxiety, stands as if rooted to the spot and whispers*]. He was capable of doing it. He will do it. He will do it in spite of everything. No, not that! Never, never! Anything rather than that! Oh, for some help, some way out of it! [*The doorbell rings.*] Doctor Rank! Anything rather than that—anything, whatever it is! [*She puts her hands over her face, pulls herself together, goes to the door and opens it. RANK is standing without, hanging up his coat. During the following dialogue it begins to grow dark.*]

NORA. Good day, Doctor Rank. I knew your ring. But you mustn't go in to Torvald now; I think he is busy with something.

RANK. And you?

NORA [*brings him in and shuts the door after him*]. Oh, you know very well I always have time for you.

RANK. Thank you. I shall make use of as much of it as I can.

NORA. What do you mean by that? As much of it as you can?

RANK. Well, does that alarm you?

NORA. It was such a strange way of putting it. Is anything likely to happen?

RANK. Nothing but what I have long been prepared for. But I certainly didn't expect it to happen so soon.

NORA [*gripping him by the arm*]. What have you found out? Doctor Rank, you must tell me.

RANK [*sitting down by the stove*]. It is all up with me. And it can't be helped.

NORA [*with a sigh of relief*]. Is it about yourself?

RANK. Who else? It is no use lying to one's self. I am the most wretched of all my patients, Mrs Helmer. Lately I have been taking stock of my internal economy. Bankrupt! Probably within a month I shall lie rotting in the churchyard.

NORA. What an ugly thing to say!

RANK. The thing itself is cursedly ugly, and the worst of it is that I shall have to face so much more that is ugly before that. I shall only make one more examination of myself; when I have done that I shall know pretty certainly when it will be that the horrors of dissolution will begin. There is something I want to tell you. Helmer's refined nature gives him an unconquerable disgust at everything that is ugly; I won't have him in my sickroom.

NORA. Oh, but, Doctor Rank—

RANK. I won't have him there. Not on any account. I bar my door to him. As soon as I am quite certain that the worst has come I shall send you my card with a black cross on it, and then you will know that the loathsome end has begun.

NORA. You are quite absurd today. And I wanted you so much to be in a really good humor.

RANK. With death stalking beside me? To have to pay this penalty for another man's sin! Is there any justice in that? And in every single family, in one way or another, some such inexorable retribution is being exacted.

NORA [*putting her hands over her ears*]. Rubbish! Do talk of something cheerful.

RANK. Oh, it's a mere laughing matter, the whole thing.

My poor innocent spine has to suffer for my father's youthful amusements.

NORA [*sitting at the table on the left*]. I suppose you mean that he was too partial to asparagus and pâté de foie gras, don't you?

RANK. Yes, and to truffles.

NORA. Truffles, yes. And oysters too, I suppose?

RANK. Oysters, of course; that goes without saying.

NORA. And heaps of port and champagne. It is sad that all these nice things should take their revenge on our bones.

RANK. Especially that they should revenge themselves on the unlucky bones of those who have not had the satisfaction of enjoying them.

NORA. Yes, that's the saddest part of it all.

RANK [*with a searching look at her*]. Hm!

NORA [*after a short pause*]. Why did you smile?

RANK. No, it was you that laughed.

NORA. No, it was you that smiled, Doctor Rank!

RANK [*rising*]. You are a greater rascal than I thought.

NORA. I am in a silly mood today.

RANK. So it seems.

NORA [*putting her hands on his shoulders*]. Dear, dear Doctor Rank, death mustn't take you away from Torvald and me.

RANK. It is a loss you would easily recover from. Those who are gone are soon forgotten.

NORA [*looking at him anxiously*]. Do you believe that?

RANK. People form new ties, and then—

NORA. Who will form new ties?

RANK. Both you and Helmer, when I am gone. You yourself are already on the highroad to it, I think. What did that Mrs Linde want here last night?

NORA. Oho! You don't mean to say that you are jealous of poor Christine?

RANK. Yes, I am. She will be my successor in this house. When I am done for, this woman will—

NORA. Hush! Don't speak so loud. She is in that room.

RANK. Today again. There, you see.

NORA. She has only come to sew my dress for me. Bless
my soul, how unreasonable you are! [*Sits down on
the sofa.*] Be nice now, Doctor Rank, and tomorrow
you will see how beautifully I shall dance, and you
can imagine I am doing it all for you—and for Torvald too, of course. [*Takes various things out of the
box.*] Doctor Rank, come and sit down here, and I
will show you something.

RANK [*sitting down*]. What is it?

NORA. Just look at those!

RANK. Silk stockings.

NORA. Flesh colored. Aren't they lovely? It is so dark
here now, but tomorrow— No, no, no! You must only
look at the feet. Oh well, you may have leave to look
at the legs too.

RANK. Hm!

NORA. Why are you looking so critical? Don't you think
they will fit me?

RANK. I have no means of forming an opinion about
that.

NORA [*looks at him for a moment*]. For shame! [*Hits
him lightly on the ear with the stockings.*] That's to
punish you. [*Folds them up again.*]

RANK. And what other nice things am I to be allowed
to see?

NORA. Not a single thing more, for being so naughty.
[*She looks among the things, humming to herself.*]

RANK [*after a short silence*]. When I am sitting here
talking to you as intimately as this I cannot imagine
for a moment what would have become of me if
I had never come into this house.

NORA [*smiling*]. I believe you do feel thoroughly at
home with us.

RANK [*in a lower voice, looking straight in front of
him*]. And to be obliged to leave it all—

NORA. Nonsense, you are not going to leave it.

RANK [*as before*]. And not be able to leave behind one the slightest token of one's gratitude, scarcely even a fleeting regret—nothing but an empty place which the firstcomer can fill as well as any other.

NORA. And if I asked you now for a— No!

RANK. For what?

NORA. For a big proof of your friendship—

RANK. Yes, yes!

NORA. I mean a tremendously big favor—

RANK. Would you really make me so happy for once?

NORA. Ah, but you don't know what it is yet.

RANK. No—but tell me.

NORA. I really can't, Doctor Rank. It is something out of all reason; it means advice and help and a favor—

RANK. The bigger a thing it is, the better. I can't conceive what it is you mean. Do tell me. Haven't I your confidence?

NORA. More than anyone else. I know you are my truest and best friend, and so I will tell you what it is. Well, Doctor Rank, it is something you must help me to prevent. You know how devotedly, how inexpressibly deeply Torvald loves me; he would never for a moment hesitate to give his life for me.

RANK [*leaning toward her*]. Nora—do you think he is the only one—

NORA [*with a slight start*]. The only one—?

RANK. The only one who would gladly give his life for your sake.

NORA [*sadly*]. Is that it?

RANK. I was determined you should know it before I went away, and there will never be a better opportunity than this. Now you know it, Nora. And now you know, too, that you can trust me as you would trust no one else.

NORA [*rises deliberately and quietly*]. Let me pass.

RANK [*makes room for her to pass him but sits still*]. Nora!

NORA [*at the hall door*]. Helen, bring in the lamp.
[*Goes over to the stove.*] Dear Doctor Rank, that was
really horrid of you.

RANK. To have loved you as much as anyone else does?
Was that horrid?

NORA. No, but to go and tell me so. There was really
no need—

RANK. What do you mean? Did you know? [MAID *enters
with lamp, puts it down on the table and goes out.*]
Nora—Mrs Helmer—tell me, had you any idea of
this?

NORA. Oh, how do I know whether I had or whether I
hadn't? I really can't tell you. To think you could
be so clumsy, Doctor Rank! We were getting on so
nicely.

RANK. Well, at all events you know that you can command me body and soul. So won't you speak out?

NORA [*looking at him*]. After what happened?

RANK. I beg you to let me know what it is.

NORA. I can't tell you anything now.

RANK. Yes, yes. You mustn't punish me in that way.
Let me have permission to do for you whatever a
man may do.

NORA. You can do nothing for me now. Besides, I really
don't need any help at all. You will find that the
whole thing is merely fancy on my part. It really is
so—of course it is! [*Sits down in the rocking chair
and looks at him with a smile.*] You are a nice sort
of man, Doctor Rank! Don't you feel ashamed of
yourself now the lamp has come?

RANK. Not a bit. But perhaps I had better go—forever?

NORA. No indeed, you shall not. Of course you must
come here just as before. You know very well Torvald can't do without you.

RANK. Yes, but you?

NORA. Oh, I am always tremendously pleased when you
come.

RANK. It is just that that put me on the wrong track.

You are a riddle to me. I have often thought that
you would almost as soon be in my company as in
Helmer's.

NORA. Yes—you see, there are some people one loves
best and others whom one would almost always
rather have as companions.

RANK. Yes, there is something in that.

NORA. When I was at home of course I loved Papa best.
But I always thought it tremendous fun if I could
steal down into the maids' room, because they never
moralized at all and talked to each other about such
entertaining things.

RANK. I see—it is *their* place I have taken.

NORA [*jumping up and going to him*]. Oh, dear, nice
Doctor Rank, I never meant that at all. But surely
you can understand that being with Torvald is a
little like being with Papa—

[*Enter* MAID *from the hall.*]

MAID. If you please, ma'am. [*Whispers and hands her
a card.*]

NORA [*glancing at the card*]. Oh! [*Puts it in her pocket.*]

RANK. Is there anything wrong?

NORA. No, no, not in the least. It is only something—
it is my new dress—

RANK. What? Your dress is lying there.

NORA. Oh yes, that one; but this is another. I ordered
it. Torvald mustn't know about it.

RANK. Oho! Then that was the great secret.

NORA. Of course. Just go in to him; he is sitting in the
inner room. Keep him as long as—

RANK. Make your mind easy; I won't let him escape.
[*Goes into* HELMER'S *room.*]

NORA [*to the* MAID]. And he is standing waiting in the
kitchen?

MAID. Yes; he came up the back stairs.

NORA. But didn't you tell him no one was in?

MAID. Yes, but it was no good.

NORA. He won't go away?

MAID. No; he says he won't until he has seen you, ma'am.

NORA. Well, let him come in—but quietly. Helen, you mustn't say anything about it to anyone. It is a surprise for my husband.

MAID. Yes, ma'am, I quite understand. [*Exit.*]

NORA. This dreadful thing is going to happen! It will happen in spite of me! No, no, no, it can't happen—it shan't happen! [*She bolts the door of* HELMER'S *room. The* MAID *opens the hall door for* KROGSTAD *and shuts it after him. He is wearing a fur coat, high boots and a fur cap.*]

NORA [*advancing toward him*]. Speak low—my husband is at home.

KROGSTAD. No matter about that.

NORA. What do you want of me?

KROGSTAD. An explanation of something.

NORA. Make haste then. What is it?

KROGSTAD. You know, I suppose, that I have got my dismissal.

NORA. I couldn't prevent it, Mr Krogstad. I fought as hard as I could on your side, but it was no good.

KROGSTAD. Does your husband love you so little then? He knows what I can expose you to, and yet he ventures—

NORA. How can you suppose that he has any knowledge of the sort?

KROGSTAD. I didn't suppose so at all. It would not be the least like our dear Torvald Helmer to show so much courage—

NORA. Mr Krogstad, a little respect for my husband, please.

KROGSTAD. Certainly—all the respect he deserves. But since you have kept the matter so carefully to yourself, I make bold to suppose that you have a little clearer idea than you had yesterday of what it actually is that you have done?

NORA. More than you could ever teach me.

KROGSTAD. Yes, such a bad lawyer as I am.

NORA. What is it you want of me?

KROGSTAD. Only to see how you were, Mrs Helmer. I have been thinking about you all day long. A mere cashier, a quill driver, a—well, a man like me—even he has a little of what is called feeling, you know.

NORA. Show it then; think of my little children.

KROGSTAD. Have you and your husband thought of mine? But never mind about that. I only wanted to tell you that you need not take this matter too seriously. In the first place there will be no accusation made on my part.

NORA. No, of course not; I was sure of that.

KROGSTAD. The whole thing can be arranged amicably; there is no reason why anyone should know anything about it. It will remain a secret between us three.

NORA. My husband must never get to know anything about it.

KROGSTAD. How will you be able to prevent it? Am I to understand that you can pay the balance that is owing?

NORA. No, not just at present.

KROGSTAD. Or perhaps that you have some expedient for raising the money soon?

NORA. No expedient that I mean to make use of.

KROGSTAD. Well, in any case it would have been of no use to you now. If you stood there with ever so much money in your hand, I would never part with your bond.

NORA. Tell me what purpose you mean to put it to.

KROGSTAD. I shall only preserve it—keep it in my possession. No one who is not concerned in the matter shall have the slightest hint of it. So that if the thought of it has driven you to any desperate resolution—

NORA. It has.

KROGSTAD. If you had it in your mind to run away from
your home—

NORA. I had.

KROGSTAD. Or even something worse—

NORA. How could you know that?

KROGSTAD. Give up the idea.

NORA. How did you know I had thought of *that?*

KROGSTAD. Most of us think of that at first. I did too—
but I hadn't the courage.

NORA [*faintly*]. No more than I.

KROGSTAD [*in a tone of relief*]. No, that's it, isn't it—
—you hadn't the courage either?

NORA. No, I haven't—I haven't.

KROGSTAD. Besides, it would have been a great piece of
folly. Once the first storm at home is over— I have a
letter for your husband in my pocket.

NORA. Telling him everything?

KROGSTAD. In as lenient a manner as I possibly could.

NORA [*quickly*]. He mustn't get the letter. Tear it up.
I will find some means of getting money.

KROGSTAD. Excuse me, Mrs Helmer, but I think I told
you just now—

NORA. I am not speaking of what I owe you. Tell me
what sum you are asking my husband for, and I will
get the money.

KROGSTAD. I am not asking your husband for a penny.

NORA. What do you want then?

KROGSTAD. I will tell you. I want to rehabilitate myself,
Mrs Helmer; I want to get on, and in that your husband must help me. For the last year and a half I
have not had a hand in anything dishonorable, and
all that time I have been struggling in most re-
stricted circumstances. I was content to work my
way up step by step. Now I am turned out, and I
am not going to be satisfied with merely being taken
into favor again. I want to get on, I tell you. I want
to get into the bank again, in a higher position. Your
husband must make a place for me—

NORA. That he will never do!

KROGSTAD. He will; I know him; he dare not protest. And as soon as I am in there again with him then you will see! Within a year I shall be the manager's right hand. It will be Nils Krogstad and not Torvald Helmer who manages the bank.

NORA. That's a thing you will never see!

KROGSTAD. Do you mean that you will—

NORA. I have courage enough for it now.

KROGSTAD. Oh, you can't frighten me. A fine, spoilt lady like you—

NORA. You will see, you will see.

KROGSTAD. Under the ice, perhaps? Down into the cold, coal-black water? And then, in the spring, to float up to the surface, all horrible and unrecognizable, with your hair fallen out—

NORA. You can't frighten me.

KROGSTAD. Nor you me. People don't do such things, Mrs Helmer. Besides, what use would it be? I should have him completely in my power all the same.

NORA. Afterward? When I am no longer—

KROGSTAD. Have you forgotten that it is I who have the keeping of your reputation? [NORA *stands speechlessly looking at him.*] Well, now, I have warned you. Do not do anything foolish. When Helmer has had my letter I shall expect a message from him. And be sure you remember that it is your husband himself who has forced me into such ways as this again. I will never forgive him for that. Good-by, Mrs Helmer. [*Exit through the hall.*]

NORA [*goes to the hall door, opens it slightly and listens*]. He is going. He is not putting the letter in the box. Oh no, no! that's impossible! [*Opens the door by degrees.*] What is that? He is standing outside. He is not going downstairs. Is he hesitating? Can he— [*A letter drops in the box; then* KROGSTAD'S *footsteps are heard, till they die away as he goes downstairs.* NORA *utters a stifled cry and runs across the room to the table by the sofa. A short pause.*]

NORA. In the letter box. [*Steals across to the hall door.*] There it lies—Torvald, Torvald, there is no hope for us now!

[MRS LINDE *comes in from the room on the left, carrying the dress.*]

MRS LINDE. There, I can't see anything more to mend now. Would you like to try it on?

NORA [*in a hoarse whisper*]. Christine, come here.

MRS LINDE [*throwing the dress down on the sofa*]. What is the matter with you? You look so agitated!

NORA. Come here. Do you see that letter? There, look—you can see it through the glass in the letter box.

MRS LINDE. Yes, I see it.

NORA. That letter is from Krogstad.

MRS LINDE. Nora—it was Krogstad who lent you the money!

NORA. Yes, and now Torvald will know all about it.

MRS LINDE. Believe me, Nora, that's the best thing for both of you.

NORA. You don't know all. I forged a name.

MRS LINDE. Good heavens!

NORA. I only want to say this to you, Christine—you must be my witness.

MRS LINDE. Your witness? What do you mean? What am I to—

NORA. If I should go out of my mind—and it might easily happen—

MRS LINDE. Nora!

NORA. Or if anything else should happen to me—anything, for instance, that might prevent my being here—

MRS LINDE. Nora! Nora! you are quite out of your mind.

NORA. And if it should happen that there were someone who wanted to take all the responsibility, all the blame, you understand—

MRS LINDE. Yes, yes—but how can you suppose—

NORA. Then you must be my witness, that it is not true,

Christine. I am not out of my mind at all; I am in my right senses now, and I tell you no one else has known anything about it; I, and I alone, did the whole thing. Remember that.

MRS LINDE. I will, indeed. But I don't understand all this.

NORA. How should you understand it? A wonderful thing is going to happen.

MRS LINDE. A wonderful thing?

NORA. Yes, a wonderful thing! But it is so terrible. Christine, it *mustn't* happen, not for all the world.

MRS LINDE. I will go at once and see Krogstad.

NORA. Don't go to him; he will do you some harm.

MRS LINDE. There was a time when he would gladly do anything for my sake.

NORA. He?

MRS LINDE. Where does he live?

NORA. How should I know? Yes— [*feeling in her pocket*] —here is his card. But the letter, the letter!

HELMER [*calls from his room, knocking at the door*]. Nora!

NORA [*cries out anxiously*]. Oh, what's that? What do you want?

HELMER. Don't be so frightened. We are not coming in; you have locked the door. Are you trying on your dress?

NORA. Yes, that's it. I look so nice, Torvald.

MRS LINDE [*who has read the card*]. I see he lives at the corner here.

NORA. Yes, but it's no use. It is hopeless. The letter is lying there in the box.

MRS LINDE. And your husband keeps the key?

NORA. Yes, always.

MRS LINDE. Krogstad must ask for his letter back unread, he must find some pretense—

NORA. But it is just at this time that Torvald generally—

MRS LINDE. You must delay him. Go in to him in the

meantime. I will come back as soon as I can. [*She goes out hurriedly through the hall door.*]

NORA [*goes to* HELMER'S *door, opens it and peeps in*]. Torvald!

HELMER [*from the inner room*]. Well? May I venture at last to come into my own room again? Come along, Rank, now you will see— [*Halting in the doorway.*] But what is this?

NORA. What is what, dear?

HELMER. Rank led me to expect a splendid transformation.

RANK [*in the doorway*]. I understood so, but evidently I was mistaken.

NORA. Yes, nobody is to have the chance of admiring me in my dress until tomorrow.

HELMER. But, my dear Nora, you look so worn out. Have you been practicing too much?

NORA. No, I have not practiced at all.

HELMER. But you will need to—

NORA. Yes, indeed I shall, Torvald. But I can't get on a bit without you to help me; I have absolutely forgotten the whole thing.

HELMER. Oh, we will soon work it up again.

NORA. Yes, help me, Torvald. Promise that you will! I am so nervous about it—all the people— You must give yourself up to me entirely this evening. Not the tiniest bit of business—you mustn't even take a pen in your hand. Will you promise, Torvald dear?

HELMER. I promise. This evening I will be wholly and absolutely at your service, you helpless little mortal. Ah, by the way, first of all I will just— [*Goes toward the hall door.*]

NORA. What are you going to do there?

HELMER. Only see if any letters have come.

NORA. No, no! Don't do that, Torvald!

HELMER. Why not?

NORA. Torvald, please don't. There is nothing there.

HELMER. Well, let me look. [*Turns to go to the letter

box. NORA, *at the piano, plays the first bars of the tarantella.* HELMER *stops in the doorway.*] Aha!

NORA. I can't dance tomorrow if I don't practice with you.

HELMER [*going up to her*]. Are you really so afraid of it, dear?

NORA. Yes, so dreadfully afraid of it. Let me practice at once; there is time now, before we go to dinner. Sit down and play for me, Torvald dear; criticize me and correct me as you play.

HELMER. With great pleasure, if you wish me to. [*Sits down at the piano.*]

NORA [*takes out of the box a tambourine and a long variegated shawl. She hastily drapes the shawl round her. Then she springs to the front of the stage and calls out*]. Now play for me! I am going to dance!

[HELMER *plays and* NORA *dances.* RANK *stands by the piano behind* HELMER *and looks on.*]

HELMER [*as he plays*]. Slower, slower!

NORA. I can't do it any other way.

HELMER. Not so violently, Nora!

NORA. This is the way.

HELMER [*stops playing*]. No, no—that is not a bit right.

NORA [*laughing and swinging the tambourine*]. Didn't I tell you so?

RANK. Let me play for her.

HELMER [*getting up*]. Yes, do. I can correct her better then.

[RANK *sits down at the piano and plays.* NORA *dances more and more wildly.* HELMER *has taken up a position by the stove and during her dance gives her frequent instructions. She does not seem to hear him; her hair comes down and falls over her shoulders; she pays no attention to it but goes on dancing. Enter* MRS LINDE.]

MRS LINDE [*standing as if spellbound in the doorway*]. Oh!

NORA [*as she dances*]. Such fun, Christine!

HELMER. My dear darling Nora, you are dancing as if your life depended on it.

NORA. So it does.

HELMER. Stop, Rank; this is sheer madness. Stop, I tell you! [RANK *stops playing, and* NORA *suddenly stands still.* HELMER *goes up to her.*] I could never have believed it. You have forgotten everything I taught you.

NORA [*throwing away the tambourine*]. There, you see.

HELMER. You will want a lot of coaching.

NORA. Yes, you see how much I need it. You must coach me up to the last minute. Promise me that, Torvald!

HELMER. You can depend on me.

NORA. You must not think of anything but me, either today or tomorrow; you mustn't open a single letter —not even open the letter box—

HELMER. Ah, you are still afraid of that fellow—

NORA. Yes, indeed I am.

HELMER. Nora, I can tell from your looks that there is a letter from him lying there.

NORA. I don't know; I think there is; but you must not read anything of that kind now. Nothing horrid must come between us till this is all over.

RANK [*whispers to* HELMER]. You musn't contradict her.

HELMER [*taking her in his arms*]. The child shall have her way. But tomorrow night, after you have danced—

NORA. Then you will be free. [*The* MAID *appears in the doorway to the right.*]

MAID. Dinner is served, ma'am.

NORA. We will have champagne, Helen.

MAID. Very good, ma'am. [*Exit.*]

HELMER. Hullo!—are we going to have a banquet?

NORA. Yes, a champagne banquet till the small hours. [*Calls out.*] And a few macaroons, Helen—lots, just for once!

HELMER. Come, come, don't be so wild and nervous. Be my own little skylark, as you used.

NORA. Yes, dear, I will. But go in now, and you too,

Doctor Rank. Christine, you must help me to do up my hair.

RANK [*whispers to* HELMER *as they go out*]. I suppose there is nothing—she is not expecting anything?

HELMER. Far from it, my dear fellow; it is simply nothing more than this childish nervousness I was telling you of. [*They go into the right-hand room.*]

NORA. Well!

MRS LINDE. Gone out of town.

NORA. I could tell from your face.

MRS LINDE. He is coming home tomorrow evening. I wrote a note for him.

NORA. You should have let it alone; you must prevent nothing. After all, it is splendid to be waiting for a wonderful thing to happen.

MRS LINDE. What is it that you are waiting for?

NORA. Oh, you wouldn't understand. Go in to them, I will come in a moment. [MRS LINDE *goes into the dining room.* NORA *stands still for a little while, as if to compose herself. Then she looks at her watch.*] Five o'clock. Seven hours till midnight; and then four-and-twenty hours till the next midnight. Then the tarantella will be over. Twenty-four and seven? Thirty-one hours to live.

HELMER [*from the doorway on the right.*] Where's my little skylark?

NORA [*going to him with her arms outstretched.*] Here she is!

ACT THREE

THE SAME SCENE—*The table has been placed in the middle of the stage with chairs round it. A lamp is burning on the table. The door into the hall stands open. Dance music is heard in the room above.* MRS LINDE *is sitting at the table idly turning over the leaves of a book; she tries to read but does not seem able to collect her thoughts. Every now and then she listens intently for a sound at the outer door.*

MRS LINDE [*looking at her watch*]. Not yet—and the time is nearly up. If only he does not— [*Listens again.*] Ah, there he is. [*Goes into the hall and opens the outer door carefully. Light footsteps are heard on the stairs. She whispers.*] Come in. There is no one here.

KROGSTAD [*in the doorway*]. I found a note from you at home. What does this mean?

MRS LINDE. It is absolutely necessary that I should have a talk with you.

KROGSTAD. Really? And it is absolutely necessary that it should be here?

MRS LINDE. It is impossible where I live; there is no private entrance to my rooms. Come in; we are quite alone. The maid is asleep, and the Helmers are at the dance upstairs.

KROGSTAD [*coming into the room*]. Are the Helmers really at a dance tonight?

MRS LINDE. Yes, why not?

KROGSTAD. Certainly—why not?

MRS LINDE. Now, Nils, let us have a talk.

KROGSTAD. Can we two have anything to talk about?

MRS LINDE. We have a great deal to talk about.

KROGSTAD. I shouldn't have thought so.

MRS LINDE. No, you have never properly understood me.

KROGSTAD. Was there anything else to understand except what was obvious to all the world—a heartless woman jilts a man when a more lucrative chance turns up?

MRS LINDE. Do you believe I am as absolutely heartless as all that? And do you believe it with a light heart?

KROGSTAD. Didn't you?

MRS LINDE. Nils, did you really think that?

KROGSTAD. If it were as you say, why did you write to me as you did at the time?

MRS LINDE. I could do nothing else. As I had to break with you, it was my duty also to put an end to all that you felt for me.

KROGSTAD [*wringing his hands*]. So that was it. And all this—only for the sake of money!

MRS LINDE. You mustn't forget that I had a helpless mother and two little brothers. We couldn't wait for you, Nils; your prospects seemed hopeless then.

KROGSTAD. That may be so, but you had no right to throw me over for anyone else's sake.

MRS LINDE. Indeed, I don't know. Many a time did I ask myself if I had the right to do it.

KROGSTAD [*more gently*]. When I lost you it was as if all the solid ground went from under my feet. Look at me now—I am a shipwrecked man clinging to a bit of wreckage.

MRS LINDE. But help may be near.

KROGSTAD. It *was* near, but then you came and stood in my way.

MRS LINDE. Unintentionally, Nils. It was only today that I learned it was your place I was going to take in the bank.

KROGSTAD. I believe you, if you say so. But now that you know it, are you not going to give it up to me?

MRS LINDE. No, because that would not benefit you in the least.

KROGSTAD. Oh, benefit, benefit—I would have done it whether or no.

MRS LINDE. I have learned to act prudently. Life and hard, bitter necessity have taught me that.

KROGSTAD. And life has taught me not to believe in fine speeches.

MRS LINDE. Then life has taught you something very reasonable. But deeds you must believe in.

KROGSTAD. What do you mean by that?

MRS LINDE. You said you were like a shipwrecked man clinging to some wreckage.

KROGSTAD. I had good reason to say so.

MRS LINDE. Well, I am like a shipwrecked woman clinging to some wreckage—no one to mourn for, no one to care for.

KROGSTAD. It was your own choice.

MRS LINDE. There was no other choice—then.

KROGSTAD. Well, what now?

MRS LINDE. Nils, how would it be if we two shipwrecked people could join forces?

KROGSTAD. What are you saying?

MRS LINDE. Two on the same piece of wreckage would stand a better chance than each on their own.

KROGSTAD. Christine!

MRS LINDE. What do you suppose brought me to town?

KROGSTAD. Do you mean that you gave me a thought?

MRS LINDE. I could not endure life without work. All my life, as long as I can remember, I have worked, and it has been my greatest and only pleasure. But now I am quite alone in the world—my life is so dreadfully empty and I feel so forsaken. There is not

the least pleasure in working for one's self. Nils, give
me someone and something to work for.

KROGSTAD. I don't trust that. It is nothing but a
woman's overstrained sense of generosity that
prompts you to make such an offer of yourself.

MRS LINDE. Have you ever noticed anything of the sort
in me?

KROGSTAD. Could you really do it? Tell me—do you
know all about my past life?

MRS LINDE. Yes.

KROGSTAD. And do you know what they think of me
here?

MRS LINDE. You seemed to me to imply that with me
you might have been quite another man.

KROGSTAD. I am certain of it.

MRS LINDE. Is it too late now?

KROGSTAD. Christine, are you saying this deliberately?
Yes, I am sure you are. I see it in your face. Have
you really the courage, then—

MRS LINDE. I want to be a mother to someone, and your
children need a mother. We two need each other.
Nils, I have faith in your real character—I can dare
anything with you.

KROGSTAD [grasps her hands]. Thanks, thanks, Christine! Now I shall find a way to clear myself in the
eyes of the world. Ah, but I forgot—

MRS LINDE [listening]. Hush! The tarantella! Go, go!

KROGSTAD. Why? What is it?

MRS LINDE. Do you hear them up there? When that is
over we may expect them back.

KROGSTAD. Yes, yes—I will go. But it is all no use. Of
course you are not aware what steps I have taken in
the matter of the Helmers.

MRS LINDE. Yes, I know all about that.

KROGSTAD. And in spite of that have you the courage
to—

MRS LINDE. I understand very well to what lengths a
man like you might be driven by despair.

KROGSTAD. If I could only undo what I have done!

MRS LINDE. You cannot. Your letter is lying in the letter box now.

KROGSTAD. Are you sure of that?

MRS LINDE. Quite sure, but—

KROGSTAD [*with a searching look at her*]. Is that what it all means?—that you want to save your friend at any cost? Tell me frankly. Is that it?

MRS LINDE. Nils, a woman who has once sold herself for another's sake doesn't do it a second time.

KROGSTAD. I will ask for my letter back.

MRS LINDE. No, no.

KROGSTAD. Yes, of course I will. I will wait here till Helmer comes; I will tell him he must give me my letter back—that it only concerns my dismissal—that he is not to read it—

MRS LINDE. No, Nils, you must not recall your letter.

KROGSTAD. But, tell me, wasn't it for that very purpose that you asked me to meet you here?

MRS LINDE. In my first moment of fright it was. But twenty-four hours have elapsed since then, and in that time I have witnessed incredible things in this house. Helmer must know all about it. This unhappy secret must be disclosed; they must have a complete understanding between them, which is impossible with all this concealment and falsehood going on.

KROGSTAD. Very well, if you will take the responsibility. But there is one thing I can do in any case, and I shall do it at once.

MRS LINDE [*listening*]. You must be quick and go! The dance is over; we are not safe a moment longer.

KROGSTAD. I will wait for you below.

MRS LINDE. Yes, do. You must see me back to my door.

KROGSTAD. I have never had such an amazing piece of good fortune in my life! [*Goes out through the outer door. The door between the room and the hall remains open.*]

MRS LINDE [*tidying up the room and laying her hat and cloak ready*]. What a difference! What a difference! Someone to work for and live for—a home to bring comfort into. That I will do, indeed. I wish they would be quick and come. [*Listens.*] Ah, there they are now. I must put on my things. [*Takes up her hat and cloak.* HELMER'S *and* NORA'S *voices are heard outside; a key is turned, and* HELMER *brings* NORA *almost by force into the hall. She is in an Italian costume with a large black shawl round her; he is in evening dress and a black domino which is flying open.*]

NORA [*hanging back in the doorway and struggling with him*]. No, no, no!—don't take me in. I want to go upstairs again; I don't want to leave so early.

HELMER. But, my dearest Nora—

NORA. Please, Torvald dear—please, *please*—only an hour more.

HELMER. Not a single minute, my sweet Nora. You know that was our agreement. Come along into the room; you are catching cold standing there. [*He brings her gently into the room in spite of her resistance.*]

MRS LINDE. Good evening.

NORA. Christine!

HELMER. You here so late, Mrs Linde?

MRS LINDE. Yes, you must excuse me; I was so anxious to see Nora in her dress.

NORA. Have you been sitting here waiting for me?

MRS LINDE. Yes; unfortunately I came too late—you had already gone upstairs—and I thought I couldn't go away again without having seen you.

HELMER [*taking off* NORA'S *shawl*]. Yes, take a good look at her. I think she is worth looking at. Isn't she charming, Mrs Linde?

MRS LINDE. Yes, indeed she is.

HELMER. Doesn't she look remarkably pretty? Everyone thought so at the dance. But she is terribly self-willed, this sweet little person. What are we to do

with her? You will hardly believe that I had almost
to bring her away by force.

NORA. Torvald, you will repent not having let me stay,
even if it were only for half an hour.

HELMER. Listen to her, Mrs Linde! She had danced her
tarantella, and it had been a tremendous success, as
it deserved—although possibly the performance was
a trifle too realistic—a little more so, I mean, than
was strictly compatible with the limitations of art.
But never mind about that! The chief thing is, she
had made a success—she had made a tremendous
success. Do you think I was going to let her remain
there after that and spoil the effect? No indeed! I
took my charming little Capri maiden—my capri-
cious little Capri maiden, I should say—on my arm,
took one quick turn round the room, a curtsey on
either side, and, as they say in novels, the beautiful
apparition disappeared. An exit ought always to be
effective, Mrs Linde; but that is what I cannot make
Nora understand. Pooh! this room is hot. [*Throws
his domino on a chair and opens the door of his
room.*] Hullo! it's all dark in here. Oh, of course—
excuse me. [*He goes in and lights some candles.*]

NORA [*in a hurried and breathless whisper*]. Well?

MRS LINDE [*in a low voice*]. I have had a talk with him.

NORA. Yes, and—

MRS LINDE. Nora, you must tell your husband all about
it.

NORA [*in an expressionless voice*]. I knew it.

MRS LINDE. You have nothing to be afraid of as far as
Krogstad is concerned, but you must tell him.

NORA. I won't tell him.

MRS LINDE. Then the letter will.

NORA. Thank you, Christine. Now I know what I must
do. Hush!

HELMER [*coming in again*]. Well, Mrs Linde, have you
admired her?

MRS LINDE. Yes, and now I will say good night.

HELMER. What, already? Is this yours, this knitting?

MRS LINDE [*taking it*]. Yes, thank you. I had very nearly forgotten it.

HELMER. So you knit?

MRS LINDE. Of course.

HELMER. Do you know, you ought to embroider.

MRS LINDE. Really? Why?

HELMER. Yes, it's far more becoming. Let me show you. You hold the embroidery thus in your left hand and use the needle with the right—like this—with a long easy sweep. Do you see?

MRS LINDE. Yes, perhaps—

HELMER. Yes, but in the case of knitting—that can never be anything but ungraceful; look here—the arms close together, the knitting needles going up and down—it has a sort of Chinese effect. . . . That was really excellent champagne they gave us.

MRS LINDE. Well—good night, Nora, and don't be self-willed any more.

HELMER. That's right, Mrs Linde.

MRS LINDE. Good night, Mr Helmer.

HELMER [*accompanying her to the door*]. Good night, good night. I hope you will get home all right. I should be very happy to— But you haven't any great distance to go. Good night, good night. [*She goes out; he shuts the door after her and comes in again.*] Ah!—at last we have got rid of her. She is a frightful bore, that woman.

NORA. Aren't you very tired, Torvald?

HELMER. No, not in the least.

NORA. Nor sleepy?

HELMER. Not a bit. On the contrary I feel extraordinarily lively. And you?—you really look both tired and sleepy.

NORA. Yes, I am very tired. I want to go to sleep at once.

HELMER. There, you see it was quite right of me not to let you stay there any longer.

NORA. Everything you do is quite right, Torvald.

HELMER [*kissing her on the forehead*]. Now my little skylark is speaking reasonably. Did you notice what good spirits Rank was in this evening?

NORA. Really? Was he? I didn't speak to him at all.

HELMER. And I very little, but I have not for a long time seen him in such good form. [*Looks for a while at her and then goes nearer to her.*] It is delightful to be at home by ourselves again, to be all alone with you—you fascinating, charming little darling!

NORA. Don't look at me like that, Torvald.

HELMER. Why shouldn't I look at my dearest treasure? —at all the beauty that is mine, all my very own?

NORA [*going to the other side of the table*]. You mustn't say things like that to me tonight.

HELMER [*following her*]. You have still got the tarantella in your blood, I see. And it makes you more captivating than ever. Listen—the guests are beginning to go now. [*In a lower voice.*] Nora—soon the whole house will be quiet.

NORA. Yes, I hope so.

HELMER. Yes, my own darling Nora. Do you know that when I am out at a party with you like this why I speak so little to you, keep away from you and only send a stolen glance in your direction now and then?—do you know why I do that? It is because I make believe to myself that we are secretly in love and you are my secretly promised bride and that no one suspects there is anything between us.

NORA. Yes, yes—I know very well your thoughts are with me all the time.

HELMER. And when we are leaving and I am putting the shawl over your beautiful young shoulders—on your lovely neck—then I imagine that you are my young bride and that we have just come from our wedding and I am bringing you, for the first time, into our home—to be alone with you for the first time—quite alone with my shy little darling! All this evening I have longed for nothing but you. When I watched the seductive figures of the tarantella my blood was on fire; I could endure it no longer, and that was why I brought you down so early—

NORA. Go away, Torvald! You must let me go. I won't—

HELMER. What's that? You're joking, my little Nora! You won't—you won't? Am I not your husband? [*A knock is heard at the outer door.*]

NORA [*starting*]. Did you hear—

HELMER [*going into the hall*]. Who is it?

RANK [*outside*]. It is I. May I come in for a moment?

HELMER [*in a fretful whisper*]. Oh, what does he want now? [*Aloud.*] Wait a minute. [*Unlocks the door.*] Come, that's kind of you not to pass by our door.

RANK. I thought I heard your voice, and I felt as if I should like to look in. [*With a swift glance round.*] Ah yes!—these dear familiar rooms. You are very happy and cosy in here, you two.

HELMER. It seems to me that you looked after yourself pretty well upstairs too.

RANK. Excellently. Why shouldn't I? Why shouldn't one enjoy everything in this world?—at any rate as much as one man and as long as one can. The wine was capital—

HELMER. Especially the champagne.

RANK. So you noticed that too? It is almost incredible how much I managed to put away!

NORA. Torvald drank a great deal of champagne tonight too.

RANK. Did he?

NORA. Yes, and he is always in such good spirits afterward.

RANK. Well, why should one not enjoy a merry evening after a well-spent day?

HELMER. Well spent? I am afraid I can't take credit for that.

RANK [*clapping him on the back*]. But I can, you know!

HELMER. Exactly.

NORA. Doctor Rank, you must have been occupied with some scientific investigation today.

HELMER. Just listen!—little Nora talking about scientific investigations!

NORA. And may I congratulate you on the result?

RANK. Indeed you may.

NORA. Was it favorable, then?

RANK. The best possible, for both doctor and patient—certainty.

NORA [*quickly and searchingly*]. Certainty?

RANK. Absolute certainty. So wasn't I entitled to make a merry evening of it after that?

NORA. Yes, you certainly were, Doctor Rank.

HELMER. I think so too, so long as you don't have to pay for it in the morning.

RANK. Oh well, one can't have anything in this life without paying for it.

NORA. Doctor Rank—are you found of fancy-dress balls?

RANK. Yes, if there is a fine lot of pretty costumes.

NORA. Tell me—what shall we two wear at the next.

HELMER. Little featherbrain!—are you thinking of the next already?

RANK. We two? Yes, I can tell you. You shall go as a good fairy—

HELMER. Yes, but what do you suggest as an appropriate costume for that?

RANK. Let your wife go dressed just as she is in everyday life.

HELMER. That was really very prettily turned. But can't you tell us what you will be?

RANK. Yes, my dear friend, I have quite made up my mind about that.

HELMER. Well?

RANK. At the next fancy-dress ball I shall be invisible.

HELMER. That's a good joke!

RANK. There is a big black hat—have you ever heard

of hats that make you invisible? If you put one on, no one can see you.

HELMER [*suppressing a smile*]. Yes, you are quite right.

RANK. But I am clean forgetting what I came for. Helmer, give me a cigar—one of the dark Havanas.

HELMER. With the greatest pleasure. [*Offers him his case.*]

RANK [*takes a cigar and cuts off the end*]. Thanks.

NORA [*striking a match*]. Let me give you a light.

RANK. Thank you. [*She holds the match for him to light his cigar.*] And now good-by!

HELMER. Good-by, good-by, dear old man!

NORA. Sleep well, Doctor Rank.

RANK. Thank you for that wish.

NORA. Wish me the same.

RANK. You? Well, if you want me to sleep well! And thanks for the light. [*He nods to them both and goes out.*]

HELMER [*in a subdued voice*]. He has drunk more than he ought.

NORA [*absently*]. Maybe. [HELMER *takes a bunch of keys out of his pocket and goes into the hall.*] Torvald! What are you going to do there?

HELMER. Empty the letter box; it is quite full; there will be no room to put the newspaper in tomorrow morning.

NORA. Are you going to work tonight?

HELMER. You know quite well I'm not. What is this? Someone has been at the lock.

NORA. At the lock?

HELMER. Yes, someone has. What can it mean? I should never have thought the maid— Here is a broken hairpin. Nora, it is one of yours.

NORA [*quickly*]. Then it must have been the children.

HELMER. Then you must get them out of those ways. There, at last I have got it open. [*Takes out the contents of the letter box and calls to the kitchen.*] Helen! Helen, put out the light over the front door.

[*Goes back into the room and shuts the door into the hall. He holds out his hand full of letters.*] Look at that—look what a heap of them there are. [*Turning them over.*] What on earth is that?

NORA [*at the window*]. The letter— No! Torvald, no!

HELMER. Two cards—of Rank's.

NORA. Of Doctor Rank's?

HELMER [*looking at them*]. Doctor Rank. They were on the top. He must have put them in when he went out.

NORA. Is there anything written on them?

HELMER. There is a black cross over the name. Look there—what an uncomfortable idea! It looks as if he were announcing his own death.

NORA. It is just what he is doing.

HELMER. What? Do you know anything about it? Has he said anything to you?

NORA. Yes. He told me that when the cards came it would be his leave-taking from us. He means to shut himself up and die.

HELMER. My poor old friend. Certainly I knew we should not have him very long with us. But so soon! And so he hides himself away like a wounded animal.

NORA. If it has to happen, it is best it should be without a word—don't you think so, Torvald?

HELMER [*walking up and down*]. He had so grown into our lives. I can't think of him as having gone out of them. He, with his sufferings and his loneliness, was like a cloudy background to our sunlit happiness. Well, perhaps it is best so. For him, anyway. [*Standing still.*] And perhaps for us too, Nora. We two are thrown quite upon each other now. [*Puts his arms round her.*] My darling wife, I don't feel as if I could hold you tight enough. Do you know, Nora, I have often wished that you might be threatened by some great danger, so that I might risk my life's blood and everything for your sake.

NORA [*disengages herself and says firmly and decidedly*]: Now you must read your letters, Torvald.

HELMER. No, no; not tonight. I want to be with you, my darling wife.

NORA. With the thought of your friend's death—

HELMER. You are right; it has affected us both. Something ugly has come between us—the thought of the horrors of death. We must try and rid our minds of that. Until then—we will each go to our own room.

NORA [*hanging on his neck*]. Good night, Torvald— good night!

HELMER [*kissing her on the forehead*]. Good night, my little singing bird. Sleep sound, Nora. Now I will read my letters through. [*He takes his letters and goes into his room, shutting the door after him*].

NORA [*gropes distractedly about, seizes* HELMER'S *domino, throws it about her while she says in quick, hoarse, spasmodic whispers*]: Never to see him again. Never! Never! [*Puts her shawl over her head.*] Never to see my children again either—never again. Never! Never! Ah! the icy black water—the unfathomable depths—if only it were over! He has got it now—now he is reading it. Good-by, Torvald and my children! [*She is about to rush out through the hall when* HELMER *opens his door hurriedly and stands with an open letter in his hand.*]

HELMER. Nora!

NORA. Ah!

HELMER. What is this? Do you know what is in this letter?

NORA. Yes, I know. Let me go! Let me get out!

HELMER [*holding her back*]. Where are you going?

NORA [*trying to get free*]. You shan't save me, Torvald!

HELMER [*reeling*]. True? Is this true, that I read here? Horrible! No, no—it is impossible that it is true.

NORA. It is true. I have loved you above everything else in the world.

HELMER. Oh, don't let us have any silly excuses.

NORA [*taking a step toward him*]. Torvald!

HELMER. Miserable creature—what have you done?

NORA. Let me go. You shall not suffer for my sake. You shall not take it upon yourself.

HELMER. No tragedy airs, please. [*Locks the hall door.*] Here you shall stay and give me an explanation. Do you understand what you have done? Answer me! Do you understand what you have done?

NORA [*looks steadily at him and says with a growing look of coldness in her face*]: Yes, now I am beginning to understand thoroughly.

HELMER [*walking about the room*]. What a horrible awakening! All these eight years—she who was my joy and pride—a hypocrite, a liar—worse, worse—a criminal! The unutterable ugliness of it all! For shame! For shame! [*NORA is silent and looks steadily at him. He stops in front of her.*] I ought to have suspected that something of the sort would happen. I ought to have foreseen it. All your father's want of principle—be silent!—all your father's want of principle has come out in you. No religion, no morality, no sense of duty— How I am punished for having winked at what he did! I did it for your sake, and this is how you repay me.

NORA. Yes, that's just it.

HELMER. Now you have destroyed all my happiness. You have ruined all my future. It is horrible to think of! I am in the power of an unscrupulous man; he can do what he likes with me, ask anything he likes of me, give me any orders he pleases—I dare not refuse. And I must sink to such miserable depths because of a thoughtless woman.

NORA. When I am out of the way you will be free.

HELMER. No fine speeches, please. Your father had always plenty of those ready too. What good would it be to me if you were out of the way, as you say? Not the slightest. He can make the affair known everywhere; and if he does, I may be falsely suspected of having been a party to your criminal action. Very likely people will think I was behind it all—that it was I who prompted you! And I have to thank you for all this—you whom I have cherished during the whole of our married life. Do you understand now what it is you have done for me?

NORA [*coldly and quietly*]. Yes.

HELMER. It is so incredible that I can't take it in. But we must come to some understanding. Take off that shawl. Take it off, I tell you. I must try and appease him in some way or another. The matter must be hushed up at any cost. And as for you and me, it must appear as if everything between us were just as before—but naturally only in the eyes of the world. You will still remain in my house, that is a matter of course. But I shall not allow you to bring up the children; I dare not trust them to you. To think that I should be obliged to say so to one whom I have loved so dearly and whom I still— No, that is all over. From this moment happiness is not the question; all that concerns us is to save the remains, the fragments, the appearance—

[*A ring is heard at the front doorbell.*]

HELMER [*with a start*]. What is that? So late! Can the worst—can he— Hide yourself, Nora. Say you are ill.

[NORA *stands motionless.* HELMER *goes and unlocks the hall door.*]

MAID [*half dressed, comes to the door*]. A letter for the mistress.

HELMER. Give it to me. [*Takes the letter and shuts the door.*] Yes, it is from him. You shall not have it; I will read it myself.

NORA. Yes, read it.

HELMER [*standing by the lamp*]. I scarcely have the courage to do it. It may mean ruin for the both of us. No, I must know. [*Tears open the letter, runs his eye over a few lines, looks at a paper enclosed and gives a shout of joy.*] Nora! [*She looks at him ques-*

tioningly.] Nora! No, I must read it once again. Yes, it is true! I am saved! Nora, I am saved!

NORA. And I?

HELMER. You too, of course; we are both saved, both you and I. Look, he sends you your bond back. He says he regrets and repents—that a happy change in his life— Never mind what he says! We are saved, Nora! No one can do anything to you. Oh, Nora, Nora— No, first I must destroy these hateful things. Let me see. [*Takes a look at the bond*.] No, no, I won't look at it. The whole thing shall be nothing but a bad dream to me. [*Tears up the bond and both letters, throws them all into the stove and watches them burn*.] There—now it doesn't exist any longer. He says that since Christmas Eve you— These must have been three dreadful days for you, Nora.

NORA. I have fought a hard fight these three days.

HELMER. And suffered agonies and seen no way out, but— No, we won't call any of the horrors to mind. We will only shout with joy and keep saying, "It's all over! It's all over!" Listen to me, Nora. You don't seem to realize that it is all over. What is this?—such a cold, set face! My poor little Nora, I quite understand; you don't feel as if you could believe that I have forgiven you. But it is true, Nora, I swear it; I have forgiven you everything. I know that what you did you did out of love for me.

NORA. That is true.

HELMER. You have loved me as a wife ought to love her husband. Only you had not sufficient knowledge to judge of the means you used. But do you suppose you are any the less dear to me because you don't understand how to act on your own responsibility? No, no; only lean on me; I will advise and direct you. I should not be a man if this womanly helplessness did not just give you a double attractiveness in my eyes. You must not think any more about the hard things I said in my first moment of consternation, when I thought everything was going to overwhelm me. I have forgiven you, Nora; I swear to you I have forgiven you.

NORA. Thank you for your forgiveness. [*She goes out through the door to the right.*]

HELMER. No, don't go. [*Looks in.*] What are you doing in there?

NORA [*from within*]. Taking off my fancy dress.

HELMER [*standing at the open door*]. Yes, do. Try and calm yourself and make your mind easy again, my frightened little singing bird. Be at rest and feel secure; I have broad wings to shelter you under. [*Walks up and down by the door.*] How warm and cosy our home is, Nora. Here is shelter for you; here I will protect you like a hunted dove that I have saved from a hawk's claws; I will bring peace to your poor beating heart. It will come, little by little, Nora, believe me. Tomorrow morning you will look upon it all quite differently; soon everything will be just as it was before. Very soon you won't need me to assure you that I have forgiven you; you will yourself feel the certainty that I have done so. Can you suppose I should ever think of such a thing as repudiating you or even reproaching you? You have no idea what a true man's heart is like, Nora. There is something so indescribably sweet and satisfying, to a man, in the knowledge that he has forgiven his wife—forgiven her freely and with all his heart. It seems as if that had made her, as it were, doubly his own; he has given her a new life, so to speak, and she has in a way become both wife and child to him. So you shall be for me after this, my little scared, helpless darling. Have no anxiety about anything, Nora; only be frank and open with me, and I will serve as will and conscience both to you— What is this? Not gone to bed? Have you changed your things?

NORA [*in everyday dress*]. Yes, Torvald, I have changed my things now.

HELMER. But what for?—so late as this.

NORA. I shall not sleep tonight.

HELMER. But, my dear Nora—

NORA [*looking at her watch*]. It is not so very late. Sit down here, Torvald. You and I have much to say to one another. [*She sits down at one side of the table.*]

HELMER. Nora—what is this?—this cold, set face?

NORA. Sit down. It will take some time; I have a lot to talk over with you.

HELMER [*sits down at the opposite side of the table*]. You alarm me, Nora!—and I don't understand you.

NORA. No, that is just it. You don't understand me, and I have never understood you either—before tonight. No, you mustn't interrupt me. You must simply listen to what I say. Torvald, this is a settling of accounts.

HELMER. What do you mean by that?

NORA [*after a short silence*]. Isn't there one thing that strikes you as strange in our sitting here like this?

HELMER. What is that?

NORA. We have been married now eight years. Does it not occur to you that this is the first time we two, you and I, husband and wife, have had a serious conversation?

HELMER. What do you mean, serious?

NORA. In all these eight years—longer than that—from the very beginning of our acquaintance we have never exchanged a word on any serious subject.

HELMER. Was it likely that I would be continually and forever telling you about worries that you could not help me to bear?

NORA. I am not speaking about business matters. I say that we have never sat down in earnest together to try and get at the bottom of anything.

HELMER. But, dearest Nora, would it have been any good to you?

NORA. That is just it; you have never understood me. I

have been greatly wronged, Torvald—first by Papa
and then by you.

HELMER. What! By us two—by us two who have loved
you better than anyone else in the world?

NORA [*shaking her head*]. You have never loved me. You
have only thought it pleasant to be in love with me.

HELMER. Nora, what do I hear you saying?

NORA. It is perfectly true, Torvald. When I was at home
with Papa he told me his opinion about everything,
and so I had the same opinions; and if I differed
from him I concealed the fact, because he would not
have liked it. He called me his doll child, and he
played with me just as I used to play with my dolls.
And when I came to live with you—

HELMER. What sort of an expression is that to use about
our marriage?

NORA [*undisturbed*]. I mean that I was simply trans-
ferred from Papa's hands to yours. You arranged
everything according to your own taste, and so I got
the same tastes as you—or else I pretended to. I am
really not quite sure which—I think sometimes the
one and sometimes the other. When I look back on it
it seems to me as if I have been living here like a
poor woman—just from hand to mouth. I have ex-
isted merely to perform tricks for you, Torvald. But
you would have it so. You and Papa have committed
a great sin against me. It is your fault that I have
made nothing of my life.

HELMER. How unreasonable and how ungrateful you
are, Nora! Have you not been happy here?

NORA. No, I have never been happy. I thought I was,
but it has never really been so.

HELMER. Not—not happy!

NORA. No, only merry. And you have always been so
kind to me. But our home has been nothing but a
playroom. I have been your doll wife, just as at home
I was Papa's doll child; and here the children have

been my dolls. I thought it great fun when you played with me, just as they thought it great fun when I played with them. That is what our marriage has been, Torvald.

HELMER. There is some truth in what you say—exaggerated and strained as your view of it is. But for the future it shall be different. Playtime shall be over and lesson time shall begin.

NORA. Whose lessons? Mine or the children's?

HELMER. Both yours and the children's, my darling Nora.

NORA. Alas, Torvald, you are not the man to educate me into being a proper wife for you.

HELMER. And you can say that!

NORA. And I—how am I fitted to bring up the children?

HELMER. Nora!

NORA. Didn't you say so yourself a little while ago—that you dare not trust me to bring them up?

HELMER. In a moment of anger! Why do you pay any heed to that?

NORA. Indeed, you were perfectly right. I am not fit for the task. There is another task I must undertake first. I must try and educate myself—you are not the man to help me in that. I must do that for myself. And that is why I am going to leave you now.

HELMER [*springing up*]. What do you say?

NORA. I must stand quite alone if I am to understand myself and everything about me. It is for that reason that I cannot remain with you any longer.

HELMER. Nora, Nora!

NORA. I am going away from here now, at once. I am sure Christine will take me in for the night.

HELMER. You are out of your mind! I won't allow it! I forbid you!

NORA. It is no use forbidding me anything any longer. I will take with me what belongs to myself. I will take nothing from you, either now or later.

HELMER. What sort of madness is this?

NORA. Tomorrow I shall go home—I mean to my old home. It will be easiest for me to find something to do there.

HELMER. You blind, foolish woman!

NORA. I must try and get some sense, Torvald.

HELMER. To desert your home, your husband and your children! And you don't consider what people will say!

NORA. I cannot consider that at all. I only know that it is necessary for me.

HELMER. It's shocking. This is how you would neglect your most sacred duties.

NORA. What do you consider my most sacred duties?

HELMER. Do I need to tell you that? Are they not your duties to your husband and your children?

NORA. I have other duties just as sacred.

HELMER. That you have not. What duties could those be?

NORA. Duties to myself.

HELMER. Before all else you are a wife and a mother.

NORA. I don't believe that any longer. I believe that before all else I am a reasonable human being just as you are—or, at all events, that I must try and become one. I know quite well, Torvald, that most people would think you right and that views of that kind are to be found in books; but I can no longer content myself with what most people say or with what is found in books. I must think over things for myself and get to understand them.

HELMER. Can you understand your place in your own home? Have you not a reliable guide in such matters as that?—have you no religion?

NORA. I am afraid, Torvald, I do not exactly know what religion is.

HELMER. What are you saying?

NORA. I know nothing but what the clergyman said when I went to be confirmed. He told us that religion was this and that and the other. When I am away from all this and am alone I will look into that matter too. I will see if what the clergyman said is true, or at all events if it is true for me.

HELMER. This is unheard of in a girl of your age! But if religion cannot lead you aright, let me try and awaken your conscience. I suppose you have some moral sense? Or—answer me—am I to think you have none?

NORA. I assure you, Torvald, that is not an easy question to answer. I really don't know. The thing perplexes me altogether. I only know that you and I look at it in quite a different light. I am learning, too, that the law is quite another thing from what I supposed; but I find it impossible to convince myself that the law is right. According to it a woman has no right to spare her old dying father or to save her husband's life. I can't believe that.

HELMER. You talk like a child. You don't understand the conditions of the world in which you live.

NORA. No, I don't. But now I am going to try. I am going to see if I can make out who is right, the world or I.

HELMER. You are ill, Nora; you are delirious; I almost think you are out of your mind.

NORA. I have never felt my mind so clear and certain as tonight.

HELMER. And is it with a clear and certain mind that you forsake your husband and your children?

NORA. Yes, it is.

HELMER. Then there is only one possible explanation.

NORA. What is that?

HELMER. You do not love me any more.

NORA. No, that is just it.

HELMER. Nora!—and you can say that?

NORA. It gives me great pain, Torvald, for you have always been so kind to me, but I cannot help it. I do not love you any more.

HELMER [*regaining his composure*]. Is that a clear and
certain conviction too?

NORA. Yes, absolutely clear and certain. That is the
reason why I will not stay here any longer.

HELMER. And can you tell me what I have done to for-
feit your love?

NORA. Yes, indeed I can. It was tonight, when the wonderful thing did not happen; then I saw you were
not the man I had thought you.

HELMER. Explain yourself better—I don't understand
you.

NORA. I have waited so patiently for eight years; for,
goodness knows, I knew very well that wonderful
things don't happen every day. Then this horrible
misfortune came upon me, and then I felt quite certain that the wonderful thing was going to happen
at last. When Krogstad's letter was lying out there
never for a moment did I imagine that you would
consent to accept this man's conditions. I was so absolutely certain that you would say to him: Publish
the thing to the whole world. And when that was
done—

HELMER. Yes, what then?—when I had exposed my wife
to shame and disgrace?

NORA. When that was done I was so absolutely certain
you would come forward and take everything upon
yourself and say: I am the guilty one.

HELMER. Nora!

NORA. You mean that I would never have accepted such
a sacrifice on your part? No, of course not. But what
would my assurances have been worth against yours?
That was the wonderful thing which I hoped for and
feared, and it was to prevent that that I wanted to
kill myself.

HELMER. I would gladly work night and day for you,
Nora—bear sorrow and want for your sake. But no
man would sacrifice his honor for the one he loves.

NORA. It is a thing hundreds of thousands of women have done.

HELMER. Oh, you think and talk like a heedless child.

NORA. Maybe. But you neither think nor talk like the man I could bind myself to. As soon as your fear was over—and it was not fear for what threatened me but for what might happen to you—when the whole thing was past, as far as you were concerned it was exactly as if nothing at all had happened. Exactly as before, I was your little skylark, your doll, which you would in the future treat with doubly gentle care because it was so brittle and fragile. [*Getting up.*] Torvald—it was then it dawned upon me that for eight years I had been living here with a strange man and had borne him three children. Oh, I can't bear to think of it! I could tear myself into little bits!

HELMER [*sadly*]. I see, I see. An abyss has opened between us—there is no denying it. But, Nora, would it not be possible to fill it up?

NORA. As I am now, I am no wife for you.

HELMER. I have it in me to become a different man.

NORA. Perhaps—if your doll is taken away from you.

HELMER. But to part—to part from you! No, no, Nora; I can't understand that idea.

NORA [*going out to the right*]. That makes it all the more certain that it must be done. [*She comes back with her cloak and hat and a small bag which she puts on a chair by the table.*]

HELMER. Nora. Nora, not now! Wait till tomorrow.

NORA [*putting on her cloak*]. I cannot spend the night in a strange man's room.

HELMER. But can't we live here like brother and sister?

NORA [*putting on her hat*]. You know very well that would not last long. [*Puts the shawl round her.*] Good-by, Torvald. I won't see the little ones. I know they are in better hands than mine. As I am now, I can be of no use to them.

HELMER. But someday, Nora—someday?

NORA. How can I tell? I have no idea what is going to become of me.

HELMER. But you are my wife, whatever becomes of you.

NORA. Listen, Torvald. I have heard that when a wife deserts her husband's house, as I am doing now, he is legally freed from all obligations toward her. In any case I set you free from all your obligations. You are not to feel yourself bound in the slightest way, any more than I shall. There must be perfect freedom on both sides. See, here is your ring back. Give me mine.

HELMER. That too?

NORA. That too.

HELMER. Here it is.

NORA. That's right. Now it is all over. I have put the keys here. The maids know all about everything in the house—better than I do. Tomorrow, after I have left her, Christine will come here and pack up my own things that I brought with me from home. I will have them sent after me.

HELMER. All over! All over! Nora, shall you never think of me again?

NORA. I know I shall often think of you and the children and this house.

HELMER. May I write to you, Nora?

NORA. No—never. You must not do that.

HELMER. But at least let me send you—

NORA. Nothing—nothing.

HELMER. Let me help you if you are in want.

NORA. No. I can receive nothing from a stranger.

HELMER. Nora—can I never be anything more than a stranger to you?

NORA [taking her bag]. Ah, Torvald, the most wonderful thing of all would have to happen.

HELMER. Tell me what that would be!

NORA. Both you and I would have to be so changed
that— Oh, Torvald, I don't believe any longer in
wonderful things happening.

HELMER. But I will believe in it. Tell me. So changed
that—

NORA. That our life together would be a real wedlock.
Good-by. [*She goes out through the hall.*]

HELMER [*sinks down on a chair at the door and buries
his face in his hands*]. Nora! Nora! [*Looks round and
rises.*] Empty! She is gone. [*A hope flashes across his
mind.*] The most wonderful thing of all—?

[*The sound of a door shutting is heard from below.*]

THE WILD DUCK

PERSONS OF THE PLAY

WERLE, *a merchant*
GREGERS WERLE, *his son*
OLD EKDAL
HIALMAR EKDAL, *his son, a photographer*
GINA EKDAL, *Hialmar's wife*
HEDVIG, *their daughter, a girl of fourteen*
MRS SORBY, *Werle's housekeeper*
RELLING, *a doctor*
MOLVIK, *a student of theology*
GRABERG, *Werle's bookkeeper*
PETTERSEN, *Werle's servant*
JENSEN, *a hired waiter*
A FLABBY GENTLEMAN
A THIN-HAIRED GENTLEMAN
A SHORTSIGHTED GENTLEMAN
SIX OTHER GENTLEMEN, *guests at Werle's
dinner party*
SEVERAL HIRED WAITERS

*The action takes place in the home of
Werle and the studio of Hialmar Ekdal.*

ACT ONE

SCENE—*At* WERLE'S *house. A richly and comfortably furnished study; bookcases and upholstered furniture; a writing table, with papers and documents, in the center of the room; lighted lamps with green shades, giving a subdued light. At the back open folding doors with curtains drawn back. Within is seen a large and handsome room, brilliantly lighted with lamps and branching candlesticks. In front, on the right (in the study), a small baize door leads into* WERLE'S *office. On the left, in front, a fireplace with a glowing coal fire and farther back a double door leading into the dining room.*

 WERLE'S *servant,* PETTERSEN, *in livery, and* JENSEN, *the hired waiter, in black, are putting the study in order. In the large room two or three other hired waiters are moving about arranging things and lighting more candles. From the dining room the hum of conversation and laughter of many voices are heard; a glass is tapped with a knife; silence follows, and a toast is proposed; shouts of "Bravo!" and then again a buzz of conversation.*

PETTERSEN [*lights a lamp on the chimney place and places a shade over it*]. Hark to them, Jensen! Now the old man's on his legs holding a long palaver about Mrs Sorby.

JENSEN [*pushing forward an armchair*]. Is it true, what folks say, that they're—very good friends, eh?

PETTERSEN. Lord knows.

JENSEN. I've heard tell as he's been a lively customer in his day.

PETTERSEN. May be.

JENSEN. And he's giving this spread in honor of his son, they say.

PETTERSEN. Yes. His son came home yesterday.

JENSEN. This is the first time I ever heard as Mr Werle had a son.

PETTERSEN. Oh yes, he has a son right enough. But he's a fixture, as you might say, up at the Höidal works. He's never once come to town all the years I've been in service here.

A WAITER [*in the doorway of the other room*]. Pettersen, here's an old fellow wanting—

PETTERSEN [*mutters*]. The devil—who's this now?

[OLD EKDAL *appears from the right, in the inner room. He is dressed in a threadbare overcoat with a high collar; he wears woolen mittens and carries in his hand a stick and a fur cap. Under his arm a brown paper parcel. Dirty red-brown wig and small gray mustache.*]

PETTERSEN [*goes toward him*]. Good lord!—what do you want here?

EKDAL [*in the doorway*]. Must get into the office, Pettersen.

PETTERSEN. The office was closed an hour ago, and—

EKDAL. So they told me at the front door. But Graberg's in there still. Let me slip in this way, Pettersen; there's a good fellow. [*Points toward the baize door.*] It's not the first time I've come this way.

PETTERSEN. Well, you may pass. [*Opens the door.*] But mind you go out again the proper way, for we've got company.

EKDAL. I know, I know—h'm! Thanks, Pettersen, good old friend! Thanks! [*Mutters softly.*] Ass! [*He goes into the office;* PETTERSEN *shuts the door after him.*]

JENSEN. Is he one of the office people?

PETTERSEN. No, he's only an outside hand that does odd jobs of copying. But he's been a tiptopper in his day, has old Ekdal.

JENSEN. You can see he's been through a lot.

PETTERSEN. Yes; he was an army officer, you know.

JENSEN. You don't say so?

PETTERSEN. No mistake about it. But then he went into the timber trade or something of the sort. They say he once played Mr Werle a very nasty trick. They were partners in the Höidal works at the time. Oh, I know old Ekdal well, I do. Many a nip of bitters and bottle of ale we two have drunk at Madam Eriksen's.

JENSEN. He don't look as if he'd much to stand treat with.

PETTERSEN. Why, bless you, Jensen, it's me that stands treat. I always think there's no harm in being a bit civil to folks that have seen better days.

JENSEN. Did he go bankrupt then?

PETTERSEN. Worse than that. He went to prison.

JENSEN. To prison!

PETTERSEN. Or perhaps it was the penitentiary. [*Listens.*] Sh! They're leaving the table.

[*The dining-room door is thrown open from within by a couple of waiters.* MRS SORBY *comes out conversing with two gentlemen. Gradually the whole company follows, amongst them* WERLE. *Last come* HIALMAR EKDAL *and* GREGERS WERLE.]

MRS SORBY [*in passing, to the servant*]. Tell them to serve the coffee in the music room, Pettersen.

PETTERSEN. Very well, madam.

[*She goes with the two gentlemen into the inner room and thence out to the right.* PETTERSEN *and* JENSEN *go out the same way.*]

A FLABBY GENTLEMEN [*to a* THIN-HAIRED GENTLEMAN]. Whew! What a dinner! It was no joke to do it justice.

THE THIN-HAIRED GENTLEMAN. Oh, with a little good will one can get through a lot in three hours.

THE FLABBY GENTLEMAN. Yes, but afterward, afterward, my dear Chamberlain!

A THIRD GENTLEMAN. I hear the coffee and maraschino are to be served in the music room.

THE FLABBY GENTLEMAN. Bravo! Then perhaps Mrs Sorby will play us something.

THE THIN-HAIRED GENTLEMAN [*in a low voice*]. I hope Mrs Sorby mayn't play us a tune we don't like, one of these days!

THE FLABBY GENTLEMAN. Oh no, not she! Bertha will never turn against her old friends.

[*They laugh and pass into the inner room.*]

WERLE [*in a low voice, dejectedly*]. I don't think anybody noticed it, Gregers.

GREGERS [*looks at him*]. Noticed what?

WERLE. Did you not notice it either?

GREGERS. What do you mean?

WERLE. We were thirteen at table.

GREGERS. Indeed? Were there thirteen of us?

WERLE [*glances toward* HIALMAR EKDAL]. Our usual party is twelve. [*To the others.*] This way, gentlemen!

[WERLE *and the others, all except* HIALMAR *and* GREGERS, *go out by the back, to the right.*]

HIALMAR [*who has overheard the conversation*]. You ought not to have invited me, Gregers.

GREGERS. What! Not ask my best and only friend to a party supposed to be in my honor?

HIALMAR. But I don't think your father likes it. You see, I am quite outside his circle.

GREGERS. So I hear. But I wanted to see you and have a talk with you, and I certainly shan't be staying long. Ah, we two old schoolfellows have drifted apart from each other. It must be sixteen or seventeen years since we met.

HIALMAR. Is it so long?

GREGERS. It is indeed. Well, how goes it with you? You look well. You have put on flesh and grown almost stout.

HIALMAR. Well, "stout" is scarcely the word, but I daresay I look a little more of a man than I used to.

GREGERS. Yes, you do; your outer man is in first-rate condition.

HIALMAR [in a tone of gloom]. Ah, but the inner man! That is a very different matter, I can tell you! Of course you know of the terrible catastrophe that has befallen me and mine since last we met.

GREGERS [more softly]. How are things going with your father now?

HIALMAR. Don't let us talk of it, old fellow. Of course my poor unhappy father lives with me. He hasn't another soul in the world to care for him. But you can understand that this is a miserable subject for me. Tell me, rather, how you have been getting on up at the works.

GREGERS. I have had a delightfully lonely time of it— plenty of leisure to think and think about things. Come over here; we may as well make ourselves comfortable. [He seats himself in an armchair by the fire and draws HIALMAR down into another alongside of it.]

HIALMAR [sentimentally]. After all, Gregers, I thank you for inviting me to your father's table; for I take it as a sign that you have got over your feeling against me.

GREGERS [surprised]. How could you imagine I had any feeling against you?

HIALMAR. You had at first, you know.

GREGERS. How at first?

HIALMAR. After the great misfortune. It was natural enough that you should. Your father was within an ace of being drawn into that—well, that terrible business.

GREGERS. Why should that give me any feeling against you? Who can have put that into your head?

HIALMAR. I know it did, Gregers; your father told me so himself.

GREGERS [*starts*]. My father! Oh, indeed. H'm. Was that why you never let me hear from you?—not a single word.

HIALMAR. Yes.

GREGERS. Not even when you made up your mind to become a photographer?

HIALMAR. Your father said I had better not write to you at all, about anything.

GREGERS [*looking straight before him*]. Well, well, perhaps he was right. But tell me now, Hialmar: are you pretty well satisfied with your present position?

HIALMAR [*with a little sigh*]. Oh yes, I am; I have really no cause to complain. At first, as you may guess, I felt it a little strange. It was such a totally new state of things for me. But of course my whole circumstances were totally changed. Father's utter, irretrievable ruin—the shame and disgrace of it, Gregers—

GREGERS [*affected*]. Yes, yes; I understand.

HIALMAR. I couldn't think of remaining at college; there wasn't a shilling to spare; on the contrary, there were debts—mainly to your father, I believe—

GREGERS. H'm.

HIALMAR. In short, I thought it best to break, once for all, with my old surroundings and associations. It was your father that specially urged me to it, and since he interested himself so much in me—

GREGERS. My father did?

HIALMAR. Yes, you surely knew that, didn't you? Where do you suppose I found the money to learn photography and to furnish a studio and make a start? All that costs a pretty penny, I can tell you.

GREGERS. And my father provided the money?

HIALMAR. Yes, my dear fellow, didn't you know? I understood him to say he had written to you about it.

GREGERS. Not a word about his part in the business. He
must have forgotten it. Our correspondence has always been purely a business one. So it was my father
that—

HIALMAR. Yes, certainly. He didn't wish it to be generally known, but he it was. And of course it was he,
too, that put me in a position to marry. Don't you—
don't you know about that either?

GREGERS. No, I haven't heard a word of it. [*Shakes him
by the arm.*] But, my dear Hialmar, I can't tell you
what pleasure all this gives me—pleasure and self-
reproach. I have perhaps done my father injustice
after all—in some things. This proves that he has a
heart. It shows a sort of compunction—

HIALMAR. Compunction?

GREGERS. Yes, yes—whatever you like to call it. Oh, I
can't tell you how glad I am to hear this of Father.
So you are a married man, Hialmar! That is further
than I shall ever get. Well, I hope you are happy in
your married life?

HIALMAR. Yes, thoroughly happy. She is as good and
capable a wife as any man could wish for. And she is
by no means without culture.

GREGERS [*rather surprised*]. No, of course not.

HIALMAR. You see, life is itself an education. Her daily
intercourse with me— And then we know one or two
rather remarkable men who come a good deal about
us. I assure you, you would hardly know Gina again.

GREGERS. Gina?

HIALMAR. Yes; had you forgotten that her name was
Gina?

GREGERS. Whose name? I haven't the slightest idea—

HIALMAR. Don't you remember that she used to be in
service here?

GREGERS [*looks at him*]. Is it Gina Hansen?

HIALMAR. Yes, of course it is Gina Hansen.

GREGERS. —who kept house for us during the last year
of my mother's illness?

HIALMAR. Yes, exactly. But, my dear friend, I'm quite sure your father told you that I was married.

GREGERS [*who has risen*]. Oh yes, he mentioned it, but not that— [*Walking about the room.*] Stay—perhaps he did—now that I think of it. My father always writes such short letters. [*Half seats himself on the arm of the chair.*] Now tell me, Hialmar—this is interesting—how did you come to know Gina—your wife?

HIALMAR. The simplest thing in the world. You know Gina did not stay here long; everything was so much upset at that time, owing to your mother's illness and so forth, that Gina was not equal to it all; so she gave notice and left. That was the year before your mother died—or it may have been the same year.

GREGERS. It was the same year. I was up at the works then. But afterward?

HIALMAR. Well, Gina lived at home with her mother, Madam Hansen, an excellent, hard-working woman who kept a little eating house. She had a room to let too, a very nice comfortable room.

GREGERS. And I suppose you were lucky enough to secure it?

HIALMAR. Yes; in fact, it was your father that recommended it to me. So it was there, you see, that I really came to know Gina.

GREGERS. And then you got engaged?

HIALMAR. Yes. It doesn't take young people long to fall in love—h'm.

GREGERS [*rises and moves about a little*]. Tell me: was it after your engagement—was it then that my father— I mean was it then that you began to take up photography?

HIALMAR. Yes, precisely. I wanted to make a start and to set up house as soon as possible, and your father and I agreed that this photography business was the readiest way. Gina thought so too. Oh, and there was

another thing in its favor, by the bye; it happened
luckily, that Gina had learned to retouch.

GREGERS. That chimed in marvelously.

HIALMAR [*pleased, rises*]. Yes, didn't it? Don't you think
it was a marvelous piece of luck?

GREGERS. Oh, unquestionably. My father seems to have
been almost a kind of providence to you.

HIALMAR [*with emotion*]. He did not forsake his old
friend's son in the hour of his need. For he has a
heart, you see.

MRS SORBY [*enters arm in arm with* WERLE]. Nonsense,
my dear Mr Werle; you mustn't stop there any longer
staring at all the lights. It's very bad for you.

WERLE [*lets go her arm and passes his hand over his
eyes*]. I daresay you are right.

[PETTERSEN *and* JENSEN *carry round refreshment trays.*]

MRS SORBY [*to the guests in the other room*]. This way,
if you please, gentlemen. Whoever wants a glass of
punch must be so good as to come in here.

THE FLABBY GENTLEMAN [*comes up to* MRS SORBY]. Surely
it isn't possible that you have suspended our cherished right to smoke?

MRS SORBY. Yes. No smoking here, in Mr Werle's sanc-
tum, Chamberlain.

THE THIN-HAIRED GENTLEMAN. When did you enact these
stringent amendments on the cigar law, Mrs Sorby?

MRS SORBY. After the last dinner, Chamberlain, when
certain persons permitted themselves to overstep the
mark.

THE THIN-HAIRED GENTLEMAN. And may one never overstep the mark a little bit, Madame Bertha? Not the
least little bit?

MRS SORBY. Not in any respect whatsoever, Mr Balle.

[*Most of the guests have assembled in the study; serv-
ants hand round glasses of punch.*]

WERLE [*to* HIALMAR, *who is studying beside a table*].
What are you studying so intently, Ekdal?

HIALMAR. Only an album, Mr Werle.

THE THIN-HAIRED GENTLEMAN [*who is wandering about*]. Ah, photographs! They are quite in your line of course.

THE FLABBY GENTLEMAN [*in an armchair*]. Haven't you brought any of your own with you?

HIALMAR. No, I haven't.

THE FLABBY GENTLEMAN. You ought to have; it's very good for the digestion to sit and look at pictures.

THE THIN-HAIRED GENTLEMAN. And it contributes to the entertainment, you know.

THE SHORTSIGHTED GENTLEMAN. And all contributions are thankfully received.

MRS SORBY. The chamberlains think that when one is invited out to dinner one ought to exert oneself a little in return, Mr Ekdal.

THE FLABBY GENTLEMAN. Where one dines so well, that duty becomes a pleasure.

THE THIN-HAIRED GENTLEMAN. And when it's a case of the struggle for existence, you know—

MRS SORBY. I quite agree with you!

[*They continue the conversation with laughter and joking.*]

GREGERS [*softly*]. You must join in, Hialmar.

HIALMAR [*writhing*]. What am I to talk about?

THE FLABBY GENTLEMAN. Don't you think, Mr Werle, that Tokay may be considered one of the more wholesome sorts of wine?

WERLE [*by the fire*]. I can answer for the Tokay you had today, at any rate; it's one of the very finest seasons. Of course you would notice that.

THE FLABBY GENTLEMAN. Yes, it had a remarkably delicate flavor.

HIALMAR [*shyly*]. Is there any difference between the seasons?

THE FLABBY GENTLEMAN [*laughs*]. Come! That's good!

WERLE [*smiles*]. It really doesn't pay to set fine wine before you.

THE THIN-HAIRED GENTLEMAN. Tokay is like photographs, Mr Ekdal; they both need sunshine. Am I not right?

HIALMAR. Yes, light is important, no doubt.

MRS SORBY. And it's exactly the same with the chamberlains—they, too, depend very much on sunshine, as the saying is.

THE THIN-HAIRED GENTLEMAN. Oh, fie! That's a very threadbare sarcasm!

THE SHORTSIGHTED GENTLEMAN. Mrs Sorby is coming out—

THE FLABBY GENTLEMAN. —and at our expense too. [*Holds up his finger reprovingly.*] Oh, Madame Bertha, Madame Bertha!

MRS SORBY. Yes, and there's not the least doubt that the seasons differ greatly. The old vintages are the finest.

THE SHORTSIGHTED GENTLEMAN. Do you reckon me among the old vintages?

MRS SORBY. Oh, far from it.

THE THIN-HAIRED GENTLEMAN. There now! But me, dear Mrs Sorby—

THE FLABBY GENTLEMAN. Yes, and me? What vintage should you say that we belong to?

MRS SORBY. Why, to the sweet vintages, gentlemen. [*She sips a glass of punch. The gentlemen laugh and flirt with her.*]

WERLE. Mrs Sorby can always find a loophole—when she wants to. Fill your glasses, gentlemen! Pettersen, will you see to it? Gregers, suppose we have a glass together. [GREGERS *does not move.*] Won't you join us, Ekdal? I found no opportunity of drinking with you at table.

[GRABERG, *the bookkeeper, looks in at the baize door.*]

GRABERG. Excuse me, sir, but I can't get out.

WERLE. Have you been locked in again?

GRABERG. Yes, and Flakstad has carried off the keys.

WERLE. Well, you can pass out this way.

GRABERG. But there's someone else—

WERLE. All right; come through, both of you. Don't be afraid.

[GRABERG *and* OLD EKDAL *come out of the office.*]

WERLE [*involuntarily*]. Ugh!

[*The laughter and talk among the guests cease.* HIALMAR *starts at the sight of his father, puts down his glass and turns toward the fireplace.*]

EKDAL [*does not look up but makes little bows to both sides as he passes, murmuring*]. Beg pardon, come the wrong way. Door locked—door locked. Beg pardon. [*He and* GRABERG *go out by the back, to the right.*]

WERLE [*between his teeth*]. That idiot Graberg.

GREGERS [*open-mouthed and staring, to* HIALMAR]. Why, surely that wasn't—

THE FLABBY GENTLEMAN. What's the matter? Who was it?

GREGERS. Oh, nobody; only the bookkeeper and some-one with him.

THE SHORTSIGHTED GENTLEMAN [*to* HIALMAR]. Did you know that man?

HIALMAR. I don't know—I didn't notice—

THE FLABBY GENTLEMAN. What the deuce has come over everyone? [*He joins another group who are talking softly.*]

MRS SORBY [*whispers to the* SERVANT]. Give him some-thing to take with him—something good, mind.

PETTERSEN [*nods*]. I'll see to it. [*Goes out.*]

GREGERS [*softly and with emotion, to* HIALMAR]. So that was really he!

HIALMAR. Yes.

GREGERS. And you could stand there and deny that you knew him.

HIALMAR [*whispers vehemently*]. But how could I—

GREGERS. —acknowledge your own father?

HIALMAR [*with pain*]. Oh, if you were in my place—

[*The conversation amongst the guests, which has been carried on in a low tone, now swells into constrained joviality.*]

THE THIN-HAIRED GENTLEMAN [*approaching* HIALMAR *and* GREGERS *in a friendly manner*]. Ah! Reviving old college memories, eh? Don't you smoke, Mr Ekdal? May I give you a light? Oh, by the bye, we mustn't—

HIALMAR. No, thank you, I won't—

THE FLABBY GENTLEMAN. Haven't you a nice little poem you could recite to us, Mr Ekdal? You used to recite so charmingly.

HIALMAR. I am sorry, I can't remember anything.

THE FLABBY GENTLEMAN. Oh, that's a pity. Well, what shall we do, Balle?

[*Both gentlemen move away and pass into the other room.*]

HIALMAR [*gloomily*]. Gregers—I am going! When a man has felt the crushing hand of Fate, you see— Say good-by to your father for me.

GREGERS. Yes, yes. Are you going straight home?

HIALMAR. Yes. Why?

GREGERS. Oh, because I may perhaps look in on you later.

HIALMAR. No, you mustn't do that. You must not come to my home. Mine is a melancholy abode, Gregers; especially after a splendid banquet like this. We can always arrange to meet somewhere in the town.

MRS SORBY [*who has quietly approached*]. Are you going, Ekdal?

HIALMAR. Yes.

MRS SORBY. Remember me to Gina.

HIALMAR. Thanks.

MRS SORBY. And say I am coming up to see her one of these days.

HIALMAR. Yes, thank you. [*To* GREGERS.] Stay here; I will slip out unobserved. [*He saunters away, then into the other room and so out to the right.*]

MRS SORBY [*softly to the* SERVANT, *who has come back*]. Well, did you give the old man something?

PETTERSEN. Yes; I sent him off with a bottle of cognac.

MRS SORBY. Oh, you might have thought of something better than that.

PETTERSEN. Oh no, Mrs Sorby; cognac is what he likes best in the world.

THE FLABBY GENTLEMAN [*in the doorway with a sheet of music in his hand*]. Shall we play a duet, Mrs Sorby?

MRS SORBY. Yes, suppose we do.

THE GUESTS. Bravo, bravo!

[*She goes with all the guests through the back room out to the right.* GREGERS *remains standing by the fire.* WERLE *is looking for something on the writing table and appears to wish that* GREGERS *would go; as* GREGERS *does not move* WERLE *goes toward the door.*]

GREGERS. Father, won't you stay a moment?

WERLE [*stops*]. What is it?

GREGERS. I must have a word with you.

WERLE. Can it not wait until we are alone?

GREGERS. No, it cannot, for perhaps we shall never be alone together.

WERLE [*drawing nearer*]. What do you mean by that?

[*During what follows the pianoforte is faintly heard from the distant music room.*]

GREGERS. How has that family been allowed to go so miserably to the wall?

WERLE. You mean the Ekdals, I suppose.

GREGERS. Yes, I mean the Ekdals. Lieutenant Ekdal was once so closely associated with you.

WERLE. Much too closely; I have felt that to my cost for many a year. It is thanks to him that I—yes *I*—have had a kind of slur cast upon my reputation.

GREGERS [*softly*]. Are you sure that he alone was to blame?

WERLE. Who else do you suppose?

GREGERS. You and he acted together in that affair of the forests—

WERLE. But was it not Ekdal that drew the map of the tracts we had bought—that fraudulent map! It was he who felled all that timber illegally on government ground. In fact, the whole management was in his hands. I was quite in the dark as to what Lieutenant Ekdal was doing.

GREGERS. Lieutenant Ekdal himself seems to have been very much in the dark as to what he was doing.

WERLE. That may be. But the fact remains that he was found guilty and I acquitted.

GREGERS. Yes, I know that nothing was proved against you.

WERLE. Acquittal is acquittal. Why do you rake up these old miseries that turned my hair gray before its time? Is that the sort of thing you have been brooding over up there, all these years? I can assure you, Gregers, here in the town the whole story has been forgotten long ago—as far as *I* am concerned.

GREGERS. But that unhappy Ekdal family—

WERLE. What would you have me do for the people? When Ekdal came out of prison he was a broken-down being, past all help. There are people in the world who dive to the bottom the moment they get a couple of slugs in their body and never come to the surface again. You may take my word for it, Gregers, I have done all I could without positively laying myself open to all sorts of suspicion and gossip.

GREGERS. Suspicion? Oh, I see.

WERLE. I have given Ekdal copying to do for the office, and I pay him far, far more for it than his work is worth.

GREGERS [*without looking at him*]. H'm; that I don't doubt.

WERLE. You laugh? Do you think I am not telling you the truth? Well, I certainly can't refer you to my books, for I never enter payments of that sort.

GREGERS [*smiles coldly*]. No, there are certain payments it is best to keep no account of.

WERLE [*taken aback*]. What do you mean by that?

GREGERS [*mustering up courage*]. Have you entered what it cost you to have Hialmar Ekdal taught photography?

WERLE. I? I? How "entered" it?

GREGERS. I have learned that it was you who paid for his training. And I have learned, too, that it was you who enabled him to set up house so comfortably.

WERLE. Well, and yet you talk as though I had done nothing for the Ekdals! I can assure you these people have cost me enough in all conscience.

GREGERS. Have you entered any of these expenses in your books?

WERLE. Why do you ask?

GREGERS. Oh, I have my reasons. Now tell me: when you interested yourself so warmly in your old friend's son—it was just before his marriage, was it not?

WERLE. Why, deuce take it—after all these years how can I—

GREGERS. You wrote me a letter about that time—a business letter, of course—and in a postscript you mentioned—quite briefly—that Hialmar Ekdal had married a Miss Hansen.

WERLE. Yes, that was quite right. That was her name.

GREGERS. But you did not mention that this Miss Hansen was Gina Hansen—our former housekeeper.

WERLE [*with a forced laugh of derision*]. No; to tell the truth, it didn't occur to me that you were so particularly interested in our former housekeeper.

GREGERS. No more I was. But [*lowers his voice*] there were others in this house who were particularly interested in her.

WERLE. What do you mean by that? [*Flaring up.*] You are not alluding to me, I hope?

GREGERS [*softly but firmly*]. Yes, I am alluding to you.

WERLE. And you dare— You presume to— How can that ungrateful hound—that photographer fellow—how dare he go making such insinuations!

GREGERS. Hialmar has never breathed a word about this.

I don't believe he has the faintest suspicion of such a thing.

WERLE. Then where have you got it from? Who can have put such notions in your head?

GREGERS. My poor unhappy mother told me, and that the very last time I saw her.

WERLE. Your mother! I might have known as much! You and she—you always held together. It was she who turned you against me from the first.

GREGERS. No, it was all that she had to suffer and submit to, until she broke down and came to such a pitiful end.

WERLE. Oh, she had nothing to suffer or submit to; not more than most people, at all events. But there's no getting on with morbid, overstrained creatures—that I have learned to my cost. And you could go on nursing such a suspicion—burrowing into all sorts of slanders against your own father! I must say, Gregers, I really think at your age you might find something more useful to do.

GREGERS. Yes, it is high time.

WERLE. Then perhaps your mind would be easier than it seems to be now. What can be your object in remaining up at the works year out and year in, drudging away like a common clerk and not drawing a farthing more than the ordinary monthly wage? It is downright folly.

GREGERS. Ah, if I were only sure of that.

WERLE. I understand you well enough. You want to be independent; you won't be beholden to me for anything. Well, now there happens to be an opportunity for you to become independent, your own master in everything.

GREGERS. Indeed? In what way?

WERLE. When I wrote you insisting on your coming to town at once—h'm—

GREGERS. Yes, what is it you really want of me? I have been waiting all day to know.

WERLE. I want to propose that you should enter the firm as partner.

GREGERS. I! Join your firm? As partner?

WERLE. Yes. It would not involve our being constantly together. You could take over the business here in town, and I should move up to the works.

GREGERS. You would?

WERLE. The fact is, I am not so fit for work as I once was. I am obliged to spare my eyes, Gregers; they have begun to trouble me.

GREGERS. They have always been weak.

WERLE. Not as they are now. And besides, circumstances might possibly make it desirable for me to live up there—for a time, at any rate.

GREGERS. That is certainly quite a new idea to me.

WERLE. Listen, Gregers, there are many things that stand between us; but we are father and son after all. We ought surely to be able to come to some sort of understanding with each other.

GREGERS. Outwardly, you mean, of course?

WERLE. Well, even that would be something. Think it over, Gregers. Don't you think it ought to be possible? Eh?

GREGERS [*looking at him coldly*]. There is something behind all this.

WERLE. How so?

GREGERS. You want to make use of me in some way.

WERLE. In such a close relationship as ours the one can always be useful to the other.

GREGERS. Yes, so people say.

WERLE. I want very much to have you at home with me for a time. I am a lonely man, Gregers; I have always felt lonely all my life through, but most of all now that I am getting up in years. I feel the need of someone about me—

GREGERS. You have Mrs Sorby.

WERLE. Yes, I have her, and she has become, I may say, almost indispensable to me. She is lively and even tempered; she brightens up the house; and that is a very great thing for me.

GREGERS. Well, then, you have everything as you wish it.

WERLE. Yes, but I am afraid it can't last. A woman so situated may easily find herself in a false position in the eyes of the world. For that matter, it does a man no good either.

GREGERS. Oh, when a man gives such dinners as you give he can risk a great deal.

WERLE. Yes, but how about the woman, Gregers? I fear she won't accept the situation much longer, and even if she did—even if, out of attachment to me, she were to take her chance of gossip and scandal and all that —do you think, Gregers, you with your strong sense of justice—

GREGERS [*interrupts him*]. Tell me in one word: are you thinking of marrying her?

WERLE. Suppose I were thinking of it? What then?

GREGERS. That's what I say: What then?

WERLE. Should you be inflexibly opposed to it?

GREGERS. Not at all. Not by any means.

WERLE. I was not sure whether your devotion to your mother's memory—

GREGERS. I am not overstrained.

WERLE. Well, whatever you may or not be, at all events you have lifted a great weight from my mind. I am extremely pleased that I can reckon on your concurrence in this matter.

GREGERS [*looking intently at him*]. Now I see the use you want to put me to.

WERLE. Use to put you to? What an expression!

GREGERS. Oh, don't let us be nice in our choice of words —not when we are alone together, at any rate. [*With a short laugh.*] Well, well. So this is what made it absolutely essential that I should come to town in person. For the sake of Mrs Sorby we are to get up a pretense at family life in the house—a tableau of filial affection. That will be something new, indeed.

WERLE. How dare you speak in that tone!

GREGERS. Was there ever any family life here? Never since I can remember. But now, forsooth, your plans demand something of the sort. No doubt it will have an excellent effect when it is reported that the son has hastened home, on the wings of filial piety, to the gray-haired father's wedding feast. What will then remain of all the rumors as to the wrongs the poor dead mother had to submit to? Not a vestige. Her son annihilates them at one stroke.

WERLE. Gregers—I believe there is no one in the world you detest as you do me.

GREGERS [*softly*]. I have seen you at too close quarters.

WERLE. You have seen me with your mother's eyes. [*Lowers his voice a little.*] But you should remember that her eyes were—clouded now and then.

GREGERS [*quivering*]. I see what you are hinting at. But who was to blame for mother's unfortunate weakness? Why, you and all those— The last of them was this woman that you palmed off upon Hialmar Ekdal when you were— Ugh!

WERLE [*shrugs his shoulders*]. Word for word as if it were your mother speaking!

GREGERS [*without heeding*]. And there he is now, with his great, confiding childlike mind, compassed about with all this treachery—living under the same roof with such a creature and never dreaming that what he calls his home is built up on a lie! [*Comes a step nearer.*] When I look back upon your past I seem to see a battlefield with shattered lives on every hand.

WERLE. I begin to think that the chasm that divides us is too wide.

GREGERS [*bowing with self-command*]. So I have observed, and therefore I take my hat and go.

WERLE. You are going? Out of the house?

GREGERS. Yes. For at last I see my mission in life.

WERLE. What mission?

GREGERS. You would only laugh if I told you.

WERLE. A lonely man doesn't laugh so easily, Gregers.

GREGERS [*pointing toward the background*]. Look, Father—the chamberlains are playing blindman's buff with Mrs Sorby. Good night and good-by. [*He goes out by the back to the right. Sound of laughter and merriment from the company, who are now visible in the outer room.*]

WERLE [*muttering contemptuously after* GREGERS]. Ha! Poor wretch—and he says he is not overstrained!

ACT TWO

SCENE—HIALMAR EKDAL'S *studio, a good-sized room, evidently in the top story of the building. On the right a sloping roof of large panes of glass half covered by a blue curtain. In the right-hand corner, at the back, the entrance door; farther forward, on the same side, a door leading to the sitting room. Two doors on the opposite side and between them an iron stove. At the back a wide double sliding door. The studio is plainly but comfortably fitted up and furnished. Between the door on the right, standing out a little from the wall, a sofa with a table and some chairs; on the table a lighted lamp with a shade; beside the stove an old armchair. Photographic instruments and apparatus of different kinds lying about the room. Against the back wall, to the left of the double door, stands a bookcase containing a few books, boxes and bottles of chemicals, instruments, tools and other objects. Photographs and small articles, such as camel's-hair pencils, paper and so forth, lie on the table.*

GINA EKDAL *sits on a chair by the table, sewing.* HEDVIG *is sitting on the sofa, with her hands shading her eyes and her thumbs in her ears, reading a book.*

GINA [*glances once or twice at* HEDVIG, *as if with secret anxiety, then says*]: Hedvig!
[HEDVIG *does not hear.*]
GINA [*repeats more loudly*]. Hedvig!

HEDVIG [*takes away her hands and looks up*]. Yes, Mother?

GINA. Hedvig dear, you mustn't sit reading any longer now.

HEDVIG. Oh, Mother, mayn't I read a little more? Just a little bit?

GINA. No, no, you must put away your book now. Father doesn't like it; he never reads himself in the evening.

HEDVIG [*shuts the book*]. No, Father doesn't care much about reading.

GINA [*puts aside her sewing and takes up a lead pencil and a little account book from the table*]. Can you remember how much we paid for the butter today?

HEDVIG. It was one crown sixty-five.

GINA. That's right. [*Puts it down.*] It's terrible what a lot of butter we get through in this house. Then there was the smoked sausage and the cheese—let me see [*writes*]—and the ham [*adds up*]. Yes, that makes just—

HEDVIG. And then the beer.

GINA. Yes, to be sure. [*Writes.*] How it do mount up! But we can't manage with no less.

HEDVIG. And then you and I didn't need anything hot for dinner, as Father was out.

GINA. No, that was so much to the good. And then I took eight crowns fifty for the photographs.

HEDVIG. Really! So much as that?

GINA. Exactly eight crowns fifty.

[*Silence.* GINA *takes up her sewing again;* HEDVIG *takes paper and pencil and begins to draw, shading her eyes with her left hand.*]

HEDVIG. Isn't it jolly to think that Father is at Mr Werle's big dinner party?

GINA. You know he's not really Mr Werle's guest. It was the son invited him. [*After a pause.*] We have nothing to do with that Mr Werle.

HEDVIG. I'm longing for Father to come home. He promised to ask Mrs Sorby for something nice for me.

GINA. Yes, there's plenty of good things going in that house, I can tell you.

HEDVIG [*goes on drawing*]. And I believe I'm a little hungry too.

[OLD EKDAL, *with the paper parcel under his arm and another parcel in his coat pocket, comes in by the entrance door.*]

GINA. How late you are today, Grandfather!

EKDAL. They had locked the office door. Had to wait in Graberg's room. And then they let me through—h'm.

HEDVIG. Did you get some more copying to do, Grandfather?

EKDAL. This whole packet. Just look.

GINA. That's capital.

HEDVIG. And you have another parcel in your pocket.

EKDAL. Eh? Oh, never mind, that's nothing. [*Puts his stick away in a corner.*] This work will keep me going a long time, Gina. [*Opens one of the sliding doors in the back wall a little.*] Hush! [*Peeps into the room for a moment, then pushes the door carefully to again.*] Hee-hee! They're fast asleep, all the lot of them. And she's gone into the basket herself. Hee-hee!

HEDVIG. Are you sure she isn't cold in that basket, Grandfather?

EKDAL. Not a bit of it! Cold? With all that straw? [*Goes toward the farther door on the left.*] There are matches in here, I suppose.

GINA. The matches is on the drawers.

[EKDAL *goes into his room.*]

HEDVIG. It's nice that Grandfather has got all that copying.

GINA. Yes, poor old Father; it means a bit of pocket money for him.

HEDVIG. And he won't be able to sit the whole forenoon down at that horrid Madam Eriksen's.

GINA. No more he won't. [*Short silence.*]

HEDVIG. Do you suppose they are still at the dinner table?

GINA. Goodness knows; as like as not.

HEDVIG. Think of all the delicious things Father is having to eat! I'm certain he'll be in splendid spirits when he comes. Don't you think so, Mother?

GINA. Yes; and if only we could tell him that we'd got the room let—

HEDVIG. But we don't need that this evening.

GINA. Oh, we'd be none the worst of it, I can tell you. It's no use to us as it is.

HEDVIG. I mean we don't need it this evening, for Father will be in good humor at any rate. It is best to keep the letting of the room for another time.

GINA [*looks across at her*]. You like having some good news to tell Father when he comes home in the evening?

HEDVIG. Yes, for then things are pleasanter somehow.

GINA [*thinking to herself*]. Yes, yes, there's something in that.

[OLD EKDAL *comes in again and is going out by the foremost door to the left.*]

GINA [*half turning in her chair*]. Do you want something in the kitchen, Grandfather?

EKDAL. Yes, yes, I do. Don't you trouble. [*Goes out.*]

GINA. He's not poking away at the fire, is he? [*Waits a moment.*] Hedvig, go and see what he's about.

[EKDAL *comes in again with a small jug of steaming hot water.*]

HEDVIG. Have you been getting some hot water, Grandfather?

EKDAL. Yes, hot water. Want it for something. Want to write, and the ink has got as thick as porridge—h'm.

GINA. But you'd best have your supper first, Grandfather. It's laid in there.

EKDAL. Can't be bothered with supper, Gina. Very busy, I tell you. No one's to come to my room. No one—

h'm. [*He goes into his room;* GINA *and* HEDVIG *look at each other.*]

GINA [*softly*]. Can you imagine where he's got money from?

HEDVIG. From Graberg, perhaps.

GINA. Not a bit of it. Graberg always sends the money to me.

HEDVIG. Then he must have got a bottle on credit somewhere.

GINA. Poor Grandfather, who'd give him credit?

[HIALMAR EKDAL, *in an overcoat and gray felt hat, comes in from the right.*]

GINA [*throws down her sewing and rises*]. Why, Ekdal, is that you already?

HEDVIG [*at the same time jumping up*]. Fancy your coming so soon, Father!

HIALMAR [*taking off his hat.*] Yes, most of the people were coming away.

HEDVIG. So early?

HIALMAR. Yes, it was a dinner party, you know. [*Takes off his overcoat.*]

GINA. Let me help you.

HEDVIG. Me too.

[*They draw off his coat;* GINA *hangs it up on the back wall.*]

HEDVIG. Were there many people there, Father?

HIALMAR. Oh no, not many. We had about twelve or fourteen at table.

GINA. And you had some talk with them all?

HIALMAR. Oh yes, a little; but Gregers took me up most of the time.

GINA. Is Gregers as ugly as ever?

HIALMAR. Well, he's not very much to look at. Hasn't the old man come home?

HEDVIG. Yes, Grandfather is in his room, writing.

HIALMAR. Did he say anything?

GINA. No, what should he say?

HIALMAR. Didn't he say anything about— I heard something about his having been with Graberg. I'll go in and see him for a moment.

GINA. No, no, better not.

HIALMAR. Why not? Did he say he didn't want me to go in?

GINA. I don't think he wants to see nobody this evening.

HEDVIG [*making signs*]. H'm—h'm!

GINA [*not noticing*]. He has been in to fetch hot water—

HIALMAR. Aha! Then he's—

GINA. Yes, I suppose so.

HIALMAR. Oh God! My poor old white-haired father! Well, well, there let him sit and get all the enjoyment he can.

[OLD EKDAL, *in an indoor coat and with a lighted pipe, comes from his room.*]

EKDAL. Got home? Thought it was you I heard talking.

HIALMAR. Yes, I have just come.

EKDAL. You didn't see me, did you?

HIALMAR. No, but they told me you had passed through —so I thought I would follow you.

EKDAL. H'm, good of you, Hialmar. Who were they, all those fellows?

HIALMAR. Oh, all sorts of people. There was Chamberlain Flor and Chamberlain Balle and Chamberlain Kaspersen and Chamberlain—this, that and the other —I don't know who all.

EKDAL [*nodding*]. Hear that, Gina! Chamberlains every one of them!

GINA. Yes, I hear as they're terrible genteel in that house nowadays.

HEDVIG. Did the chamberlains sing, Father? Or did they read aloud?

HIALMAR. No, they only talked nonsense. They wanted me to recite something for them, but I knew better than that.

EKDAL. You weren't to be persuaded, eh?

GINA. Oh, you might have done it.

HIALMAR. No; one mustn't be at everybody's beck and

call. [*Walks about the room.*] That's not my way, at
any rate.

EKDAL. No, no; Hialmar's not to be had for the asking,
he isn't.

HIALMAR. I don't see why I should bother myself to
entertain people on the rare occasions when I go into
society. Let the others exert themselves. These fellows go from one great dinner table to the next and
gorge and guzzle day out and day in. It's for them to
bestir themselves and do something in return for all
the good feeding they get.

GINA. But you didn't say that?

HIALMAR [*humming*]. Ho-ho-ho; faith, I gave them a bit
of my mind.

EKDAL. Not the chamberlains?

HIALMAR. Oh, why not? [*Lightly.*] After that we had a
little discussion about Tokay.

EKDAL. Tokay! There's a fine wine for you!

HIALMAR [*comes to a standstill*]. It may be a fine wine.
But of course you know the vintages differ; it all depends on how much sunshine the grapes have had.

GINA. Why, you know everything, Ekdal.

EKDAL. And did they dispute that?

HIALMAR. They tried to, but they were requested to observe it was just the same with chamberlains—that
with them, too, different batches were of different
qualities.

GINA. What things you do think of!

EKDAL. Hee-hee! So they got that in their pipes too?

HIALMAR. Right in their teeth.

EKDAL. Do you hear that, Gina? He said it right in the
very teeth of all the chamberlains.

GINA. Fancy! Right in their teeth!

HIALMAR. Yes, but I don't want it talked about. One
doesn't speak of such things. The whole affair passed
off quite amicably, of course. They were nice genial
fellows; I didn't want to wound them—not I!

EKDAL. Right in their teeth, though!

HEDVIG [*caressingly*]. How nice it is to see you in a dress coat! It suits you so well, Father.

HIALMAR. Yes, don't you think so? And this one really fits to perfection. It fits almost as if it had been made for me—a little tight in the armholes, perhaps; help me, Hedvig [*takes off the coat*]. I think I'll put on my jacket. Where is my jacket, Gina?

GINA. Here it is. [*Brings the jacket and helps him.*]

HIALMAR. That's it! Don't forget to send the coat back to Molvik first thing tomorrow morning.

GINA [*laying it away*]. I'll be sure and see to it.

HIALMAR [*stretching himself*]. After all, there's a more homely feeling about this. A free-and-easy indoor costume suits my whole personality better. Don't you think so, Hedvig?

HEDVIG. Yes, Father.

HIALMAR. When I loosen my necktie into a pair of flowing ends—like this—eh?

HEDVIG. Yes, and that goes so well with your mustache and the sweep of your curls.

HIALMAR. I should not call them curls exactly; I should rather say locks.

HEDVIG. Yes, they are too big for curls.

HIALMAR. Locks describes them better.

HEDVIG [*after a pause, twitching his jacket*]. Father!

HIALMAR. Well, what is it?

HEDVIG. Oh, you know very well.

HIALMAR. No, really I don't.

HEDVIG. [*half laughing, half whispering*]. Oh yes, Father; now don't tease me any longer!

HIALMAR. Why, what do you mean?

HEDVIG [*shaking him*]. Oh, what nonsense! Come, where are they, Father? All the good things you promised me, you know?

HIALMAR. Oh—if I haven't forgotten all about them!

HEDVIG. Now you're only teasing me, Father! Oh, it's too bad of you! Where have you put them?

HIALMAR. No, I positively forgot to get anything. But

wait a little! I have something else for you, Hedvig. [*Goes and searches in the pockets of the coat.*]

HEDVIG [*skipping and clapping her hands*]. Oh, Mother, Mother!

HIALMAR [*with a paper*]. Look, here it is.

GINA. There, you see; if you only give him time—

HEDVIG. That? Why, that's only a paper.

HIALMAR. That is the bill of fare, my dear; the whole bill of fare. Here you see "Menu"—that means bill of fare.

HEDVIG. Haven't you anything else?

HIALMAR. I forgot the other things, I tell you. But you may take my word for it, these dainties are very unsatisfying. Sit down at the table and read the bill of fare, and then I'll describe to you how the dishes taste. Here you are, Hedvig.

HEDVIG [*gulping down her tears*]. Thank you. [*She seats herself but does not read;* GINA *makes signs to her;* HIALMAR *notices it.*]

HIALMAR [*pacing up and down the room*]. It's monstrous what absurd things the father of a family is expected to think of, and if he forgets the smallest trifle he is treated to sour faces at once. Well, well, one gets used to that too. [*Stops near the stove by the old man's chair.*] Have you peeped in there this evening, Father?

EKDAL. Yes, to be sure I have. She's gone into the basket.

HIALMAR. Ah, she has gone into the basket. Then she's beginning to get used to it.

EKDAL. Yes, just as I prophesied. But you know there are still a few little things—

HIALMAR. A few improvements, yes.

EKDAL. They've got to be made, you know.

HIALMAR. Yes, let us have a talk about the improvements, Father. Come, let us sit on the sofa.

EKDAL. All right. H'm—think I'll just fill my pipe first.

Must clean it out too. H'm. [*He goes into his room.*]

GINA [*smiling to* HIALMAR]. His pipe!

HIALMAR. Oh yes, yes, Gina; let him alone—the poor shipwrecked old man. Yes, these improvements—we had better get them out of hand tomorrow.

GINA. You'll hardly have time tomorrow, Ekdal.

HEDVIG [*interposing*]. Oh yes, he will, Mother!

GINA. —for remember them prints that has to be retouched; they've sent for them time after time.

HIALMAR. There now! Those prints again! I shall get them finished all right. Have any new orders come in?

GINA. No, worse luck; tomorrow I have nothing to do but those two sittings, you know.

HIALMAR. Nothing else? Oh no, if people won't set about things with a will—

GINA. But what more can I do? Don't I advertise in the papers as much as we can afford?

HIALMAR. Yes, the papers; you see how much good they do. And I suppose no one has been to look at the room either?

GINA. No, not yet.

HIALMAR. That was only to be expected. If people won't keep their eyes open— Nothing can be done without a real effort, Gina!

HEDVIG [*going toward him*]. Shall I fetch you the flute, Father?

HIALMAR. No; no flute for me; *I* want no pleasures in this world. [*Pacing about.*] Yes indeed, I will work tomorrow; you shall see if I don't. You may be sure I shall work as long as my strength holds out.

GINA. But, my dear good Ekdal, I didn't mean it in that way.

HEDVIG. Father, mayn't I bring in a bottle of beer?

HIALMAR. No, certainly not. I require nothing, nothing. [*Comes to a standstill.*] Beer? Was it beer you were talking about?

HEDVIG [*cheerfully*]. Yes, Father; beautiful fresh beer.

HIALMAR. Well—since you insist upon it, you may bring in a bottle.

GINA. Yes, do; and we'll be nice and cosy.

[HEDVIG *runs toward the kitchen door.*]

HIALMAR [*by the stove, stops her, looks at her, puts his arm round her neck and presses her to him*]. Hedvig, Hedvig!

HEDVIG [*with tears of joy*]. My dear, kind father!

HIALMAR. No, don't call me that. Here have I been feasting at the rich man's table—battening at the groaning board! And I couldn't even—

GINA [*sitting at the table*]. Oh, nonsense, nonsense, Ekdal.

HIALMAR. It's not nonsense! And yet you mustn't be too hard upon me. You know that I love you for all that.

HEDVIG [*throwing her arms round him*]. And we love you, oh, so dearly, Father!

HIALMAR. And if I am unreasonable once in a while—why, then—you must remember that I am a man beset by a host of cares. There, there! [*Dries his eyes.*] No beer at such a moment as this. Give me the flute.

[HEDVIG *runs to the bookcase and fetches it.*]

HIALMAR. Thanks! That's right. With my flute in my hand and you two at my side—ah!

[HEDVIG *seats herself at the table near* GINA; HIALMAR *paces backward and forward, pipes up vigorously and plays a Bohemian peasant dance, but in a slow plaintive tempo and with sentimental expression.*]

HIALMAR [*breaking off the melody, holds out his left hands to* GINA *and says with emotion*]: Our roof may be poor and humble, Gina, but it is home. And with all my heart I say: here dwells my happiness. [*He begins to play again; almost immediately after a knocking is heard at the entrance door.*]

GINA [*rising*]. Hush, Ekdal—I think there's someone at the door.

HIALMAR [*laying the flute on the bookcase*]. There! Again!

[GINA *goes and opens the door.*]

GREGERS [*in the passage*]. Excuse me—

GINA [*starting back slightly*]. Oh!

GREGERS. —does not Mr Ekdal, the photographer, live here?

GINA. Yes, he does.

HIALMAR [*going toward the door*]. Gregers! You here after all? Well, come in then.

GREGERS [*coming in*]. I told you I would come and look you up.

HIALMAR. But this evening— Have you left the party?

GREGERS. I have left both the party and my father's house. Good evening, Mrs Ekdal. I don't know whether you recognize me?

GINA. Oh yes, it's not difficult to know young Mr Werle again.

GREGERS. No, I am like my mother, and no doubt you remember her.

HIALMAR. Left your father's house, did you say?

GREGERS. Yes, I have gone to a hotel.

HIALMAR. Indeed. Well, since you're here, take off your coat and sit down.

GREGERS. Thanks. [*He takes off his overcoat. He is now dressed in a plain gray suit of a countrified cut.*]

HIALMAR. Here on the sofa. Make yourself comfortable.

GREGERS [*looking around him*]. So these are your quarters, Hialmar—this is your home.

HIALMAR. This is the studio, as you see.

GINA. But it's the largest of our rooms, so we generally sit here.

HIALMAR. We used to live in a better place, but this flat has one great advantage: there are such capital outer rooms—

GINA. And we have a room on the other side of the passage that we can let.

GREGERS [*to* HIALMAR]. Ah—so you have lodgers too?

HIALMAR. No, not yet. They're not so easy to find, you
see; you have to keep your eyes open. [*To* HEDVIG.]
How about that beer, eh?

[HEDVIG *nods and goes out into the kitchen.*]

GREGERS. So that is your daughter?

HIALMAR. Yes, that is Hedvig.

GREGERS. And she is your only child?

HIALMAR. Yes, the only one. She is the joy of our lives,
and [*lowering his voice*] at the same time our deep-
est sorrow, Gregers.

GREGERS. What do you mean?

HIALMAR. She is in serious danger of losing her eyesight.

GREGERS. Becoming blind?

HIALMAR. Yes. Only the first symptoms have appeared
as yet, and she may not feel it much for some time.
But the doctor has warned us. It is coming inexo-
rably.

GREGERS. What a terrible misfortune! How do you account for it?

HIALMAR [*sighs*]. Hereditary, no doubt.

GREGERS [*starting*]. Hereditary?

GINA. Ekdal's mother had weak eyes.

HIALMAR. Yes, so my father says; I can't remember her.

GREGERS. Poor child! And how does she take it?

HIALMAR. Oh, you can imagine we haven't the heart to
tell her of it. She dreams of no danger. Gay and care-
less and chirping like a little bird, she flutters on-
ward into a life of endless night. [*Overcome.*] Oh, it
is cruelly hard on me, Gregers.

[HEDVIG *brings a tray with beer and glasses which she
sets upon the table.*]

HIALMAR [*stroking her hair*]. Thanks, thanks, Hedvig.

[HEDVIG *puts her arm around his neck and whispers in
his ear.*]

HIALMAR. No, no bread and butter just now. [*Looks
up.*] But perhaps you would like some, Gregers?

GREGERS [*with a gesture of refusal*]. No, no thank you.

HIALMAR [*still melancholy*]. Well, you can bring in a

little all the same. If you have a crust, that is all I
want. And plenty of butter on it, mind.

[HEDVIG *nods gaily and goes out into the kitchen again.*]

GREGERS [*who has been following her with his eyes*]. She
seems quite strong and healthy otherwise.

GINA. Yes. In other ways there's nothing amiss with her,
thank goodness.

GREGERS. She promises to be very like you, Mrs Ekdal.
How old is she now?

GINA. Hedvig is close on fourteen; her birthday is the
day after tomorrow.

GREGERS. She is pretty tall for her age then.

GINA. Yes, she's shot up wonderful this last year.

GREGERS. It makes one realize one's own age to see these
young people growing up. How long is it now since
you were married?

GINA. We've been married—let me see—just on fifteen
years.

GREGERS. Is it so long as that?

GINA [*becomes attentive, looks at him*]. Yes, it is indeed.

HIALMAR. Yes, so it is. Fifteen years, all but a few
months. [*Changing his tone.*] They must have been
long years for you up at the works, Gregers.

GREGERS. They seemed long while I was living them;
now they are over, I hardly know how the time has
gone.

[OLD EKDAL *comes from his room without his pipe but
with his old-fashioned uniform cap on his head; his
gait is somewhat unsteady.*]

EKDAL. Come now, Hialmar, let's sit down and have a
good talk about this—h'm—what was it again?

HIALMAR [*going toward him*]. Father, we have a visitor
here—Gregers Werle—I don't know if you remember
him.

EKDAL [*looking at* GREGERS, *who has risen*]. Werle? Is
that the son? What does he want with me?

HIALMAR. Nothing! It's me he has come to see.

EKDAL. Oh! Then there's nothing wrong?

HIALMAR. No, no, of course not.

EKDAL [*with a large gesture*]. Not that I'm afraid, you
know; but—

GREGERS [*goes over to him*]. I bring you a greeting from
your old hunting grounds, Lieutenant Ekdal.

EKDAL. Hunting grounds?

GREGERS. Yes, up in Höidal, about the works, you know.

EKDAL. Oh, up there. Yes, I knew all those places well
in the old days.

GREGERS. You were a great sportsman then.

EKDAL. So I was, I don't deny it. You're looking at my
uniform cap. I don't ask anybody's leave to wear it
in the house. So long as I don't go out in the streets
with it—

[HEDVIG *brings a plate of bread and butter which she
puts upon the table*.]

HIALMAR. Sit down, Father, and have a glass of beer.
Help yourself, Gregers.

[EKDAL *mutters and stumbles over to the sofa.* GREGERS
seats himself on the chair nearest to him, HIALMAR *on
the other side of* GREGERS. GINA *sits a little way from
the table, sewing;* HEDVIG *stands beside her father*.]

GREGERS. Can you remember, Lieutenant Ekdal, how
Hialmar and I used to come up and visit you in the
summer and at Christmas?

EKDAL. Did you? No, no, no; I don't remember it. But,
sure enough, I've been a tidy bit of sportsman in my
day. I've shot bears too. I've shot nine of 'em no less.

GREGERS [*looking sympathetically at him*]. And now you
never get any shooting?

EKDAL. Can't say that, sir. Get a shot now and then,
perhaps. Of course not in the old way. For the woods,
you see—the woods, the woods— [*Drinks.*] Are the
woods fine up there now?

GREGERS. Not so fine as in your time. They have been
thinned out a good deal.

EKDAL. Thinned? [*More softly and as if afraid.*] It's dan-

gerous work, that. Bad things come of it. The woods
revenge themselves.

HIALMAR [*filling up his glass*]. Come—a little more,
Father.

GREGERS. How can a man like you—such a man for the
open air—live in the midst of a stuffy town, boxed
within four walls?

EKDAL [*laughs quietly and glances at* HIALMAR]. Oh, it's
not so bad here. Not at all so bad.

GREGERS. But don't you miss all the things that used to
be a part of your very being—the cool sweeping
breezes, the free life in the woods and on the up-
lands, among beasts and birds?

EKDAL [*smiling*]. Hialmar, shall we let him see it?

HIALMAR [*hastily and a little embarrassed*]. Oh no, no,
Father; not this evening.

GREGERS. What does he want to show me?

HIALMAR. Oh, it's only something—you can see it another time.

GREGERS [*continues, to the old man*]. You see, I have
been thinking, Lieutenant Ekdal, that you should
come up with me to the works; I am sure to be going
back soon. No doubt you could get some copying
there too. And here you have nothing on earth to
interest you—nothing to liven you up.

EKDAL [*stares in astonishment at him*]. Have I nothing
on earth to—

GREGERS. Of course you have Hialmar, but then he has
his own family. And a man like you, who has always
had such a passion for what is free and wild—

EKDAL [*thumps the table*]. Hialmar, he shall see it!

HIALMAR. Oh, do you think it's worth while, Father?
It's all dark.

EKDAL. Nonsense; it's moonlight. [*Rises.*] He shall see
it, I tell you. Let me pass! Come on and help me,
Hialmar.

HEDVIG. Oh yes, do, Father!

HIALMAR [*rising*]. Very well then.

GREGERS [*to* GINA]. What is it?

GINA. Oh, nothing so wonderful after all.

[EKDAL *and* HIALMAR *have gone to the back wall and are each pushing back a side of the sliding door;* HEDVIG *helps the old man;* GREGERS *remains standing by the sofa;* GINA *sits still and sews. Through the open doorway a large, deep irregular garret is seen with odd nooks and corners, a couple of stovepipes running through it from rooms below. There are skylights through which clear moonbeams shine in on some parts of the great room; others lie in deep shadow.*]

EKDAL [*to* GREGERS]. You may come close up if you like.

GREGERS [*going over to them*]. Why, what is it?

EKDAL. Look for yourself, h'm.

HIALMAR [*somewhat embarrassed*]. This belongs to Father, you understand.

GREGERS [*at the door, looks into the garret*]. Why, you keep poultry, Lieutenant Ekdal.

EKDAL. Should think we did keep poultry. They've gone to roost now. But you should see our fowls by daylight, sir!

HEDVIG. And there's a—

EKDAL. Sh—sh! Don't say anything about it yet.

GREGERS. And you have pigeons too, I see.

EKDAL. Oh yes, haven't we just got pigeons! They have their nest boxes up there under the rooftree; for pigeons like to roost high, you see.

HIALMAR. They aren't all common pigeons.

EKDAL. Common! Should think not, indeed! We have tumblers and a pair of pouters too. But come here! Can you see that hutch down there by the wall?

GREGERS. Yes; what do you use it for?

EKDAL. That's where the rabbits sleep, sir.

GREGERS. Dear me, so you have rabbits too?

EKDAL. Yes, you may take my word for it, we have rabbits! He wants to know if we have rabbits, Hialmar!

H'm! But now comes the thing, let me tell you!
Here we have it! Move away, Hedvig. Stand here;
that's right—and now look down there. Don't you
see a basket with straw in it?

GREGERS. Yes. And I can see a fowl lying in the basket.

EKDAL. H'm—"a fowl"—

GREGERS. Isn't it a duck?

EKDAL [hurt]. Why, of course it's a duck.

HIALMAR. But what kind of a duck, do you think?

HEDVIG. It's not just a common duck.

EKDAL. Sh!

GREGERS. And it's not a Muscovy duck either.

EKDAL. No, Mr—Werle; it's not a Muscovy duck, for it's
a wild duck!

GREGERS. Is it really? A wild duck?

EKDAL. Yes, that's what it is. That "fowl"—as you call it
—is the wild duck. It's our wild duck, sir.

HEDVIG. My wild duck. It belongs to me.

GREGERS. And can it live up here in the garret? Does it
thrive?

EKDAL. Of course it has a trough of water to splash
about in, you know.

HIALMAR. Fresh water every other day.

GINA [turning toward HIALMAR]. But, my dear Ekdal,
it's getting icy cold here.

EKDAL. H'm, we had better shut up then. It's as well not
to disturb their night's rest too. Close up, Hedvig.

[HIALMAR and HEDVIG push the garret doors together.]

EKDAL. Another time you shall see her properly. [Seats
himself in the armchair by the stove.] Oh, they're
curious things, these wild ducks, I can tell you.

GREGERS. How did you manage to catch it, Lieutenant
Ekdal?

EKDAL. I didn't catch it. There's a certain man in this
town whom we have to thank for it.

GREGERS [starts slightly]. That man was not my father,
was he?

EKDAL. You've hit it. Your father and no one else. H'm.

HIALMAR. Strange that you should guess that, Gregers.

GREGERS. You were telling me that you owed so many things to my father, and so I thought perhaps—

GINA. But we didn't get the duck from Mr Werle himself.

EKDAL. It's Hakon Werle we have to thank for her, all the same, Gina. [*To* GREGERS.] He was shooting from a boat, you see, and he brought her down. But your father's sight is not very good now. H'm; she was only wounded.

GREGERS. Ah! She got a couple of slugs in her body, I suppose?

HIALMAR. Yes, two or three.

HEDVIG. She was hit under the wing so that she couldn't fly.

GREGERS. And I suppose she dived to the bottom, eh?

EKDAL [*sleepily, in a thick voice*]. Of course. Always do that, wild ducks do. They shoot to the bottom as deep as they can get, sir—and bite themselves fast in the tangle and seaweed—and all the devil's own mess that grows down there. And they never come up again.

GREGERS. But your wild duck came up again, Lieutenant Ekdal.

EKDAL. He had such an amazingly clever dog, your father had. And that dog—he dived in after the duck and fetched her up again.

GREGERS [*who has turned to* HIALMAR]. And then she was sent to you here?

HIALMAR. Not at once; at first your father took her home. But she wouldn't thrive there, so Pettersen was told to put an end to her.

EKDAL [*half asleep*]. H'm—yes—Pettersen—that ass—

HIALMAR [*speaking more softly*]. That was how we got her, you see; for Father knows Pettersen a little, and when he heard about the wild duck he got him to hand her over to us.

GREGERS. And now she thrives as well as possible in the garret there?

HIALMAR. Yes, wonderfully well. She has got fat. You see, she has lived in there so long now that she has forgotten her natural wild life, and it all depends on that.

GREGERS. You are right there, Hialmar. Be sure you never let her get a glimpse of the sky and the sea. But I mustn't stay any longer; I think your father is asleep.

HIALMAR. Oh, as for that—

GREGERS. But by the bye—you said you had a room to let—a spare room?

HIALMAR. Yes; what then? Do you know of anybody?

GREGERS. Can *I* have that room?

HIALMAR. You?

GINA. Oh no, Mr Werle, you—

GREGERS. May I have the room? If so, I'll take possession first thing tomorrow morning.

HIALMAR. Yes, with the greatest pleasure.

GINA. But, Mr Werle, I'm sure it's not at all the sort of room for you.

HIALMAR. Why, Gina! how can you say that?

GINA. Why, because the room's neither large enough nor light enough, and—

GREGERS. That really doesn't matter, Mrs Ekdal.

HIALMAR. I call it quite a nice room, and not at all badly furnished either.

GINA. But remember the pair of them underneath.

GREGERS. What pair?

GINA. Well, there's one as has been a tutor.

HIALMAR. That's Molvik—Mr Molvik, B.A.

GINA. And then there's a doctor by the name of Relling.

GREGERS. Relling? I know him a little; he practiced for a time up in Höidal.

GINA. They're a regular rackety pair, they are. As often as not they're out on the loose in the evenings, and then they come home at all hours, and they are not always just—

GREGERS. One soon gets used to that sort of thing. I daresay I shall be like the wild duck.

GINA. H'm; I think you ought to sleep upon it first, anyway.

GREGERS. You seem very unwilling to have me in the house, Mrs Ekdal.

GINA. Oh no! What makes you think that?

HIALMAR. Well, you really behave strangely about it, Gina. [*To* GREGERS.] Then I suppose you intend to remain in town for the present?

GREGERS [*putting on his overcoat*]. Yes, now I intend to remain here.

HIALMAR. And yet not at your father's? What do you propose to do then?

GREGERS. Ah, if I only knew that, Hialmar, I shouldn't be so badly off! But when one has the misfortune to be called Gregers!—"Gregers"—and then "Werle" after it; did you ever hear of anything so hideous?

HIALMAR. Oh, I don't think so at all.

GREGERS. Ugh! Bah! I feel I should like to spit on the fellow that answers to such a name. But when a man is once for all doomed to be Gregers Werle—in this world—as I am—

HIALMAR [*laughs*]. Ha, ha! If you weren't Gregers Werle, what would you like to be?

GREGERS. If I should choose, I should like best to be a clever dog.

GINA. A dog!

HEDVIG [*involuntarily*]. Oh no!

GREGERS. Yes, an amazingly clever dog; one that goes to the bottom after wild ducks when they dive and bite themselves fast in tangle and seaweed down among the ooze.

HIALMAR. Upon my word now, Gregers—I don't in the least know what you are driving at.

GREGERS. Oh well, you might not be much the wiser if

you did. It's understood, then, that I move in early
tomorrow morning. [*To* GINA.] I won't give you any
trouble; I do everything for myself. [*To* HIALMAR.]
We will talk about the rest tomorrow. Good night,
Mrs Ekdal. [*Nods to* HEDVIG.] Good night.

GINA. Good night, Mr Werle.

HEDVIG. Good night.

HIALMAR [*who has lighted a candle*]. Wait a moment;
I must show you a light; the stairs are sure to be
dark.

[GREGERS *and* HIALMAR *go out by the passage door*.]

GINA [*looking straight before her with her sewing in
her lap*]. Wasn't that queer-like talk about wanting
to be a dog?

HEDVIG. Do you know, Mother—I believe he meant
something quite different by that.

GINA. Why, what should he mean?

HEDVIG. Oh, I don't know, but it seemed to me he
meant something different from what he said—all
the time.

GINA. Do you think so? Yes, it was sort of queer.

HIALMAR [*comes back*]. The lamp was still burning.
[*Puts out the candle and sets it down.*] Ah, now one
can get a mouthful of food at last. [*Begins to eat the
bread and butter.*] Well, you see, Gina—if only you
keep your eyes open—

GINA. How keep your eyes open?

HIALMAR. Why, haven't we at last had the luck to get
the room let? And just think—to a person like Gregers—a good old friend.

GINA. Well, I don't know what to say about it.

HEDVIG. Oh, Mother, you'll see; it'll be such fun!

HIALMAR. You're very strange. You were so bent upon
getting the room let before, and now you don't like
it.

GINA. Yes, I do, Ekdal; if it had only been to someone
else. But what do you suppose Mr Werle will say?

HIALMAR. Old Werle? It doesn't concern him.

GINA. But surely you can see that there's something
amiss between them again, or the young man
wouldn't be leaving home. You know very well those
two can't get on with each other.

HIALMAR. Very likely not, but—

GINA. And now Mr Werle may fancy it's you that has
edged him on—

HIALMAR. Let him fancy so, then! Mr Werle has done
a great deal for me; far be it from me to deny it.
But that doesn't make me everlastingly dependent
upon him.

GINA. But, my dear Ekdal, maybe Grandfather'll suffer
for it. He may lose the little bit of work he gets from
Graberg.

HIALMAR. I could almost say: so much the better! Is it
not humiliating for a man like me to see his gray-
haired father treated as a pariah? But now I believe
the fullness of time is at hand. [*Takes a fresh piece
of bread and butter.*] As sure as I have a mission in
life, I mean to fulfill it now!

HEDVIG. Oh yes, Father, do!

GINA. Hush! Don't wake him!

HIALMAR [*more softly*]. I will fulfill it, I say. The day
shall come when— And that is why I say it's a good
thing we have let the room, for that makes me more
independent. The man who has a mission in life
must be independent. [*By the armchair, with emotion.*] Poor old white-haired Father! Rely on your
Hialmar. He has broad shoulders—strong shoulders,
at any rate. You shall yet wake up some fine day
and— [*To* GINA.] Do you not believe it?

GINA [*rising*]. Yes, of course I do, but in the meantime
suppose we see about getting him to bed.

HIALMAR. Yes, come.

[*They take hold of the old man carefully.*]

ACT THREE

SCENE—HIALMAR EKDAL'S *studio. It is morning; the daylight shines through the large window in the slanting roof; the curtain is drawn back.*

HIALMAR is sitting at the table, busy retouching a photograph; several others lie before him. Presently GINA, wearing her hat and cloak, enters by the passage door; she has a covered basket on her arm.

HIALMAR. Back already, Gina?

GINA. Oh yes, one can't let the grass grow under one's feet. [*Sets her basket on a chair and takes off her things.*]

HIALMAR. Did you look in at Gregers' room?

GINA. Yes, that I did. It's a rare sight, I can tell you; he's made a pretty mess to start off with.

HIALMAR. How so?

GINA. He was determined to do everything for himself, he said; so he sets to work to light the stove, and what must he do but screw down the damper till the whole room is full of smoke. Ugh! There was a smell fit to—

HIALMAR. Well, really!

GINA. But that's not the worst of it; for then he thinks he'll put out the fire and goes and empties his water jug into the stove and so makes the whole floor one filthy puddle.

HIALMAR. How annoying!

GINA. I've got the porter's wife to clear up after him, pig that he is! But the room won't be fit to live in till the afternoon.

HIALMAR. What's he doing with himself in the meantime?

GINA. He said he was going out for a little while.

HIALMAR. I looked in upon him too, for a moment—after you had gone.

GINA. So I heard. You've asked him to lunch.

HIALMAR. Just to a little bit of early lunch, you know. It's his first day—we can hardly do less. You've got something in the house, I suppose?

GINA. I shall have to find something or other.

HIALMAR. And don't cut it too fine, for I fancy Relling and Molvik are coming up too. I just happened to meet Relling on the stairs, you see; so I had to—

GINA. Oh, are we to have those two as well?

HIALMAR. Good lord—a couple more or less can't make any difference.

OLD EKDAL [*opens his door and looks in*]. I say, Hialmar— [*Sees* GINA.] Oh!

GINA. Do you want anything, Grandfather?

EKDAL. Oh no, it doesn't matter. H'm! [*Retires again.*]

GINA [*takes up the basket*]. Be sure you see that he doesn't go out.

HIALMAR. All right, all right. And, Gina, a little herring salad wouldn't be a bad idea. Relling and Molvik were out on the loose again last night.

GINA. If only they don't come before I'm ready for them—

HIALMAR. No, of course they won't; take your own time.

GINA. Very well, and meanwhile you can be working a bit.

HIALMAR. Well, I am working! I am working as hard as I can!

GINA. Then you'll have that job off your hands, you see. [*She goes out to the kitchen with her basket.*

HIALMAR *sits for a time penciling away at the photo-graph in an indolent and listless manner.*]

EKDAL [*peeps in, looks round the studio and says softly*]: Are you busy?

HIALMAR. Yes, I'm toiling at these wretched pictures.

EKDAL. Well, well, never mind—since you're so busy—h'm! [*He goes out again; the door stands open.*]

HIALMAR [*continues for some time in silence, then he lays down his brush and goes over to the door*]. Are you busy, Father?

EKDAL [*in a grumbling tone within*]. If you're busy, I'm busy too. H'm!

HIALMAR. Oh, very well then. [*Goes to his work again.*]

EKDAL [*presently coming to the door again*]. H'm; I say Hialmar, I'm not so very busy, you know.

HIALMAR. I thought you were writing.

EKDAL. Oh, devil take it! Can't Graberg wait a day or two? After all, it's not a matter of life and death.

HIALMAR. No, and you're not his slave either.

EKDAL. And about that other business in there—

HIALMAR. Just what I was thinking of. Do you want to go in? Shall I open the door for you?

EKDAL. Well, it wouldn't be a bad notion.

HIALMAR [*rises*]. Then we'd have that off our hands.

EKDAL. Yes, exactly. It's got to be ready first thing to-morrow. It is tomorrow, isn't it? H'm?

HIALMAR. Yes, of course it's tomorrow.

[HIALMAR *and* EKDAL *push aside each his half of the sliding door. The morning sun is shining in through the skylights; some doves are flying about; others sit cooing upon the perches; the hens are heard clucking now and then further back in the garret.*]

HIALMAR. There; now you can get to work, Father.

EKDAL [*goes in*]. Aren't you coming too?

HIALMAR. Well, really, do you know—I almost think—
[*Sees* GINA *at the kitchen door.*] I? No; I haven't time; I must work— But now for our new contriv-

ance— [*He pulls a cord; a curtain slips down inside, the lower part consisting of a piece of old sailcloth, the upper part of a stretched fishing net. The floor of the garret is thus no longer visible.*]

HIALMAR [*goes to the table*]. So! Now perhaps I can sit in peace for a little while.

GINA. Is he rampaging in there again?

HIALMAR. Would you rather have him slip down to Madam Eriksen's? [*Seats himself.*] Do you want anything? You know you said—

GINA. I only wanted to ask if you think we can lay the table for lunch here?

HIALMAR. Yes; we have no early appointment, I suppose?

GINA. No, I expect no one today except those two sweethearts that are to be taken together.

HIALMAR. Why the deuce couldn't they be taken together another day?

GINA. Don't you know, I told them to come in the afternoon, when you are having your nap.

HIALMAR. Oh, that's capital. Very well, let us have lunch here then.

GINA. All right, but there's no hurry about laying the cloth; you can have the table for a good while yet.

HIALMAR. Do you think I am not sticking at my work? I'm at it as hard as I can!

GINA. Then you'll be free later on, you know. [*Goes out into the kitchen again. Short pause.*]

EKDAL [*in the garret doorway, behind the net*]. Hialmar!

HIALMAR. Well?

EKDAL. Afraid we shall have to move the water trough after all.

HIALMAR. What else have I been saying all along?

EKDAL. H'm—h'm—h'm. [*Goes away from the door again.* HIALMAR *goes on working a little, glances toward the garret and half rises.* HEDVIG *comes in from the kitchen.*]

HIALMAR [*sits down again hurriedly*]. What do you want?

HEDVIG. I only wanted to come in beside you, Father.

HIALMAR [*after a pause*]. What makes you go prying around like that? Perhaps you are told off to watch me?

HEDVIG. No, no.

HIALMAR. What is your mother doing out there?

HEDVIG. Oh, Mother's in the middle of making the herring salad. [*Goes to the table.*] Isn't there any little thing I could help you with, Father?

HIALMAR. Oh no. It is right that I should bear the whole burden—so long as my strength holds out. Set your mind at rest, Hedvig; if only your father keeps his health—

HEDVIG. Oh no, Father! You mustn't talk in that horrid way. [*She wanders about a little, stops by the doorway and looks into the garret.*]

HIALMAR. Tell me, what is he doing?

HEDVIG. I think he's making a new path to the water trough.

HIALMAR. He can never manage that by himself! And here am I doomed to sit!

HEDVIG [*goes to him*]. Let me take the brush, Father; I can do it quite well.

HIALMAR. Oh, nonsense; you will only hurt your eyes.

HEDVIG. Not a bit. Give me the brush.

HIALMAR [*rising*]. Well, it won't take more than a minute or two.

HEDVIG. Pooh, what harm can it do then? [*Takes the brush.*] There! [*Seats herself.*] I can begin upon this one.

HIALMAR. But mind you don't hurt your eyes! Do you hear? *I* won't be answerable; you do it on your own responsibility—understand that.

HEDVIG [*retouching*]. Yes, yes, I understand.

HIALMAR. You are quite clever at it, Hedvig. Only a minute or two, you know. [*He slips through by the edge of the curtain into the garret.* HEDVIG *sits at her work.* HIALMAR *and* EKDAL *are heard disputing inside.*]

HIALMAR [*appears behind the net*]. I say, Hedvig—give me those pincers that are lying on the shelf. And the chisel. [*Turns away inside.*] Now you shall see, Father. Just let me show you first what I mean!

[HEDVIG *has fetched the required tools from the shelf and hands them to him through the net.*]

HIALMAR. Ah, thanks. I didn't come a moment too soon.

[*Goes back from the curtain again; they are heard carpentering and talking inside.* HEDVIG *stands looking in at them. A moment later there is a knock at the passage door; she does not notice it.*]

GREGERS WERLE [*bareheaded, in indoor dress, enters and stops near the door*]. H'm!

HEDVIG [*turns and goes toward him*]. Good morning. Please come in.

GREGERS. Thank you. [*Looking toward the garret.*] You seem to have work-people in the house.

HEDVIG. No, it's only Father and Grandfather. I'll tell them you are here.

GREGERS. No, no, don't do that; I would rather wait a little. [*Seats himself on the sofa.*]

HEDVIG. It looks so untidy here— [*Begins to clear away the photographs.*]

GREGERS. Oh, don't take them away. Are those prints that have to be finished off?

HEDVIG. Yes, they are a few I was helping Father with.

GREGERS. Please don't let me disturb you.

HEDVIG. Oh no. [*She gathers the things to her and sits down to work;* GREGERS *looks at her meanwhile in silence.*]

GREGERS. Did the wild duck sleep well last night?

HEDVIG. Yes, I think so, thanks.

GREGERS [*turning toward the garret*]. It looks quite different by day from what it did last night in the moonlight.

HEDVIG. Yes, it changes ever so much. It looks different in the morning and in the afternoon, and it's different on rainy days from what it is in fine weather.

GREGERS. Have you noticed it?

HEDVIG. Yes, how could I help it?

GREGERS. Are you too fond of being in there with the wild duck?

HEDVIG. Yes, when I can manage it.

GREGERS. But I suppose you haven't much spare time; you go to school, no doubt.

HEDVIG. No, not now; Father is afraid of my hurting my eyes.

GREGERS. Oh, then he reads with you himself?

HEDVIG. Father has promised to read with me, but he has never had time yet.

GREGERS. Then is there nobody else to give you a little help?

HEDVIG. Yes, there is Mr Molvik, but he is not always exactly—quite—

GREGERS. Sober?

HEDVIG. Yes, I suppose that's it!

GREGERS. Why, then, you must have any amount of time on your hands. And in there I suppose it is a sort of world by itself?

HEDVIG. Oh yes, quite. And there are such lots of wonderful things.

GREGERS. Indeed?

HEDVIG. Yes, there are big cupboards full of books, and a great many of the books have pictures in them.

GREGERS. Aha!

HEDVIG. And there's an old bureau with drawers and flaps and a big clock with figures that go out and in. But the clock isn't going now.

GREGERS. So time has come to a standstill in there—in the wild duck's domain?

HEDVIG. Yes. And then there's an old paintbox and things of that sort, and all the books.

GREGERS. And you read the books, I suppose.

HEDVIG. Oh yes, when I get the chance. Most of them are English, though, and I don't understand English. But then I look at the pictures. There is one great book called *Harrison's History of London*. It must be a hundred years old, and there are such heaps of pictures in it. At the beginning there is Death with an hourglass and a woman. I think that is horrid. But then there are all the other pictures of churches and castles and streets and great ships sailing on the sea.

GREGERS. But tell me, where did all those wonderful things come from?

HEDVIG. Oh, an old sea captain once lived here, and he brought them home with him. They used to call him "The Flying Dutchman." That was curious, because he wasn't a Dutchman at all.

GREGERS. Was he not?

HEDVIG. No. But at last he was drowned at sea, and so he left all those things behind him.

GREGERS. Tell me now—when you are sitting in there looking at the pictures don't you wish you could travel and see the real world for yourself?

HEDVIG. Oh no! I mean always to stay at home and help Father and Mother.

GREGERS. To retouch photographs?

HEDVIG. No, not only that. I should love above everything to learn to engrave pictures like those in the English books.

GREGERS. H'm. What does your father say to that?

HEDVIG. I don't think Father likes it; Father is strange about such things. Only think, he talks of my learning basketmaking and straw plaiting! But I don't think that would be much good.

GREGERS. Oh no, I don't think so either.

HEDVIG. But Father was right in saying that if I had learned basketmaking I could have made the new basket for the wild duck.

GREGERS. So you could; and it was you that ought to have done it, wasn't it?

HEDVIG. Yes, for it's my wild duck.

GREGERS. Of course it is.

HEDVIG. Yes, it belongs to me. But I lend it to Father and Grandfather as often as they please.

GREGERS. Indeed? What do they do with it?

HEDVIG. Oh, they look after it and build places for it and so on.

GREGERS. I see; for no doubt the wild duck is by far the most distinguished inhabitant of the garret?

HEDVIG. Yes, indeed she is; for she is a real wild fowl, you know. And then she is so much to be pitied; she has no one to care for, poor thing.

GREGERS. She has no family, as the rabbits have.

HEDVIG. No. The hens too, many of them, were chickens together; but she has been taken right away from all her friends. And then there is so much that is strange about the wild duck. Nobody knows her, and nobody knows where she came from either.

GREGERS. And she has been down in the depths of the sea.

HEDVIG [*with a quick glance at him, represses a smile and asks*]: Why do you say "depths of the sea"?

GREGERS. What else should I say?

HEDVIG. You could say "the bottom of the sea."

GREGERS. Oh, mayn't I just as well say the depths of the sea?

HEDVIG. Yes, but it sounds so strange to me when other people speak of the depths of the sea.

GREGERS. Why so? Tell me why?

HEDVIG. No, I won't; it's so stupid.

GREGERS. Oh no, I am sure it's not. Do tell me why you smiled.

HEDVIG. Well, this is the reason: whenever I come to realize suddenly—in a flash—what is in there, it always seems to me that the whole room and everything in it should be called "the depths of the sea." But that is so stupid.

GREGERS. You mustn't say that.

HEDVIG. Oh yes, for you know it is only a garret.

GREGERS [*looks fixedly at her*]. Are you so sure of that?

HEDVIG [*astonished*]. That it's a garret?

GREGERS. Are you quite certain of it?

[HEDVIG *is silent and looks at him open-mouthed.* GINA *comes in from the kitchen with the table things.*]

GREGERS [*rising*]. I have come in upon you too early.

GINA. Oh, you must be somewhere, and we're nearly ready now anyway. Clear the table, Hedvig.

[HEDVIG *clears away her things; she and* GINA *lay the cloth during what follows.* GREGERS *seats himself in the armchair and turns over an album.*]

GREGERS. I hear you can retouch, Mrs Ekdal.

GINA [*with a side glance*]. Yes, I can.

GREGERS. That was exceedingly lucky.

GINA. How—lucky?

GREGERS. Since Ekdal took to photography, I mean.

HEDVIG. Mother can take photographs too.

GINA. Oh yes, I was bound to learn that.

GREGERS. So it is really you that carry on the business, I suppose?

GINA. Yes, when Ekdal hasn't time himself—

GREGERS. He is a great deal taken up with his old father, I daresay.

GINA. Yes; and then you can't expect a man like Ekdal to do nothing but take car-de-visits of Dick, Tom and Harry.

GREGERS. I quite agree with you, but having once gone in for the thing—

GINA. You can surely understand, Mr Werle, that Ekdal's not like one of your common photographers.

GREGERS. Of course not, but still—

[*A shot is fired within the garret.*]

GREGERS [*starting up*]. What's that?

GINA. Ugh! Now they're firing again!

GREGERS. Have they firearms in there?

HEDVIG. They are out shooting.

GREGERS. What! [*At the door of the garret.*] Are you shooting, Hialmar?

HIALMAR [*inside the net*]. Are you there? I didn't know; I was so taken up— [*To* HEDVIG.] Why did you not let us know? [*Comes into the studio.*]

GREGERS. Do you go shooting in the garret?

HIALMAR [*showing a double-barreled pistol*]. Oh, only with this thing.

GINA. Yes, you and Grandfather will do yourselves a mischief someday with that there pigstol.

HIALMAR [*with irritation*]. I believe I have told you that this kind of firearm is called a pistol.

GINA. Oh, that doesn't make it much better that I can see.

GREGERS. So you have become a sportsman too, Hialmar?

HIALMAR. Only a little rabbit shooting now and then. Mostly to please Father, you understand.

GINA. Men are strange beings; they must always have something to pervert theirselves with.

HIALMAR [*snappishly*]. Just so; we must always have something to divert ourselves with.

GINA. Yes, that's just what I say.

HIALMAR. H'm. [*To* GREGERS.] You see, the garret is fortunately so situated that no one can hear us shooting. [*Lays the pistol on the top shelf of the bookcase.*] Don't touch the pistol, Hedvig! One of the barrels is loaded; remember that.

GREGERS [*looking through the net*]. You have a fowling piece too, I see.

HIALMAR. That is Father's old gun. It's of no use now. Something has gone wrong with the lock. But it's fun to have it all the same, for we can take it to pieces now and then and clean and grease it and screw it together again. Of course it's mostly Father that fiddle-faddles with all that sort of thing.

HEDVIG [*beside* GREGERS]. Now you can see the wild duck properly.

GREGERS. I was just looking at her. One of her wings seems to me to droop a bit.

HEDVIG. Well, no wonder; her wing was broken, you know.

GREGERS. And she trails one foot a little. Isn't that so?

HIALMAR. Perhaps a very little bit.

HEDVIG. Yes, it was by that foot the dog took hold of her.

HIALMAR. But otherwise she hasn't the least thing the matter with her, and that is simply marvelous for a creature that has a charge of shot in her body and has been between a dog's teeth—

GREGERS [*with a glance at* HEDVIG]. —and that has lain in the depths of the sea—so long.

HEDVIG [*smiling*]. Yes.

GINA [*laying the table*]. That blessed wild duck! What a lot of fuss you do make over her.

HIALMAR. H'm—will lunch soon be ready?

GINA. Yes, directly. Hedvig, you must come and help me now.

[GINA *and* HEDVIG *go out into the kitchen.*]

HIALMAR [*in a low voice*]. I think you had better not stand there looking in at Father; he doesn't like it. [GREGERS *moves away from the garret door.*] Besides, I may as well shut up before the others come. [*Claps his hands to drive the fowls back.*] Shh—shh, in with you! [*Draws up the curtain and pulls the doors together.*] All the contrivances are my own invention. It's really quite amusing to have things of this sort to potter with and to put to rights when they get out of order. And its absolutely necessary too, for Gina objects to having rabbits and fowls in the studio.

GREGERS. To be sure, and I suppose the studio is your wife's special department?

HIALMAR. As a rule I leave the everyday details of busi-

ness to her, for then I can take refuge in the parlor
and give my mind to more important things.

GREGERS. What things may they be, Hialmar?

HIALMAR. I wonder you have not asked that question
sooner. But perhaps you haven't heard of the invention?

GREGERS. The invention? No.

HIALMAR. Really? Have you not? Oh no, out there in
the wilds—

GREGERS. So you have invented something, have you?

HIALMAR. It is not quite completed yet, but I am working at it. You can easily imagine that when I resolved
to devote myself to photography it wasn't simply
with the idea of taking likenesses of all sorts of com-
monplace people.

GREGERS. No; your wife was saying the same thing just
now.

HIALMAR. I swore that if I concentrated my powers to
this handicraft I would so exalt it that it should become both an art and a science. And to that end I
determined to make this great invention.

GREGERS. And what is the nature of the invention?
What purpose does it serve?

HIALMAR. Oh, my dear fellow, you mustn't ask for details yet. It takes time, you see. And you must not
think that my motive is vanity. It is not for my own
sake that I am working. Oh no; it is my life's mission that stands before me night and day.

GREGERS. What is you life's mission?

HIALMAR. Do you forget the old man with the silver
hair?

GREGERS. Your poor father? Well, but what can you do
for him?

HIALMAR. I can raise up his self-respect from the dead
by restoring the name of Ekdal to honor and dignity.

GREGERS. Then that is your life's mission?

HIALMAR. Yes. I will rescue the shipwrecked man. For shipwrecked he was, by the very first blast of the storm. Even while those terrible investigations were going on he was no longer himself. That pistol there —the one we used to shoot rabbits with—has played its part in the tragedy of the house of Ekdal.

GREGERS. The pistol? Indeed?

HIALMAR. When the sentence of imprisonment was passed—he had the pistol in his hand.

GREGERS. Had he?

HIALMAR. Yes, but he dared not use it. His courage failed him. So broken, so demoralized was he even then! Oh, can you understand it? He, a soldier; he, who had shot nine bears and who was descended from two lieutenant colonels—one after the other, of course. Can you understand it, Gregers?

GREGERS. Yes, I understand it well enough.

HIALMAR. I cannot. And once more the pistol played a part in the history of our house. When he had put on the gray clothes and was under lock and key—oh, that was a terrible time for me, I can tell you. I kept the blinds drawn down over both my windows. When I peeped out I saw the sun shining as if nothing had happened. I could not understand it. I saw people going along the street, laughing and talking about indifferent things. I could not understand it. It seemed to me that the whole of existence must be at a standstill—as if under an eclipse.

GREGERS. I felt that too, when my mother died.

HIALMAR. It was in such an hour that Hialmar Ekdal pointed the pistol at his own breast.

GREGERS. You, too, thought of—

HIALMAR. Yes.

GREGERS. But you did not fire?

HIALMAR. No. At the decisive moment I won the victory over myself. I remained in life. But I can assure you it takes some courage to choose life under circumstances like those.

GREGERS. Well, that depends on how you look at it.

HIALMAR. Yes indeed, it takes courage. But I am glad I was firm, for now I shall soon perfect my invention; and Doctor Relling thinks, as I do myself, that Father may be allowed to wear his uniform again. I will demand that as my sole reward.

GREGERS. So that is what he meant about his uniform?

HIALMAR. Yes, that is what he most yearns for. You can't think how my heart bleeds for him. Every time we celebrate any little family festival—Gina's and my wedding day or whatever it may be—in comes the old man in the lieutenant's uniform of happier days. But if he only hears a knock at the door—for he daren't show himself to strangers, you know—he hurries back to his room again as fast as his old legs can carry him. Oh, it's heart-rending for a son to see such things!

GREGERS. How long do you think it will take you to finish your invention?

HIALMAR. Come now, you mustn't expect me to enter into particulars like that. An invention is not a thing completely under one's own control. It depends largely on inspiration—on intuition—and it is almost impossible to predict when the inspiration may come.

GREGERS. But it's advancing?

HIALMAR. Yes, certainly it is advancing. I turn it over in my mind every day; I am full of it. Every afternoon, when I have had my dinner, I shut myself up in the parlor where I can ponder undisturbed. But I can't be goaded to it; it's not a bit of good. Relling says so too.

GREGERS. And you don't think that all that business in the garret draws you off and distracts you too much?

HIALMAR. No, no, no; quite the contrary. You mustn't say that. I cannot be everlastingly absorbed in the same laborious train of thought. I must have something alongside of it to fill up the time of waiting.

The inspiration, the intuition, you see—when it comes it comes, and there's an end of it.

GREGERS. My dear Hialmar, I almost think you have something of the wild duck in you.

HIALMAR. Something of the wild duck? How do you mean?

GREGERS. You have dived down and bitten yourself fast in the undergrowth.

HIALMAR. Are you alluding to the well-nigh fatal shot that has broken my father's wing—and mine too?

GREGERS. Not exactly to that. I don't say that your wing has been broken, but you have strayed into a poisonous marsh, Hialmar; an insidious disease has taken hold of you, and you have sunk down to die in the dark.

HIALMAR. I? To die in the dark? Look here, Gregers, you must really leave off talking such nonsense.

GREGERS. Don't be afraid; I shall find a way to help you up again. I, too, have a mission in life now; I found it yesterday.

HIALMAR. That's all very well, but you will please leave me out of it. I can assure you that—apart from my very natural melancholy, of course—I am as contented as anyone can wish to be.

GREGERS. Your contentment is an effect of the marsh poison.

HIALMAR. Now, my dear Gregers, pray do not go on about disease and poison; I am not used to that sort of talk. In my house nobody ever speaks to me about unpleasant things.

GREGERS. Ah, that I can easily believe.

HIALMAR. It's not good for me, you see. And there are no marsh poisons here, as you express it. The poor photographer's roof is lowly, I know—and my circumstances are narrow. But I am an inventor, and I am the breadwinner of a family. That exalts me above my mean surroundings. Ah, here comes lunch!

[GINA *and* HEDVIG *bring bottles of ale, a decanter of*

brandy, glasses, etc. At the same time RELLING *and*
MOLVIK *enter from the passage; they are both with-*
out hat or overcoat. MOLVIK *is dressed in black.*]

GINA [*placing the things upon the table*]. Ah, you two
have come in the nick of time.

RELLING. Molvik got it into his head that he could
smell herring salad, and then there was no holding
him. Good morning again, Ekdal.

HIALMAR. Gregers, let me introduce you to Mr Molvik
—Doctor— Oh, you know Relling, don't you?

GREGERS. Yes, slightly.

RELLING. Oh, Mr Werle junior! Yes, we two have had
one or two little skirmishes up at the Höidal works.
You've just moved in?

GREGERS. I moved in this morning.

RELLING. Molvik and I live right under you, so you
haven't far to go for the doctor and the clergyman
if you should need anything in that line.

GREGERS. Thanks; it's not quite unlikely, for yesterday
we were thirteen at table.

HIALMAR. Oh, come now, don't let us get upon unpleasant subjects again!

RELLING. You may make your mind easy, Ekdal; I'll
be hanged if the finger of fate points to you.

HIALMAR. I should hope not, for the sake of my family.
But let us sit down now and eat and drink and be
merry.

GREGERS. Shall we not wait for your father?

HIALMAR. No, his lunch will be taken in to him later.
Come along!

[*The men seat themselves at table and eat and drink.*
GINA *and* HEDVIG *go in and out and wait upon them.*]

RELLING. Molvik was frightfully screwed yesterday, Mrs
Ekdal.

GINA. Really? Yesterday again?

RELLING. Didn't you hear him when I brought him
home last night?

GINA. No, I can't say I did.

RELLING. That was a good thing, for Molvik was disgusting last night.

GINA. Is that true, Molvik?

MOLVIK. Let us draw a veil over last night's proceedings. That sort of thing is totally foreign to my better self.

RELLING [*to* GREGERS]. It comes over him like a sort of possession, and then I have to go out on the loose with him. Mr Molvik is demonic, you see.

GREGERS. Demonic?

RELLING. Molvik is demonic, yes.

GREGERS. H'm.

RELLING. And demonic natures are not made to walk straight through the world; they must meander a little now and then. Well, so you still stick up there at those horrible grimy works?

GREGERS. I have stuck there until now.

RELLING. And did you ever manage to collect that claim you went about presenting?

GREGERS. Claim? [*Understands him.*] Ah, I see.

HIALMAR. Have you been presenting claims, Gregers?

GREGERS. Oh, nonsense.

RELLING. Faith, but he has, though! He went round to all the cotters' cabins presenting something he called "the claim of the ideal."

GREGERS. I was young then.

RELLING. You're right; you were very young. And as for the claim of the ideal—you never got it honored while *I* was up there.

GREGERS. Nor since either.

RELLING. Ah, then you've learned to knock a little discount off, I expect.

GREGERS. Never, when I have a true man to deal with.

HIALMAR. No, I should think not, indeed. A little butter, Gina.

RELLING. And a slice of bacon for Molvik.

MOLVIK. Ugh! not bacon!

[*A knock at the garret door.*]

HIALMAR. Open the door, Hedvig; Father wants to come out.

[HEDVIG *goes over and opens the door a little way;* EK-DAL *enters with a fresh rabbitskin; she closes the door after him.*]

EKDAL. Good morning, gentlemen! Good sport today. Shot a big one.

HIALMAR. And you've gone and skinned it without waiting for me!

EKDAL. Salted it too. It's good tender meat, is rabbit; it's sweet; it tastes like sugar. Good appetite to you, gentlemen! [*Goes into his room.*]

MOLVIK [*rising*]. Excuse me—I can't—I must get downstairs immediately—

RELLING. Drink some soda water, man!

MOLVIK [*hurrying away*]. Ugh—ugh. [*Goes out by the passage door.*]

RELLING [*to* HIALMAR]. Let us drain a glass to the old hunter.

HIALMAR [*clinks glasses with him*]. To the undaunted sportsman who has looked death in the face!

RELLING. To the gray-haired— [*Drinks.*] By the bye, is his hair gray or white?

HIALMAR. Something between the two, I fancy; for that matter, he has very few hairs left of any color.

RELLING. Well, well, one can get through the world with a wig. After all, you are a happy man, Ekdal; you have your noble mission to labor for—

HIALMAR. And I do labor, I can tell you.

RELLING. And then you have your excellent wife, shuffling quietly in and out in her felt slippers, with that seesaw walk of hers, and making everything cosy and comfortable about you.

HIALMAR. Yes, Gina [*nods to her*]—you were a good helpmate on the path of life.

GINA. Oh, don't sit there cricketizing me.

RELLING. And your Hedvig too, Ekdal!

HIALMAR [*affected*]. The child, yes! The child before

everything! Hedvig, come here to me. [*Strokes her hair.*] What day is it tomorrow, eh?

HEDVIG [*shaking him*]. Oh no, you're not to say anything, Father.

HIALMAR. It cuts me to the heart when I think what a poor affair it will be; only a little festivity in the garret.

HEDVIG. Oh, but that's just what I like!

RELLING. Just you wait till the wonderful invention sees the light, Hedvig!

HIALMAR. Yes indeed—then you shall see! Hedvig, I have resolved to make your future secure. You shall live in comfort all your days. I will demand something or other—on your behalf. That shall be the poor inventor's sole reward.

HEDVIG [*whispering, with her arms round his neck*]. Oh, you dear, kind father!

RELLING [*to* GREGERS]. Come now, don't you find it pleasant, for once in a way, to sit at a well-spread table in a happy family circle?

HIALMAR. Ah yes, I really prize these social hours.

GREGERS. For my part, I don't thrive in marsh vapors.

RELLING. Marsh vapors?

HIALMAR. Oh, don't begin with that stuff again!

GINA. Goodness knows there's no vapors in this house, Mr Werle; I give the place a good airing every blessed day.

GREGERS [*leaves the table*]. No airing you can give will drive out the taint I mean.

HIALMAR. Taint!

GINA. Yes, what do you say to that, Ekdal!

RELLING. Excuse me—may it not be you yourself that have brought the taint from those mines up there?

GREGERS. It is like you to call what I bring into this house a taint.

RELLING [*goes up to him*]. Look here, Mr Werle junior: I have a strong suspicion that you are still carrying about that "claim of the ideal" large as life in your coattail pocket.

GREGERS. I carry it in my breast.

RELLING. Well, wherever you carry it, I advise you not to come dunning us with it here as long as *I* am on the premises.

GREGERS. And if I do so nonetheless?

RELLING. Then you'll go headforemost down the stairs; now I've warned you.

HIALMAR [*rising*]. Oh, but, Relling—

GREGERS. Yes, you may turn me out.

GINA [*interposing between them*]. We can't have that, Relling. But I must say, Mr Werle, it ill becomes you to talk about vapors and taints after all the mess you made with your stove.

[*A knock at the passage door.*]

HEDVIG. Mother, there's somebody knocking.

HIALMAR. There now, we're going to have a whole lot of people!

GINA. I'll go. [*Goes over and opens the door, starts and draws back.*] Oh—oh dear!

[WERLE, *in a fur coat, advances one step into the room.*]

WERLE. Excuse me, but I think my son is staying here.

GINA [*with a gulp*]. Yes.

HIALMAR [*approaching him*]. Won't you do us the honor to—

WERLE. Thank you, I merely wish to speak to my son.

GREGERS. What is it? Here I am.

WERLE. I want a few words with you in your room.

GREGERS. In my room? Very well. [*About to go.*]

GINA. No, no, your room's not in a fit state.

WERLE. Well, then, out in the passage here; I want to have a few words with you alone.

HIALMAR. You can have them here, sir. Come into the parlor, Relling.

[HIALMAR *and* RELLING *go off to the right;* GINA *takes* HEDVIG *with her into the kitchen.*]

GREGERS [*after a short pause*]. Well, now we are alone.

WERLE. From something you let fall last evening, and from your coming to lodge with the Ekdals, I can't help inferring that you intend to make yourself unpleasant to me in one way or another.

GREGERS. I intend to open Hialmar Ekdal's eyes. He shall see his position as it really is—that is all.

WERLE. Is that the mission in life you spoke of yesterday?

GREGERS. Yes. You have left me no other.

WERLE. Is it I, then, that have crippled your mind, Gregers?

GREGERS. You have crippled my whole life. I am not thinking of all that about Mother—but it's thanks to you that I am continually haunted and harassed by a guilty conscience.

WERLE. Indeed! It is your conscience that troubles you, is it?

GREGERS. I ought to have taken a stand against you when the trap was set for Lieutenant Ekdal. I ought to have cautioned him, for I had a misgiving as to what was in the wind.

WERLE. Yes, that was the time to have spoken.

GREGERS. I did not dare to, I was so cowed and spiritless. I was mortally afraid of you—not only then, but long afterward.

WERLE. You have got over that fear now, it appears.

GREGERS. Yes, fortunately. The wrong done to old Ekdal, both by me and by others, can never be undone; but Hialmar I can rescue from all the falsehood and deception that are bringing him to ruin.

WERLE. Do you think that will be doing him a kindness?

GREGERS. I have not the least doubt of it.

WERLE. You think our worthy photographer is the sort of man to appreciate such friendly offices?

GREGERS. Yes, I do.

WERLE. H'm—we shall see.

GREGERS. Besides, if I am to go on living, I must try to find some cure for my sick conscience.

WERLE. It will never be sound. Your conscience has been sickly from childhood. That is a legacy from your mother, Gregers—the only one she left you.

GREGERS [with a scornful half-smile]. Have you not yet forgiven her for the mistake you made in supposing she would bring you a fortune?

WERLE. Don't let us wander from the point. Then you hold to your purpose of setting young Ekdal upon what you imagine to be the right scent?

GREGERS. Yes, that is my fixed resolve.

WERLE. Well, in that case I might have spared myself this visit, for of course it is useless to ask whether you will return home with me?

GREGERS. Quite useless.

WERLE. And I suppose you won't enter the firm either?

GREGERS. No.

WERLE. Very good. But as I am thinking of marrying again, your share in the property will fall to you at once.

GREGERS [quickly]. No, I do not want that.

WERLE. You don't want it?

GREGERS. No, I dare not take it, for conscience' sake.

WERLE [after a pause]. Are you going up to the works again?

GREGERS. No; I consider myself released from your service.

WERLE. But what are you going to do?

GREGERS. Only to fulfill my mission, nothing more.

WERLE. Well, but afterward? What are you going to live upon?

GREGERS. I have laid by a little out of my salary.

WERLE. How long will that last?

GREGERS. I think it will last my time.

WERLE. What do you mean?

GREGERS. I shall answer no more questions.

WERLE. Good-by, then, Gregers.

GREGERS. Good-by.

[WERLE *goes.*]

HIALMAR [*peeping in*]. He's gone, isn't he?

GREGERS. Yes.

[HIALMAR *and* RELLING *enter; also* GINA *and* HEDVIG *from the kitchen.*]

RELLING. That luncheon party was a failure.

GREGERS. Put on your coat, Hialmar; I want you to come for a long walk with me.

HIALMAR. With pleasure. What was it your father wanted? Had it anything to do with me?

GREGERS. Come along. We must have a talk. I'll go and put on my overcoat. [*Goes out by the passage door.*]

GINA. You shouldn't go out with him, Ekdal.

RELLING. No, don't you do it. Stay where you are.

HIALMAR [*gets his hat and overcoat*]. Oh, nonsense! When a friend of my youth feels impelled to open his mind to me in private—

RELLING. But devil take it—don't you see that the fellow's mad, cracked, demented!

GINA. There, what did I tell you! His mother before him had crazy fits like that sometimes.

HIALMAR. The more need for a friend's watchful eye. [*To* GINA.] Be sure you have dinner ready in good time. Good-by for the present. [*Goes out by the passage door.*]

RELLING. It's a thousand pities the fellow didn't go to hell through one of the Höidal mines.

GINA. Good lord! What makes you say that?

RELLING [*muttering*]. Oh, I have my own reasons.

GINA. Do you think young Werle is really mad?

RELLING. No, worse luck; he's no madder than most other people. But one disease he has certainly got in his system.

GINA. What is it that's the matter with him?

RELLING. Well, I'll tell you, Mrs Ekdal. He is suffering from an acute attack of integrity.

GINA. Integrity?

HEDVIG. Is that a kind of disease?

RELLING. Yes, it's a national disease, but it only appears
  sporadically. [*Nods to* GINA.] Thanks for your hos-
  pitality. [*He goes out by the passage door.*]

GINA [*moving restlessly to and fro*]. Ugh, that Gregers
  Werle—he was always a wretched creature.

HEDVIG [*standing by the table and looking searchingly
  at her*]. I think all this is very strange.

ACT FOUR

SCENE—HIALMAR EKDAL'S *studio. A photograph has just been taken; a camera with the cloth over it, a pedestal, two chairs, a folding table, etc., are standing out in the room. Afternoon light; the sun is going down; a little later it begins to grow dusk.*

GINA stands in the passage doorway with a little box and a wet glass plate in her hand and is speaking to somebody outside.

GINA. Yes, certainly. When I make a promise I keep it. The first dozen shall be ready on Monday. Good afternoon.

[*Someone is heard going downstairs.* GINA *shuts the door, slips the plate into the box and puts it into the covered camera.*]

HEDVIG [*comes in from the kitchen*]. Are they gone?

GINA [*tidying up*]. Yes, thank goodness. I've got rid of them at last.

HEDVIG. But can you imagine why Father hasn't come home yet?

GINA. Are you sure he's not down in Relling's room?

HEDVIG. No, he's not; I ran down the kitchen stair just now and asked.

GINA. And his dinner standing and getting cold too.

HEDVIG. Yes, I can't understand it. Father's always so careful to be home to dinner!

GINA. Oh, he'll be here directly, you'll see.

HEDVIG. I wish he would come; everything seems so queer today.

GINA [*calls out*]. There he is!

[HIALMAR EKDAL *comes in at the passage door.*]

HEDVIG [*going to him*]. Father! Oh, what a time we've been waiting for you!

GINA [*glancing sidelong at him*]. You've been out a long time, Ekdal.

HIALMAR [*without looking at her*]. Rather long, yes. [*He takes off his overcoat;* GINA *and* HEDVIG *go to help him; he motions them away.*]

GINA. Perhaps you've had dinner with Werle?

HIALMAR [*hanging up his coat*]. No.

GINA [*going toward the kitchen door*]. Then I'll bring some in for you.

HIALMAR. No; let the dinner alone. I want nothing to eat.

HEDVIG [*going nearer to him*]. Are you not well, Father?

HIALMAR. Well? Oh yes, well enough. We have had a tiring walk, Gregers and I.

GINA. You didn't ought to have gone so far, Ekdal; you're not used to it.

HIALMAR. H'm; there's many a thing a man must get used to in this world. [*Wanders about the room.*] Has anyone been here whilst I was out?

GINA. Nobody but the two sweethearts.

HIALMAR. No new orders?

GINA. No, not today.

HEDVIG. There will be some tomorrow, Father, you'll see.

HIALMAR. I hope there will, for tomorrow I am going to set to work in real earnest.

HEDVIG. Tomorrow! Don't you remember what day it is tomorrow?

HIALMAR. Oh yes, by the bye— Well, the day after, then. Henceforth I mean to do everything myself; I shall take all the work into my own hands.

GINA. Why, what can be the good of that, Ekdal? It'll

only make your life a burden to you. I can manage the photography all right, and you can go on working at your invention.

HEDVIG. And think of the wild duck, Father, and all the hens and rabbits and—

HIALMAR. Don't talk to me of all that trash! From to-morrow I will never set foot in the garret again.

HEDVIG. Oh, but, Father, you promised that we should have a little party.

HIALMAR. H'm, true. Well, then, from the day after to-morrow. I should almost like to wring that cursed wild duck's neck!

HEDVIG [*shrieks*]. The wild duck!

GINA. Well, I never!

HEDVIG [*shaking him*]. Oh no, Father; you know it's my wild duck!

HIALMAR. That is why I don't do it. I haven't the heart to—for your sake, Hedvig. But in my inmost soul I feel that I ought to do it. I ought not to tolerate under my roof a creature that has been through those hands.

GINA. Why, good gracious, even if Grandfather did get it from that poor creature Pettersen—

HEDVIG [*going after him*]. But think of the wild duck —the poor wild duck!

HIALMAR [*stops*]. I tell you I will spare it—for your sake. Not a hair of its head shall be—I mean, it shall be spared. There are greater problems than that to be dealt with. But you should go out a little now, Hedvig, as usual; it is getting dusk enough for you now.

HEDVIG. No, I don't care about going out now.

HIALMAR. Yes, do; it seems to me your eyes are blinking a great deal; all these vapors in here are bad for you. The air is heavy under this roof.

HEDVIG. Very well then, I'll run down the kitchen stair and go for a little walk. My cloak and hat? Oh, they're in my own room. Father—be sure you don't do the wild duck any harm whilst I'm out.

HIALMAR. Not a feather of its head shall be touched.
[*Draws her to him.*] You and I, Hedvig—we two—
Well, go along.

[HEDVIG *nods to her parents and goes out through the kitchen.*]

HIALMAR [*walks about without looking up*]. Gina.

GINA. Yes?

HIALMAR. From tomorrow—or say from the day after
tomorrow—I should like to keep the household account book myself.

GINA. Do you want to keep the accounts too now?

HIALMAR. Yes; or to check the receipts at any rate.

GINA. Lord help us; that's soon done.

HIALMAR. One would hardly think so; at any rate you
seem to make the money go a very long way. [*Stops
and looks at her.*] How do you manage it?

GINA. It's because me and Hedvig, we need so little.

HIALMAR. Is it the case that Father is very liberally
paid for the copying he does for Mr Werle?

GINA. I don't know as he gets anything out of the way.
I don't know the rates for that sort of work.

HIALMAR. Well, what does he get, about? Let me hear!

GINA. Oh, it varies; I daresay it'll come to about as
much as he costs us, with a little pocket money
over.

HIALMAR. As much as he costs us! And you have never
told me this before.

GINA. No, how could I tell you? It pleased you so much
to think he got everything from you.

HIALMAR. And he gets it from Mr Werle.

GINA. Oh well, he has plenty and to spare, he has.

HIALMAR. Light the lamp for me, please!

GINA [*lighting the lamp*]. And of course we don't know
as it's Mr Werle himself; it may be Graberg.

HIALMAR. Why attempt such an evasion?

GINA. I don't know; I only thought—

HIALMAR. H'm!

GINA. It wasn't me that got Grandfather that copying.

It was Bertha, when she used to come about us.

HIALMAR. It seems to me your voice is trembling.

GINA [*putting the lamp shade on*]. Is it?

HIALMAR. And your hands are shaking, are they not?

GINA [*firmly*]. Come right out with it, Ekdal. What has he been saying about me?

HIALMAR. Is it true—can it be true that—that there was an—an understanding between you and Mr Werle while you were in service there?

GINA. That's not true. Not at that time. Mr Werle did come after me, that's a fact. And his wife thought there was something in it, and then she made such a hocus-pocus and hurly-burly, and she hustled me and bustled me about so that I left her service.

HIALMAR. But afterward, then?

GINA. Well, then I went home. And Mother—well, she wasn't the woman you took her for, Ekdal; she kept on worrying and worrying at me about one thing and another—for Mr Werle was a widower by that time.

HIALMAR. Well, and then?

GINA. I suppose you've got to know it. He gave me no peace until he'd had his way.

HIALMAR [*striking his hands together*]. And this is the mother of my child! How could you hide this from me?

GINA. Yes, it was wrong of me; I ought certainly to have told you long ago.

HIALMAR. You should have told me at the very first— then I should have known the sort of woman you were.

GINA. But would you have married me all the same?

HIALMAR. How can you dream that I would?

GINA. That's just why I didn't dare tell you anything then. For I'd come to care for you so much, you see, and I couldn't go and make myself utterly miserable.

HIALMAR [*walks about*]. And this is my Hedvig's

mother! And to know that all I see before me [*kicks at chair*]—all that I call my home—I owe to a favored predecessor! Oh, that scoundrel Werle!

GINA. Do you repent of the fourteen—the fifteen years we've lived together?

HIALMAR [*placing himself in front of her*]. Have you not every day, every hour, repented of the spider's web of deceit you have spun around me? Answer me that! How could you help writhing with penitence and remorse?

GINA. Oh, my dear Ekdal, I've had all I could do to look after the house and get through the day's work.

HIALMAR. Then you never think of reviewing your past?

GINA. No; heaven knows I'd almost forgotten those old stories.

HIALMAR. Oh, this dull, callous contentment! To me there is something revolting about it. Think of it—never so much as a twinge of remorse!

GINA. But tell me, Ekdal—what would have become of you if you hadn't had a wife like me?

HIALMAR. Like you!

GINA. Yes; for you know I've always been a bit more practical and wide awake than you. Of course I'm a year or two older.

HIALMAR. What would have become of me!

GINA. You'd got into all sorts of bad ways when first you met me; that you can't deny.

HIALMAR. "Bad ways," do you call them? Little do you know what a man goes through when he is in grief and despair—especially a man of my fiery temperament.

GINA. Well, well, that may be so. And I've no reason to crow over you neither, for you turned a moral of a husband, that you did, as soon as ever you had a house and home of your own. And now we'd got everything so nice and cosy about us, and me and

Hedvig was just thinking we'd soon be able to let ourselves go a bit in the way of both food and clothes.

HIALMAR. In the swamp of deceit, yes.

GINA. I wish to goodness that detestable thing had never set his foot inside our doors!

HIALMAR. And I, too, thought my home such a pleasant one. That was a delusion. Where shall I now find the elasticity of spirit to bring my invention into the world of reality? Perhaps it will die with me, and then it will be your past, Gina, that will have killed it.

GINA [*nearly crying*]. You mustn't say such things, Ekdal. Me, that has only wanted to do the best I could for you all my days!

HIALMAR. I ask you, what becomes of the breadwinner's dream? When I used to lie in there on the sofa and brood over my invention I had a clear enough presentiment that it would sap my vitality to the last drop. I felt even then that the day when I held the patent in my hand—that day—would bring my—release. And then it was my dream that you should live on after me, the dead inventor's well-to-do widow.

GINA [*drying her tears*]. No, you mustn't talk like that, Ekdal. May the Lord never let me see the day I am left a widow!

HIALMAR. Oh, the whole dream has vanished. It is all over now. All over!

[GREGERS WERLE *opens the passage door cautiously and looks in.*]

GREGERS. May I come in?

HIALMAR. Yes, come in.

GREGERS [*comes forward, his face beaming with satisfaction, and holds out both his hands to them.*] Well, dear friends! [*Looks from one to the other and whispers to* HIALMAR.] Have you not done it yet?

HIALMAR [*aloud*]. It is done.

GREGERS. It is?

HIALMAR. I have passed through the bitterest moments of my life.

GREGERS. But also, I trust, the most ennobling.

HIALMAR. Well, at any rate, we have got through it for the present.

GINA. God forgive you, Mr Werle.

GREGERS [*in great surprise*]. But I don't understand this.

HIALMAR. What don't you understand?

GREGERS. After so great a crisis—a crisis that is to be the starting point of an entirely new life—of a communion founded on truth and free from all taint of deception—

HIALMAR. Yes, yes, I know; I know that quite well.

GREGERS. I confidently expected, when I entered the room, to find the light of transfiguration shining upon me from both husband and wife. And now I see nothing but dullness, oppression, gloom—

GINA. Oh, is that it? [*Takes off the lamp shade.*]

GREGERS. You will not understand me, Mrs Ekdal. Ah well, you, I suppose, need time to— But you, Hialmar? Surely you feel a new consecration after the great crisis?

HIALMAR. Yes, of course I do. That is—in a sort of way.

GREGERS. For surely nothing in the world can compare with the joy of forgiving one who has erred and raising her up to oneself in love.

HIALMAR. Do you think a man can so easily throw off the bitter cup I have drained?

GREGERS. No, not a common man, perhaps. But a man like you—

HIALMAR. Good God! I know that well enough. But you must keep me up to it, Gregers. It takes time, you know.

GREGERS. You have much of the wild duck in you, Hialmar.

[RELLING *has come in at the passage door.*]

RELLING. Oho! Is the wild duck to the fore again?

HIALMAR. Yes; Mr Werle's wing-broken victim.

RELLING. Mr Werle? So it's him you are talking about?

HIALMAR. Him and—ourselves.

RELLING [*in an undertone to* GREGERS]. May the devil fly away with you!

HIALMAR. What is that you are saying?

RELLING. Only uttering a heartfelt wish that this quack-salver would take himself off. If he stays here he is quite equal to making an utter mess of life for both of you.

GREGERS. These two will not make a mess of life, Mr Relling. Of course I won't speak to Hialmar—him we know. But she too, in her innermost heart, has certainly something loyal and sincere—

GINA [*almost crying*]. You might have let me alone for what I was then.

RELLING [*to* GREGERS]. Is it rude to ask what you really want in this house?

GREGERS. To lay the foundations of a true marriage.

RELLING. So you don't think Ekdal's marriage is good enough as it is?

GREGERS. No doubt it is as good a marriage as most others, worse luck. But a true marriage it has yet to become.

HIALMAR. You have never had eyes for the claims of the ideal, Relling.

RELLING. Rubbish, my boy! But excuse me, Mr Werle; how many—in round numbers—how many true marriages have you seen in the course of your life?

GREGERS. Scarcely a single one.

RELLING. Nor I either.

GREGERS. But I have seen innumerable marriages of the opposite kind. And it has been my fate to see at close quarters what ruin such a marriage can work in two human souls.

HIALMAR. A man's whole moral basis may give away beneath his feet; that is the terrible part of it.

RELLING. Well, I can't say I've ever been exactly married, so I don't pretend to speak with authority. But this I know, that the child enters into the marriage problem. And you must leave the child in peace.

HIALMAR. Oh—Hedvig! My poor Hedvig!

RELLING. Yes, you must be good enough to keep Hedvig outside of all this. You two are grown-up people; you are free, in God's name, to make what mess and muddle you please of your life. But you must deal cautiously with Hedvig, I tell you; else you may do her a great injury.

HIALMAR. An injury!

RELLING. Yes, or she may do herself an injury—and perhaps others too.

GINA. How can you know that, Relling?

HIALMAR. Her sight is in no immediate danger, is it?

RELLING. I am not talking about her sight. Hedvig is at a critical age. She may be getting all sorts of mischief into her head.

GINA. That's true—I've noticed it already! She's taken to carrying on with the fire out in the kitchen. She calls it playing at house on fire. I'm often scared for fear she really sets fire to the house.

RELLING. You see, I thought as much.

GREGERS [to RELLING]. But how do you account for that?

RELLING [sullenly]. Her constitution's changing, sir.

HIALMAR. So long as the child has me—so long as I am above ground— [A knock at the door.]

GINA. Hush, Ekdal, there's someone in the passage. [Calls out.] Come in!

[MRS SORBY, in walking dress, comes in.]

MRS SORBY. Good evening.

GINA [going toward her]. Is it really you, Bertha?

MRS SORBY. Yes, of course it is. But I'm disturbing you, I'm afraid.

HIALMAR. No, not at all; an emissary from that house—

MRS SORBY [to GINA]. To tell the truth, I hoped your menfolk would be out at this time. I just ran up to have a little chat with you and to say good-by.

GINA. Good-by? Are you going away then?

MRS SORBY. Yes, tomorrow morning—up to Höidal. Mr
Werle started this afternoon. [*Lightly to* GREGERS.]
He asked me to say good-by for him.

GINA. Only fancy!

HIALMAR. I say: beware!

GREGERS. I must explain the situation. My father and
Mrs Sorby are going to be married.

HIALMAR. Going to be married!

GINA. Oh, Bertha! So it's come to that at last!

RELLING [*his voice quivering a little*]. This is surely not
true?

MRS SORBY. Yes, my dear Relling, it's true enough.

RELLING. You are going to marry again?

MRS SORBY. Yes, it looks like it. Werle has got a special
license, and we are going to be married quietly up at
the works.

GREGERS. Then I must wish you all happiness, like a
dutiful stepson.

MRS SORBY. Thank you very much—if you mean what
you say. I certainly hope it will lead to happiness,
both for Werle and for me.

RELLING. You have every reason to hope that. Mr Werle
never gets drunk—so far as I know; and I don't suppose he's in the habit of thrashing his wives, like the
late lamented horse doctor.

MRS SORBY. Come now, let Sorby rest in peace. He had
his good points too.

RELLING. Mr Werle has better ones, I have no doubt.

MRS SORBY. He hasn't frittered away all that was good
in him, at any rate. The man who does that must
take the consequences.

RELLING. I shall go out with Molvik this evening.

MRS SORBY. You mustn't do that, Relling. Don't do it—
for my sake.

RELLING. There's nothing else for it. [*To* HIALMAR.] If
you're going with us, come along.

GINA. No, thank you. Ekdal doesn't go in for that sort of dissertation.

HIALMAR [*half aloud, in vexation*]. Oh, do hold your tongue!

RELLING. Good-by, Mrs—Werle. [*Goes out through the passage door.*]

GREGERS [*to* MRS SORBY]. You seem to know Doctor Relling pretty intimately.

MRS SORBY. Yes, we have known each other for many years. At one time it seemed as if things might have gone further between us.

GREGERS. It was surely lucky for you that they did not.

MRS SORBY. You may well say that. But I have always been wary of acting on impulse. A woman can't afford absolutely to throw herself away.

GREGERS. Are you not in the least afraid that I may let my father know about this old friendship?

MRS SORBY. Why, of course I have told him all about it myself.

GREGERS. Indeed?

MRS SORBY. Your father knows every single thing that can, with any truth, be said about me. I have told him all; it was the first thing I did when I saw what was in his mind.

GREGERS. Then you have been franker than most people, I think.

MRS SORBY. I have always been frank. We women find that the best policy.

HIALMAR. What do you say to that, Gina?

GINA. Oh, we're not all alike, us women aren't. Some are made one way, some another.

MRS SORBY. Well, for my part, Gina, I believe it's wisest to do as I've done. And Werle has no secrets either, on his side. That's really the great bond between us, you see. Now he can talk to me as openly as a child. He has never had the chance to do that before. Fancy a man like him, full of health and vigor, passing his

286 The Wild Duck

whole youth and the best years of his life in listening
to nothing but penitential sermons! And very often
the sermons had for their text the most imaginary of-
fenses—at least so I understand.

GINA. That's true enough.

GREGERS. If you ladies are going to follow up this topic,
I had better withdraw.

MRS SORBY. You can stay as far as that's concerned. I
shan't say a word more. But I wanted you to know
that I had done nothing secretly or in an under-
hand way. I may seem to have come in for a great
piece of luck, and so I have, in a sense. But after all,
I don't think I am getting any more than I am giving. I shall stand by him always, and I can tend and
care for him as no one else can, now that he is getting helpless.

HIALMAR. Getting helpless?

GREGERS [to MRS SORBY]. Hush, don't speak of that here.

MRS SORBY. There is no disguising it any longer, however much he would like to. He is going blind.

HIALMAR [starts]. Going blind? That's strange. He, too,
going blind!

GINA. Lots of people do.

MRS SORBY. And you can imagine what that means to
a businessman. Well, I shall try as well as I can to
make my eyes take the place of his. But I mustn't
stay any longer; I have heaps of things to do. Oh, by
the bye, Ekdal, I was to tell you that if there is anything Werle can do for you, you must just apply to
Graberg.

GREGERS. That offer I am sure Hialmar Ekdal will decline with thanks.

MRS SORBY. Indeed? I don't think he used to be so—

GINA. No, Bertha, Ekdal doesn't need anything from
Mr Werle now.

HIALMAR [slowly and with emphasis]. Will you present
my compliments to your future husband and say that
I intend very shortly to call upon Mr Graberg—

GREGERS. What! You don't really mean that?

HIALMAR. To call upon Mr Graberg, I say, and obtain an account of the sum I owe his principal. I will pay that debt of honor—ha, ha, ha! a debt of honor, let us call it! In any case I will pay the whole with five per cent interest.

GINA. But, my dear Ekdal, God knows we haven't got the money to do it.

HIALMAR. Be good enough to tell your future husband that I am working assiduously at my invention. Please tell him that what sustains me in this laborious task is the wish to free myself from a torturing burden of debt. That is my reason for proceeding with the invention. The entire profits shall be devoted to releasing me from my pecuniary obligations to your future husband.

MRS SORBY. Something has happened here.

HIALMAR. Yes, you are right.

MRS SORBY. Well, good-by. I had something else to speak to you about, Gina, but it must keep till another time. Good-by.

[HIALMAR and GREGERS bow silently. GINA follows MRS SORBY to the door.]

HIALMAR. Not beyond the threshold, Gina!

[MRS SORBY goes; GINA shuts the door after her.]

HIALMAR. There now, Gregers, I have got that burden of debt off my mind.

GREGERS. You soon will, at all events.

HIALMAR. I think my attitude may be called correct.

GREGERS. You are the man I have always taken you for.

HIALMAR. In certain cases it is impossible to disregard the claim of the ideal. Yes, as the breadwinner of a family, I cannot but writhe and groan under it. I can tell you it is no joke for a man without capital to attempt the repayment of a long-standing obligation over which, so to speak, the dust of oblivion has gathered. But it cannot be helped; the man in me demands his rights.

GREGERS [*laying his hand on* HIALMAR's *shoulder*]. My dear Hialmar—was it not a good thing I came?

HIALMAR. Yes.

GREGERS. Are you not glad to have had your true position made clear to you?

HIALMAR [*somewhat impatiently*]. Yes, of course I am. But there is one thing that is revolting to my sense of justice.

GREGERS. And what is that?

HIALMAR. It is that— But I don't know whether I ought to express myself so unreservedly about your father.

GREGERS. Say what you please so far as I am concerned.

HIALMAR. Well, then, is it not exasperating to think that it is not I, but he, who will realize the true marriage?

GREGERS. How can you say such a thing?

HIALMAR. Because it is clearly the case. Isn't the marriage between your father and Mrs Sorby founded upon complete confidence, upon entire and unreserved candor on both sides? They hide nothing from each other, they keep no secrets in the background; their relation is based, if I may put it so, on mutual confession and absolution.

GREGERS. Well, what then?

HIALMAR. Well, is not that the whole thing? Did you not yourself say that this was precisely the difficulty that had to be overcome in order to found a true marriage?

GREGERS. But this is a totally different matter, Hialmar. You surely don't compare either yourself or your wife with those two— Oh, you understood me well enough.

HIALMAR. Say what you like, there is something in all this that hurts and offends my sense of justice. It really looks as if there were no just Providence to rule the world.

GINA. Oh no, Ekdal; for God's sake don't say such things.

GREGERS. H'm; don't let us get upon those questions.

HIALMAR. And yet, after all, I cannot but recognize the guiding finger of Fate. He is going blind.

GINA. Oh, you can't be sure of that.

HIALMAR. There is no doubt about it. At all events there ought not to be, for in that very fact lies the righteous retribution. He has hoodwinked a confiding fellow creature in days gone by—

GREGERS. I fear he has hoodwinked many.

HIALMAR. And now comes inexorable, mysterious Fate and demands Werle's own eyes.

GINA. Oh, how dare you say such dreadful things! You make me quite scared.

HIALMAR. It is profitable, now and then, to plunge deep into the night side of existence.

[HEDVIG, *in her hat and cloak, comes in by the passage door. She is pleasurably excited and out of breath.*]

GINA. Are you back already?

HEDVIG. Yes, I didn't care to go any farther. It was a good thing, too, for I've just met someone at the door.

HIALMAR. It must have been that Mrs Sorby.

HEDVIG. Yes.

HIALMAR [*walks up and down*]. I hope you have seen her for the last time.

[*Silence.* HEDVIG, *discouraged, looks first at one and then at the other, trying to divine their frame of mind.*]

HEDVIG [*approaching, coaxingly*]. Father.

HIALMAR. Well—what is it, Hedvig?

HEDVIG. Mrs Sorby had something with her for me.

HIALMAR [*stops*]. For you?

HEDVIG. Yes. Something for tomorrow.

GINA. Bertha has always given you some little thing on your birthday.

HIALMAR. What is it?

HEDVIG. Oh, you mustn't see it now. Mother is to give it to me tomorrow morning before I'm up.

HIALMAR. What is all this hocus-pocus that I am to be in the dark about?

HEDVIG [*quickly*]. Oh no, you may see it if you like. It's a big letter. [*Takes the letter out of her cloak pocket.*]

HIALMAR. A letter too?

HEDVIG. Yes, it is only a letter. The rest will come afterward, I suppose. But fancy—a letter! I've never had a letter before. And there's "Miss" written upon it. [*Reads.*] "Miss Hedvig Ekdal." Only fancy—that's me!

HIALMAR. Let me see that letter.

HEDVIG [*hands it to him*]. There it is.

HIALMAR. That is Mr Werle's hand.

GINA. Are you sure of that, Ekdal?

HIALMAR. Look for yourself.

GINA. Oh, what do I know about suchlike things?

HIALMAR. Hedvig, may I open the letter—and read it?

HEDVIG. Yes, of course you may, if you want to.

GINA. No, not tonight, Ekdal; it's to be kept till tomorrow.

HEDVIG [*softly*]. Oh, can't you let him read it! It's sure to be something good, and then Father will be glad and everything will be nice again.

HIALMAR. I may open it then?

HEDVIG. Yes, do, Father. I'm so anxious to know what it is.

HIALMAR. Well and good. [*Opens the letter, takes out a paper, reads it through and appears bewildered.*] What is this?

GINA. What does it say?

HEDVIG. Oh yes, Father—tell us!

HIALMAR. Be quiet. [*Reads it through again; he has turned pale but says with self-control.*] It is a deed of gift, Hedvig.

HEDVIG. Is it? What sort of gift am I to have?

HIALMAR. Read for yourself.

[HEDVIG *goes over and reads for a time by the lamp.*]

HIALMAR [*half aloud, clenching his hands*]. The eyes! The eyes—and then that letter!

HEDVIG [*leaves off reading*]. Yes, but it seems to me that it's Grandfather that's to have it.

HIALMAR [*takes letter from her*]. Gina—can you understand this?

GINA. I know nothing whatever about it; tell me what's the matter.

HIALMAR. Mr Werle writes to Hedvig that her old grandfather need not trouble himself any longer with the copying but that he can henceforth draw on the office for a hundred crowns a month—

GREGERS. Aha!

HEDVIG. A hundred crowns, Mother! I read that.

GINA. What a good thing for Grandfather!

HIALMAR. —a hundred crowns a month so long as he needs it—that means, of course, so long as he lives.

GINA. Well, so he's provided for, poor dear.

HIALMAR. But there is more to come. You didn't read that, Hedvig. Afterward this gift is to pass on to you.

HEDVIG. To me! The whole of it?

HIALMAR. He says that the same amount is assured to you for the whole of your life. Do you hear that, Gina?

GINA. Yes, I hear.

HEDVIG. Fancy—all that money for me! [*Shakes him.*] Father, Father, aren't you glad?

HIALMAR [*eluding her*]. Glad! [*Walks about.*] Oh, what vistas—what perspectives open up before me! It is Hedvig, Hedvig that he showers these benefactions upon!

GINA. Yes, because it's Hedvig's birthday.

HEDVIG. And you'll get it all the same, Father! You know quite well I shall give all the money to you and Mother.

HIALMAR. To Mother, yes! There we have it.

GREGERS. Hialmar, this is a trap he is setting for you.

HIALMAR. Do you think it's another trap?

GREGERS. When he was here this morning he said: Hialmar Ekdal is not the man you imagine him to be.

HIALMAR. Not the man—

GREGERS. That you shall see, he said.

HIALMAR. He meant you should see that I would let myself be bought off!

HEDVIG. Oh, Mother, what does all this mean?

GINA. Go and take off your things.

[HEDVIG *goes out by the kitchen door, half crying.*]

GREGERS. Yes, Hialmar—now is the time to show who was right, he or I.

HIALMAR [*slowly tears the paper across, lays both pieces on the table and says*]: Here is my answer.

GREGERS. Just what I expected.

HIALMAR [*goes over to* GINA, *who stands by the stove and says in a low voice*]: Now please make a clean breast of it. If the connection between you and him was quite over when you—came to care for me, as you call it—why did he place us in a position to marry?

GINA. I suppose he thought as he could come and go in our house.

HIALMAR. Only that? Was he not afraid of a possible contingency?

GINA. I don't know what you mean.

HIALMAR. I want to know whether—your child has the right to live under my roof.

GINA [*draws herself up; her eyes flash*]. You ask that!

HIALMAR. You shall answer me this one question: Does Hedvig belong to me—or—? Well?

GINA [*looking at him with cold defiance*]. I don't know.

HIALMAR [*quivering a little*]. You don't know!

GINA. How should I know. A creature like me—

HIALMAR [*quietly turning away from her*]. Then I have nothing more to do in this house.

GREGERS. Take care, Hialmar! Think what you are doing!

HIALMAR [*puts on his overcoat*]. In this case there is nothing for a man like me to think twice about.

GREGERS. Yes indeed, there are endless things to be considered. You three must be together if you are to attain the true frame of mind for self-sacrifice and forgiveness.

HIALMAR. I don't want to attain it. Never, never! My hat! [*Takes his hat.*] My home has fallen into ruins about me. [*Bursts into tears.*] Gregers, I have no child!

HEDVIG [*who has opened the kitchen door*]. What is that you're saying? [*Coming to him.*] Father, Father!

GINA. There, you see!

HIALMAR. Don't come near me, Hedvig! Keep far away. I cannot bear to see you. Oh! those eyes! Good-by. [*Makes for the door.*]

HEDVIG [*clinging close to him and screaming loudly*]. No! No! Don't leave me!

GINA [*cries out*]. Look at the child, Ekdal! Look at the child!

HIALMAR. I will not! I cannot! I must get out—away from all this! [*He tears himself away from* HEDVIG *and goes out by the passage door.*]

HEDVIG [*with despairing eyes*]. He is going away from us, Mother! He is going away from us! He will never come back again!

GINA. Don't cry, Hedvig. Father's sure to come back again.

HEDVIG [*throws herself sobbing on the sofa*]. No, no, he'll never come home to us any more.

GREGERS. Do you believe I meant all for the best, Mrs Ekdal?

GINA. Yes, I daresay you did, but God forgive you all the same.

HEDVIG [*lying on the sofa*]. Oh, this will kill me! What have I done to him? Mother, you must fetch him home again!

GINA. Yes, yes, yes; only be quiet, and I'll go out and look for him. [*Puts on her outdoor things.*] Perhaps he's gone into Relling's. But you mustn't lie there and cry. Promise me!

HEDVIG [*weeping convulsively*]. Yes, I'll stop, I'll stop; if only Father comes back!

GREGERS. [*to* GINA, *who is going*]. After all, had you not better leave him to fight out his bitter fight to the end?

GINA. Oh, he can do that afterward. First of all we must get the child quieted. [*Goes out by the passage door.*]

HEDVIG [*sits up and dries her tears*]. Now you must tell me what all this means. Why doesn't Father want me any more?

GREGERS. You mustn't ask that till you are a big girl— quite grown up.

HEDVIG [*sobs*]. But I can't go on being as miserable as this till I'm grown up. I think I know what it is. Perhaps I'm not really Father's child.

GREGERS [*uneasily*]. How could that be?

HEDVIG. Mother might have found me. And perhaps Father has just got to know it; I've read of such things.

GREGERS. Well, but if it were so—

HEDVIG. I think he might be just as fond of me for all that. Yes, fonder almost. We got the wild duck in a present, you know, and I love it so dearly all the same.

GREGERS [*turning the conversation*]. Ah, the wild duck, by the bye! Let us talk about the wild duck a little, Hedvig.

HEDVIG. The poor wild duck! He doesn't want to see it any more either. Only think, he wanted to wring its neck!

GREGERS. Oh, he won't do that.

HEDVIG. No, but he said he would like to. And I think it was horrid of Father to say it, for I pray for the wild duck every night and ask that it may be preserved from death and all that is evil.

GREGERS [*looking at her*]. Do you say your prayers every night?

HEDVIG. Yes.

GREGERS. Who taught you to do that?

HEDVIG. I myself—one time when Father was very ill and had leeches on his neck and said that death was staring him in the face.

GREGERS. Well?

HEDVIG. Then I prayed for him as I lay in bed, and since then I have always kept it up.

GREGERS. And now you pray for the wild duck too?

HEDVIG. I thought it best to bring in the wild duck, for she was so weakly at first.

GREGERS. Do you pray in the morning too?

HEDVIG. No, of course not.

GREGERS. Why not in the morning as well?

HEDVIG. In the morning it's light, you know, and there's nothing in particular to be afraid of.

GREGERS. And your father was going to wring the neck of the wild duck that you love so dearly?

HEDVIG. No; he said he ought to wring its neck but he would spare it for my sake, and that was kind of Father.

GREGERS [*coming a little nearer*]. But suppose you were to sacrifice the wild duck of your own free will for his sake?

HEDVIG [*rising*]. The wild duck!

GREGERS. Suppose you were to make a free-will offering, for his sake, of the dearest treasure you have in the world?

HEDVIG. Do you think that would do any good?

GREGERS. Try it, Hedvig.

HEDVIG [*softly, with flashing eyes.*] Yes, I will try it.

GREGERS. Have you really the courage for it, do you think?

HEDVIG. I'll ask Grandfather to shoot the wild duck for me.

GREGERS. Yes, do. But not a word to your mother about it.

HEDVIG. Why not?

GREGERS. She doesn't understand us.

HEDVIG. The wild duck! I'll try it tomorrow morning. [GINA *comes in by the passage door.*]

HEDVIG [*going toward her*]. Did you find him, Mother?

GINA. No, but I heard as he had called and taken Relling with him.

GREGERS. Are you sure of that?

GINA. Yes, the porter's wife said so. Molvik went with them too, she said.

GREGERS. This evening, when his mind so sorely needs to wrestle in solitude!

GINA [*takes off her things*]. Yes, men are strange creatures, so they are. The Lord only knows where Relling has dragged him to! I ran over to Madam Eriksen's, but they weren't there.

HEDVIG [*struggling to keep back her tears*]. Oh, if he should never come home any more!

GREGERS. He will come home again. I shall have news to give him tomorrow, and then you shall see how he comes home. You may rely upon that, Hedvig, and sleep in peace. Good night. [*He goes out by the passage door.*]

HEDVIG [*throws herself sobbing on* GINA'S *neck*]. Mother, Mother!

GINA [*pats her shoulder and sighs*]. Ah yes, Relling was right, he was. That's what comes of it when crazy creatures go about presenting the claim of the—what-you-may-call-it.

ACT FIVE

SCENE—HIALMAR EKDAL's *studio. Cold gray morning light. Wet snow lies upon the large panes of the sloping roof window.*

GINA *comes from the kitchen with an apron and bib on and carrying a dusting brush and a duster; she goes toward the sitting-room door. At the same moment* HEDVIG *comes hurriedly in from the passage.*

GINA [*stops*]. Well?

HEDVIG. Oh, Mother, I almost think he's down at Relling's—

GINA. There, you see!

HEDVIG. —because the porter's wife says she could hear that Relling had two people with him when he came home last night.

GINA. That's just what I thought.

HEDVIG. But it's no use his being there if he won't come up to us.

GINA. I'll go down and speak to him at all events.

[OLD EKDAL, *in dressing gown and slippers and with a lighted pipe, appears at the door of his room.*]

EKDAL. Hialmar—isn't Hialmar at home?

GINA. No, he's gone out.

EKDAL. So early? And in such a tearing snowstorm? Well, well, just as he pleases; I can take my morning walk alone. [*He slides the garret door aside;* HEDVIG *helps him; he goes in; she closes it after him.*]

HEDVIG [*in an undertone*]. Only think, Mother, when

poor Grandfather hears that Father is going to leave us.

GINA. Oh, nonsense; Grandfather mustn't hear anything about it. It was a heaven's mercy he wasn't at home yesterday in all that hurly-burly.

HEDVIG. Yes, but—

[GREGERS *comes in by the passage door.*]

GREGERS. Well, have you any news of him?

GINA. They say he's down at Relling's.

GREGERS. At Relling's! Has he really been out with those creatures?

GINA. Yes, like enough.

GREGERS. When he ought to have been yearning for solitude, to collect and clear his thoughts—

GINA. Yes, you may well say so.

[RELLING *enters from the passage.*]

HEDVIG [*going to him*]. Is Father in your room?

GINA [*at the same time*]. Is he there?

RELLING. Yes, to be sure he is.

HEDVIG. And you never let us know!

RELLING. Yes, I'm a brute. But in the first place I had to look after the other brute; I mean our demonic friend, of course; and then I fell so dead asleep that—

GINA. What does Ekdal say today?

RELLING. He says nothing whatever.

HEDVIG. Doesn't he speak?

RELLING. Not a blessed word.

GREGERS. No, no; I can understand that very well.

GINA. But what's he doing then?

RELLING. He's lying on the sofa, snoring.

GINA. Oh, is he? Yes, Ekdal's a rare one to snore.

HEDVIG. Asleep? Can he sleep?

RELLING. Well, it certainly looks like it.

GREGERS. No wonder, after the spiritual conflict that has rent him—

GINA. And then he's never been used to gadding about out of doors at night.

HEDVIG. Perhaps it's a good thing that he's getting sleep, Mother.

GINA. Of course it is, and we must take care we don't wake him up too early. Thank you, Relling. I must get the house cleaned up a bit now, and then— Come and help me, Hedvig.

[GINA *and* HEDVIG *go into the sitting room.*]

GREGERS [*turning to* RELLING]. What is your explanation of the spiritual tumult that is now going on in Hialmar Ekdal?

RELLING. Devil a bit of a spiritual tumult have I noticed in him.

GREGERS. What! Not at such a crisis, when his whole life has been placed on a new foundation? How can you think that such an individuality as Hialmar's—

RELLING. Oh, individuality—he! If he ever had any tendency to the abnormal developments you call individuality, I can assure you it was rooted out of him while he was still in his teens.

GREGERS. That would be strange indeed—considering the loving care with which he was brought up.

RELLING. By those two high-flown, hysterical maiden aunts, you mean?

GREGERS. Let me tell you that they were women who never forgot the claim of the ideal—but of course you will only jeer at me again.

RELLING. No, I'm in no humor for that. I know all about those ladies, for he has ladled out no end of rhetoric on the subject of his "two soul mothers." But I don't think he has much to thank them for. Ekdal's misfortune is that in his own circle he has always been looked upon as a shining light.

GREGERS. Not without reason, surely. Look at the depth of his mind!

RELLING. I have never discovered it. That his father believed in it I don't so much wonder; the old lieutenant has been an ass all his days.

GREGERS. He has had a childlike mind all his days; that is what you cannot understand.

RELLING. Well, so be it. But then when our dear sweet Hialmar went to college he at once passed for the great light of the future amongst his comrades too! He was handsome, the rascal—red and white—a shop-girl's dream of manly beauty; and with his superficially emotional temperament and his sympathetic voice and his talent for declaiming other people's verses and other people's thoughts—

GREGERS [*indignantly*]. Is it Hialmar Ekdal you are talking about in this strain?

RELLING. Yes, with your permission; I am simply giving you an inside view of the idol you are groveling before.

GREGERS. I should hardly have thought I was quite stone-blind.

RELLING. Yes, you are—or not far from it. You are a sick man too, you see.

GREGERS. You are right there.

RELLING. Yes. Yours is a complicated case. First of all there is that plaguy integrity fever, and then—what's worse—you are always in a delirium of hero worship; you must always have something to adore, outside yourself.

GREGERS. Yes, I must certainly seek it outside myself.

RELLING. But you make such shocking mistakes about every new phoenix you think you have discovered. Here again you have come to a cotter's cabin with your claim of the ideal, and the people of the house are insolvent.

GREGERS. If you don't think better than that of Hialmar Ekdal, what pleasure can you find in being everlastingly with him?

RELLING. Well, you see, I'm supposed to be a sort of a doctor—save the mark! I can't but give a hand to the poor sick folk who live under the same roof with me.

GREGERS. Oh, indeed! Hialmar Ekdal is sick too, is he?

RELLING. Most people are, worse luck.

GREGERS. And what remedy are you applying in Hialmar's case?

RELLING. My usual one. I am cultivating the life illusion in him.

GREGERS. Life—illusion? I didn't catch what you said.

RELLING. Yes, I said illusion. For illusion, you know, is the stimulating principle.

GREGERS. May I ask with what illusion Hialmar is inoculated?

RELLING. No, thank you; I don't betray professional secrets to quacksalvers. You would probably go and muddle his case still more than you have already. But my method is infallible. I have applied it to Molvik as well. I have made him "demonic." That's the blister I have to put on his neck.

GREGERS. Is he not really demonic then?

RELLING. What the devil do you mean by demonic? It's only a piece of gibberish I've invented to keep up a spark of life in him. But for that, the poor harmless creature would have succumbed to self-contempt and despair many a long year ago. And then the old lieutenant! But he has hit upon his own cure, you see.

GREGERS. Lieutenant Ekdal? What of him?

RELLING. Just think of the old bear hunter shutting himself up in that dark garret to shoot rabbits! I tell you there is not a happier sportsman in the world than that old man pottering about in there among all that rubbish. The four or five withered Christmas trees he has saved up are the same to him as the whole great fresh Höidal forest; the cock and the hens are big game birds in the fir tops, and the rabbits that flop about the garret floor are the bears he has to battle with—the mighty hunter of the mountains!

GREGERS. Poor unfortunate old man! Yes, he has indeed had to narrow the ideals of his youth.

RELLING. While I think of it, Mr Werle junior—don't use that foreign word: ideals. We have the excellent native word: lies.

GREGERS. Do you think the two things are related?

RELLING. Yes, just about as closely as typhus and putrid fever.

GREGERS. Doctor Relling, I shall not give up the struggle until I have rescued Hialmar from your clutches!

RELLING. So much the worse for him. Rob the average man of his life illusion and you rob him of his happiness at the same stroke. [*To* HEDVIG, *who comes in from the sitting room.*] Well, little wild-duck mother. I'm just going down to see whether Papa is still lying meditating upon that wonderful invention of his. [*Goes out by passage door.*]

GREGERS [*approaches* HEDVIG]. I can see by your face that you have not yet done it.

HEDVIG. What? Oh, that about the wild duck! No.

GREGERS. I suppose your courage failed when the time came?

HEDVIG. No, that wasn't it. But when I awoke this morning and remembered what he had been talking about it seemed so strange.

GREGERS. Strange?

HEDVIG. Yes, I don't know— Yesterday evening, at the moment, I thought there was something so delightful about it; but since I have slept and thought of it again, it somehow doesn't seem worth while.

GREGERS. Ah, I thought you could not have grown up quite unharmed in this house.

HEDVIG. I don't care about that, if only Father would come up—

GREGERS. Oh, if only your eyes had been opened to that which gives life its value—if you possessed the true, joyous, fearless spirit of sacrifice you would soon see how he would come up to you. But I believe in you still, Hedvig. [*He goes out by the passage door.* HEDVIG *wanders about the room for a time; she is on the*

*point of going into the kitchen when a knock is
heard at the garret door.* HEDVIG *goes over and opens
it a little;* OLD EKDAL *comes out; she pushes the door
to again.*]

EKDAL. H'm, it's not much fun to take one's morning
walk alone.

HEDVIG. Wouldn't you like to go shooting, Grandfather?

EKDAL. It's not the weather for it today. It's so dark
there you can scarcely see where you're going.

HEDVIG. Do you never want to shoot anything besides
the rabbits?

EKDAL. Do you think the rabbits aren't good enough?

HEDVIG. Yes, but what about the wild duck?

EKDAL. Ho-ho! Are you afraid I shall shoot your wild
duck? Never in the world. Never!

HEDVIG. No, I suppose you couldn't; they say it's very
difficult to shoot wild ducks.

EKDAL. Couldn't! Should rather think I could.

HEDVIG. How would you set about it, Grandfather? I
don't mean with my wild duck, but with others.

EKDAL. I should take care to shoot them in the breast,
you know; that's the surest place. And then you
must shoot against the feathers, you see—not the way
of the feathers.

HEDVIG. Do they die then, Grandfather?

EKDAL. Yes they die right enough—when you shoot
properly. Well, I must go and brush up a bit. H'm—
understand—h'm. [*Goes into his room.*]

[HEDVIG *waits a little, glances toward the sitting-room
door, goes over to the bookcase, stands on tiptoe,
takes the double-barreled pistol down from the shelf
and looks at it.* GINA, *with brush and duster, comes
from the sitting room.* HEDVIG *hastily lays down the
pistol unobserved.*]

GINA. Don't stand raking amongst Father's things, Hedvig.

HEDVIG [*goes away from the bookcase*]. I was only going
to tidy up a little.

GINA. You'd better go into the kitchen and see if the coffee's keeping hot; I'll take his breakfast on a tray when I go down to him.

[HEDVIG *goes out.* GINA *begins to sweep and clean up the studio. Presently the passage door is opened with hesitation and* HIALMAR EKDAL *looks in. He has on his overcoat but not his hat; he is unwashed, and his hair is disheveled and unkempt. His eyes are dull and heavy.*]

GINA [*standing with the brush in her hand and looking at him*]. Oh, there now, Ekdal—so you've come after all?

HIALMAR [*comes in and answers in a toneless voice*]. I come—only to depart immediately.

GINA. Yes, yes, I suppose so. But, Lord help us! what a sight you are!

HIALMAR. A sight?

GINA. And your nice winter coat too! Well, that's done for.

HEDVIG [*at the kitchen door*]. Mother, hadn't I better— [*Sees* HIALMAR, *gives a loud scream of joy and runs to him.*] Oh, Father, Father!

HIALMAR [*turns away and makes a gesture of repulsion*]. Away, away, away! [*To* GINA.] Keep her away from me, I say!

GINA [*in a low tone*]. Go into the sitting room, Hedvig. [HEDVIG *does so without a word.*]

HIALMAR [*fussily pulls out the table drawer*]. I must have my books with me. Where are my books?

GINA. Which books?

HIALMAR. My scientific books, of course; the technical magazines I require for my invention.

GINA [*searches in the bookcase*]. Is it these here paper-covered ones?

HIALMAR. Yes, of course.

GINA [*lays a heap of magazines on the table*]. Shan't I get Hedvig to cut them for you?

HIALMAR. I don't require to have them cut for me. [*Short silence.*]

GINA. Then you're still set on leaving us, Ekdal?

HIALMAR [*rummaging amongst the books*]. Yes, that is a matter of course, I should think.

GINA. Well, well.

HIALMAR [*vehemently*]. How can I live here, to be stabbed to the heart every hour of the day?

GINA. God forgive you for thinking such vile things of me.

HIALMAR. Prove—

GINA. I think it's you as has got to prove.

HIALMAR. After a past like yours? There are certain claims—I may almost call them claims of the ideal—

GINA. But what about Grandfather? What's to become of him, poor dear?

HIALMAR. I know my duty; my helpless father will come with me. I am going out into the town to make arrangements— H'm [*hesitatingly*]—has anyone found my hat on the stairs?

GINA. No. Have you lost your hat?

HIALMAR. Of course I had it on when I came in last night—there's no doubt about that—but I couldn't find it this morning.

GINA. Lord help us! Where have you been to with those two ne'er-do-wells?

HIALMAR. Oh, don't bother me about trifles. Do you suppose I am in the mood to remember details?

GINA. If only you haven't caught cold, Ekdal— [*Goes out into the kitchen.*]

HIALMAR [*talks to himself in a low tone of irritation while he empties the table drawer*]. You're a scoundrel, Relling! You're a low fellow! Ah, you shameless tempter! I wish I could get someone to stick a knife into you! [*He lays some old letters on one side, finds the torn document of yesterday, takes it up and looks at the pieces, puts it down hurriedly as* GINA *enters.*]

GINA [*sets a tray with coffee, etc., on the table*]. Here's a drop of something hot, if you'd fancy it. And there's some bread and butter and a snack of salt meat.

HIALMAR [*glancing at the tray*]. Salt meat? Never under this roof! It's true I have not had a mouthful of solid food for nearly twenty-four hours, but no matter. My memoranda! The commencement of my autobiography! What has become of my diary and all my important papers? [*Opens the sitting-room door but draws back.*] She is there too!

GINA. Good lord! the child must be somewhere!

HIALMAR. Come out. [*He makes room; HEDVIG comes, scared, into the studio.*]

HIALMAR [*with his hand on the door handle, says to GINA*]: In these, the last moments I spend in my former home, I wish to be spared from interlopers. [*Goes into the room.*]

HEDVIG [*with a bound toward her mother, asks softly, trembling*]: Does that mean me?

GINA. Stay out in the kitchen, Hedvig; or, no—you'd best go into your own room. [*Speaks to HIALMAR as she goes in to him.*] Wait a bit, Ekdal; don't rummage so in the drawers. I know where everything is.

HEDVIG [*stands a moment immovable, in terror and perplexity, biting her lips to keep back the tears; then she clenches her hands convulsively and says softly*]: The wild duck! [*She steals over and takes the pistol from the shelf, opens the garret door a little way, creeps in and draws the door to after her. HIALMAR and GINA can be heard disputing in the sitting room.*]

HIALMAR [*comes in with some manuscript books and old loose papers which he lays upon the table*]. That portmanteau is of no use! There are a thousand and one things I must drag with me.

GINA [*following with the portmanteau*]. Why not leave all the rest for the present and only take a shirt and a pair of woolen drawers with you?

HIALMAR. Whew! All these exhausting preparations! [*Pulls off his overcoat and throws it upon the sofa.*]

GINA. And there's the coffee getting cold.

HIALMAR. H'm. [*Drinks a mouthful without thinking of it and then another.*]

GINA [*dusting the backs of the chairs*]. A nice job you'll have to find such another big garret for the rabbits.

HIALMAR. What! Am I to drag all those rabbits with me too?

GINA. You don't suppose Grandfather can get on without his rabbits.

HIALMAR. He must just get used to doing without them. Have not *I* to sacrifice very much greater things than rabbits!

GINA [*dusting the bookcase*]. Shall I put the flute in the portmanteau for you?

HIALMAR. No. No flute for me. But give me the pistol!

GINA. Do you want to take the pigstol with you?

HIALMAR. Yes. My loaded pistol.

GINA [*searching for it*]. It's gone. He must have taken it in with him.

HIALMAR. Is he in the garret?

GINA. Yes, of course he's in the garret.

HIALMAR. H'm—poor lonely old man. [*He takes a piece of bread and butter, eats it and finishes his cup of coffee.*]

GINA. And if we hadn't have let that room, you could have moved in there.

HIALMAR. And continued to live under the same roof with— Never—never!

GINA. But couldn't you put up with the sitting room for a day or two? You could have it all to yourself.

HIALMAR. Never within these walls!

GINA. Well, then, down with Relling and Molvik.

HIALMAR. Don't mention those wretches' names to me! The very thought of them almost takes away my appetite. Oh no, I must go out into the storm and the

308 The Wild Duck

snowdrift—go from house to house and seek shelter
for my father and myself.

GINA. But you've got no hat, Ekdal! You've been and
lost your hat, you know.

HIALMAR. Oh, those two brutes, those slaves of all the
vices! A hat must be procured. [*Takes another piece
of bread and butter.*] Some arrangements must be
made. For I have no mind to throw away my life
either. [*Looks for something on the tray.*]

GINA. What are you looking for?

HIALMAR. Butter.

GINA. I'll get some at once. [*Goes out into the kitchen.*]

HIALMAR [*calls after her*]. Oh, it doesn't matter; dry
bread is good enough for me.

GINA [*brings a dish of butter*]. Look here; this is fresh
churned. [*She pours out another cup of coffee for
him; he seats himself on the sofa, spreads more butter on the already buttered bread and eats and drinks
a while in silence.*]

HIALMAR. Could I, without being subject to intrusion—
intrusion of any sort—could I live in the sitting room
there for a day or two?

GINA. Yes, to be sure you could, if you only would.

HIALMAR. For I see no possibility of getting all Father's
things out in such a hurry.

GINA. And, besides, you've surely got to tell him first as
you don't mean to live with us others no more.

HIALMAR [*pushes away his coffee cup*]. Yes, there is that
too; I shall have to lay bare the whole tangled story
to him— I must turn matters over; I must have
breathing time. I cannot take all these burdens on
my shoulders in a single day.

GINA. No, especially in such horrible weather as it is
outside.

HIALMAR [*touching* WERLE's *letter*]. I see that paper still
lying about here.

GINA. Yes, *I* haven't touched it.

HIALMAR. So far as I am concerned it is mere waste-paper—

GINA. Well, *I* have certainly no notion of making any use of it.

HIALMAR. —but we had better not let it get lost all the same; in all the upset when I move it might easily—

GINA. I'll take good care of it, Ekdal.

HIALMAR. The donation is in the first instance made to Father, and it rests with him to accept or decline it.

GINA [*sighs*]. Yes, poor old Father—

HIALMAR. To make quite safe— Where shall I find some gum?

GINA [*goes to the bookcase*]. Here's the gum pot.

HIALMAR. And a brush?

GINA. The brush is here too. [*Brings him the things.*]

HIALMAR [*takes a pair of scissors*]. Just a strip of paper at the back— [*Clips and gums.*] Far be it from me to lays hands upon what is not my own—and least of all upon what belongs to a destitute old man—and to— the other as well. There now! Let it lie there for a time, and when it is dry take it away. I wish never to see that document again. Never!

[GREGERS WERLE *enters from the passage.*]

GREGERS [*somewhat surprised*]. What—are you sitting here, Hialmar?

HIALMAR [*rises hurriedly*]. I had sunk down from fatigue.

GREGERS. You have been having breakfast, I see.

HIALMAR. The body sometimes makes its claims felt too.

GREGERS. What have you decided to do?

HIALMAR. For a man like me there is only one course possible. I am just putting my most important things together. But it takes time, you know.

GINA [*with a touch of impatience*]. Am I to get the room ready for you or am I to pack your portmanteau?

HIALMAR [*after a glance of annoyance at* GREGERS]. Pack
—and get the room ready!

GINA [*takes the portmanteau*]. Very well; then I'll put
in the shirt and the other things. [*Goes into the sitting room and draws the door to after her.*]

GREGERS [*after a short silence*]. I never dreamed that
this would be the end of it. Do you really feel it a
necessity to leave house and home?

HIALMAR [*wanders about restlessly*]. What would you
have me do? I am not fitted to bear unhappiness,
Gregers. I must feel secure and at peace in my surroundings.

GREGERS. But can you not feel that here? Just try it. I
should have thought you had firm ground to build
upon now—if only you start afresh. And, remember,
you have your invention to live for.

HIALMAR. Oh, don't talk about my invention. It's perhaps still in the dim distance.

GREGERS. Indeed!

HIALMAR. Why, great heavens, what would you have
one invent? Other people have invented almost everything already. It becomes more and more difficult
every day—

GREGERS. And you have devoted so much labor to it.

HIALMAR. It was that blackguard Relling that urged me
to it.

GREGERS. Relling?

HIALMAR. Yes, it was he that first made me realize my
aptitude for making some notable discovery in photography.

GREGERS. Aha—it was Relling!

HIALMAR. Oh, I have been so truly happy over it! Not
so much for the sake of the invention itself as because Hedvig believed in it—believed in it with a
child's whole eagerness of faith. At least I have been
fool enough to go and imagine that she believed in
it.

GREGERS. Can you really think Hedvig has been false toward you?

HIALMAR. I can think anything now. It is Hedvig that stands in my way. She will blot out the sunlight from my whole life.

GREGERS. Hedvig! Is it Hedvig you are talking of? How should she blot out your sunlight?

HIALMAR [*without answering*]. How unutterably I have loved that child! How unutterably happy I have felt every time I came home to my humble room and she flew to meet me with her sweet little blinking eyes. Oh, confiding fool that I have been! I loved her unutterably—and I yielded myself up to the dream, the delusion, that she loved me unutterably in return.

GREGERS. Do you call that a delusion?

HIALMAR. How should I know? I can get nothing out of Gina; and besides, she is totally blind to the ideal side of these complications. But to you I feel impelled to open my mind, Gregers. I cannot shake off this frightful doubt—perhaps Hedvig has never really and honestly loved me.

GREGERS. What would you say if she were to give you a proof of her love? [*Listens.*] What's that? I thought I heard the wild duck—

HIALMAR. It's the wild duck quacking. Father's in the garret.

GREGERS. Is he? [*His face lights up with joy.*] I say you may yet have proof that your poor misunderstood Hedvig loves you!

HIALMAR. Oh, what proof can she give me? I dare not believe in any assurance from that quarter.

GREGERS. Hedvig does not know what deceit means.

HIALMAR. Oh, Gregers, that is just what I cannot be sure of. Who knows what Gina and that Mrs Sorby may many a time have sat here whispering and tattling about? And Hedvig usually has her ears open, I can tell you. Perhaps the deed of gift was not such a surprise to her after all. In fact, I'm not sure but that I noticed something of the sort.

GREGERS. What spirit is this that has taken possession of you?

HIALMAR. I have had my eyes opened. Just you notice— you'll see, the deed of gift is only a beginning. Mrs Sorby has always been a good deal taken up with Hedvig, and now she has the power to do whatever she likes for the child. They can take her from me whenever they please.

GREGERS. Hedvig will never, never leave you.

HIALMAR. Don't be so sure of that. If only they beckon to her and throw out a golden bait— And oh! I have loved her so unspeakably! I would have counted it my highest happiness to take her tenderly by the hand and lead her, as one leads a timid child through a great dark empty room! I am cruelly certain now that the poor photographer in his humble attic has never really and truly been anything to her. She has only cunningly contrived to keep on a good footing with him until the time came.

GREGERS. You don't believe that yourself, Hialmar.

HIALMAR. That is just the terrible part of it— I don't know what to believe— I never can know it. But can you really doubt that it must be as I say? Ho-ho, you have far too much faith in the claim of the ideal, my good Gregers! If those others came, with the glamour of wealth about them, and called to the child: "Leave him; come to us; here life awaits you—"

GREGERS [*quickly*]. Well, what then?

HIALMAR. If I then asked her: "Hedvig, are you willing to renounce that life for me?" [*Laughs scornfully.*] No, thank you! You would soon hear what answer I should get.

[*A pistol shot is heard from within the garret.*]

GREGERS [*loudly and joyfully*]. Hialmar!

HIALMAR. There now; he must needs go shooting too.

GINA [*comes in*]. Oh, Ekdal, I can hear Grandfather blazing away in the garret by himself.

HIALMAR. I'll look in—

GREGERS [*eagerly, with emotion*]. Wait a moment! Do you know what that was?

HIALMAR. Yes, of course I know.

GREGERS. No, you don't know. But *I* do. That was the proof!

HIALMAR. What proof?

GREGERS. It was a child's free-will offering. She has got your father to shoot the wild duck.

HIALMAR. To shoot the wild duck!

GINA. Oh, think of that!

HIALMAR. What was that for?

GREGERS. She wanted to sacrifice to you her most cherished possession, for then she thought you would surely come to love her again.

HIALMAR [*tenderly, with emotion*]. Oh, poor child!

GINA. What things she does think of!

GREGERS. She only wanted your love again, Hialmar. She could not live without it.

GINA [*struggling with her tears*]. There, you can see for yourself, Ekdal.

HIALMAR. Gina, where is she?

GINA [*sniffs*]. Poor dear, she's sitting out in the kitchen, I daresay.

HIALMAR [*goes over, tears open the kitchen door and says*]: Hedvig, come, come in to me! [*Looks around.*] No, she's not here.

GINA. Then she must be in her own little room.

HIALMAR [*without*]. No, she's not here either. [*Comes in.*] She must have gone out.

GINA. Yes, you wouldn't have her anywheres in the house.

HIALMAR. Oh, if she would only come home quickly, so that I can tell her— Everything will come right now, Gregers; now I believe we can begin life afresh.

GREGERS [*quietly*]. I knew it; I knew the child would make amends.

[OLD EKDAL *appears at the door of his room; he is in full uniform and is busy buckling on his sword.*]

HIALMAR [*astonished*]. Father! Are you there?

GINA. Have you been firing in your room?

EKDAL [*resentfully, approaching*]. So you go shooting alone, do you, Hialmar?

HIALMAR [*excited and confused*]. Then it wasn't you that fired that shot in the garret?

EKDAL. Me that fired? H'm.

GREGERS [*calls out to* HIALMAR]. She has shot the wild duck herself!

HIALMAR. What can it mean? [*Hastens to the garret door, tears it aside, looks in and calls loudly.*] Hedvig!

GINA [*runs to the door*]. Good God! what's that?

HIALMAR [*goes in*]. She's lying on the floor!

GREGERS. Hedvig! Lying on the floor! [*Goes in to* HIALMAR.]

GINA [*at the same time*]. Hedvig! [*Inside the garret.*] No, no, no!

EKDAL. Ho-ho! Does she go shooting too now?

[HIALMAR, GINA *and* GREGERS *carry* HEDVIG *into the studio; in her dangling right hand she holds the pistol fast clasped in her fingers.*]

HIALMAR [*distracted*]. The pistol has gone off. She has wounded herself. Call for help! Help!

GINA [*runs into the passage and calls down*]. Relling! Relling! Doctor Relling, come up as quick as you can!

[HIALMAR *and* GREGERS *lay* HEDVIG *down on the sofa.*]

EKDAL [*quietly*]. The woods avenge themselves.

HIALMAR [*on his knees beside* HEDVIG]. She'll soon come to now. She's coming to; yes, yes, yes.

GINA [*who has come in again*]. Where has she hurt herself? I can't see anything.

[RELLING *comes hurriedly, and immediately after him*

MOLVIK; *the latter without his waistcoat and necktie and with his coat open.*]

RELLING. What's the matter here?

GINA. They say Hedvig shot herself.

HIALMAR. Come and help us!

RELLING. Shot herself! [*He pushes the table aside and begins to examine her.*]

HIALMAR [*kneeling and looking anxiously up at him.*] It can't be dangerous? Speak, Relling! She is scarcely bleeding at all. It can't be dangerous?

RELLING. How did it happen?

HIALMAR. Oh, we don't know—

GINA. She wanted to shoot the wild duck.

RELLING. The wild duck?

HIALMAR. The pistol must have gone off.

RELLING. H'm. Indeed.

EKDAL. The woods avenge themselves. But I'm not afraid all the same. [*Goes into the garret and closes the door after him.*]

HIALMAR. Well, Relling, why don't you say something?

RELLING. The ball has entered the breast.

HIALMAR. Yes, but she's coming to!

RELLING. Surely you can see that Hedvig is dead.

GINA [*bursts into tears*]. Oh, my child, my child—

GREGERS [*huskily*]. In the depths of the sea—

HIALMAR [*jumps up*]. No, no, she must live! Oh, for God's sake, Relling—only a moment—only just till I can tell her how unspeakably I loved her all the time.

RELLING. The bullet has gone through her heart. Internal hemorrhage. Death must have been instantaneous.

HIALMAR. And I! I hunted her from me like an animal! And she crept terrified into the garret and died for love of me! [*Sobbing.*] I can never atone to her! I can never tell her— [*Clenches his hands and cries upward.*] Oh, Thou above—if Thou be indeed! Why hast Thou done this thing to me?

GINA. Hush, hush, you mustn't go on that awful way. We had no right to keep her, I suppose.

MOLVIK. The child is not dead but sleepeth.

RELLING. Bosh!

HIALMAR [*becomes calm, goes over to the sofa, folds his arms and looks at* HEDVIG]. There she lies so stiff and still.

RELLING [*tries to loosen the pistol*]. She's holding it so tight, so tight.

GINA. No, no, Relling; don't break her fingers; let the pistol be.

HIALMAR. She shall take it with her.

GINA. Yes, let her. But the child mustn't lie here for a show. She shall go to her own room, so she shall. Help me, Ekdal.

[HIALMAR *and* GINA *take* HEDVIG *between them.*]

HIALMAR [*as they are carrying her*]. Oh, Gina, Gina, can you survive this?

GINA. We must help each other to bear it. For now, at least, she belongs to both of us.

MOLVIK [*stretches out his arms and mumbles*]. Blessed be the Lord; to earth thou shalt return; to earth thou shalt return—

RELLING [*whispers*]. Hold your tongue, you fool; you're drunk.

[HIALMAR *and* GINA *carry the body out through the kitchen door.* RELLING *shuts it after them.* MOLVIK *slinks out into the passage.*]

RELLING [*goes over to* GREGERS *and says*]: No one shall ever convince me that the pistol went off by accident.

GREGERS [*who has stood terrified, with convulsive twitchings*]. Who can say how the dreadful thing happened?

RELLING. The powder has burned the body of her dress. She must have pressed the pistol right against her breast and fired.

GREGERS. Hedvig has not died in vain. Did you not see how sorrow set free what is noble in him?

RELLING. Most people are ennobled by the actual presence of death. But how long do you suppose this nobility will last in him?

GREGERS. Why should it not endure and increase throughout his life?

RELLING. Before a year is over, little Hedvig will be nothing to him but a pretty theme for declamation.

GREGERS. How dare you say that of Hialmar Ekdal?

RELLING. We will talk of this again, when the grass has first withered on her grave. Then you'll hear him spouting about "the child too early torn from her father's heart"; then you'll see him steep himself in a syrup of sentiment and self-admiration and self-pity. Just you wait!

GREGERS. If you are right and I am wrong, then life is not worth living.

RELLING. Oh, life would be quite tolerable, after all, if only we could be rid of the confounded duns that keep on pestering us, in our poverty, with the claim of the ideal.

GREGERS [looking straight before him]. In that case I am glad that my destiny is what it is.

RELLING. May I inquire—what is your destiny?

GREGERS [going]. To be the thirteenth at table.

RELLING. The devil it is.

LAUREL LITERATURE SERIES

Distinguished, inexpensive

LAUREL GREAT LITERATURE SERIES

THE LAUREL HENRY JAMES

THE LAUREL JANE AUSTEN

Pride and Prejudice	LC-122	50c
Sense and Sensibility	LC-128	50c
Persuasion and *Lady Susan*	LC-144	50c

With a general introduction by Mark Schorer

THE LAUREL DREISER

An American Tragedy	LY-101	95c
The Titan	LX-109	75c
Sister Carrie	LX-118	75c

With a general introduction by Alfred Kazin

THE LAUREL DOSTOYEVSKY

Crime and Punishment	LX-106	75c
The House of the Dead	LC-131	50c
Notes from Underground, Poor People and *The Friend of the Family*	LX-121	75c

With a general introduction by Ernest J. Simmons

THE LAUREL CONRAD

The Nigger of the Narcissus and *The End of the Tether*	LC-142	50c
Heart of Darkness, Almayer's Folly, The Lagoon	LC-147	50c

With a general introduction by Albert J. Guerard.

THE SUNRISE SEMESTER LIBRARY

Moby Dick by Herman Melville Introduction by William M. Gibson.	LX-105	75c
Madame Bovary by Gustave Flaubert Translated by Gerard Hopkins. Introduction by Floyd Zulli, Jr.	LC-118	50c
Crime and Punishment by Fyodor Dostoyevsky Introduction by Ernest J. Simmons.	LX-106	75c
Three Plays by Ibsen *The Wild Duck, Hedda Gabler, A Doll's House.* Introduction by Seymour L. Flaxman.	LC-123	50c
Jude the Obscure by Thomas Hardy Introduction by William E. Buckler.	LX-108	75c
Great Stories by Chekhov Selected and introduced by David H. Greene.	LC-126	50c
Centuries of Great Poetry Edited, with an introduction, by Robert Penn Warren and Albert Erskine.	LX-110	75c

THE LAUREL DRAMA SERIES

If you cannot obtain these books locally, send the price of the book
10c per book to cover handling and postage to Dell Publishing Co
321 West 44th Street, New York 36, N.Y. If order is for 5 or mor
no handling and postage charge is necessary.